## PRAISE FOR MAGDA SZUBANSKI AND *RECKONING*

**WINNER** ABIA Book of the Year 2016

**WINNER** ABIA Biography of the Year 2016

**WINNER** NSW Premier's Literary Awards Douglas Stewart Prize for Non-Fiction 2016

**WINNER** Indie Award for Non-Fiction 2016

**WINNER** Nielsen BookData Booksellers' Choice Award 2016

**BEST BOOKS OF 2015 LISTINGS**

'It is impossible not to be moved…Let's hope Szubanski writes more. She shines just as brightly as a serious writer as she does as a comedian.' *Guardian*

'Compelling author, compelling premise, compelling writing.' Graeme Simsion, *Age / Sydney Morning Herald*

'She has great stories to draw on but it is her very fine writing that makes it such a joy to read.' Christos Tsiolkas, *Age / Sydney Morning Herald*

'A beautiful and moving story of a serious, thoughtful and complex person.' Paul Barclay, Radio National *Books and Arts*

'Captures wonderfully well the strange dissonance of history.' Sophie Cunningham, *Australian*

'Moving and grave.' Peter Craven, *Australian*

'Brave, compassionate—and hilarious…may be some sort of masterpiece of the form.' Stephen Romei, *Australian*

'Magda Szubanski blew us away with her writing chops in this remarkable, fearless and deeply personal memoir.' Booktopia

'Do not, repeat, do not underestimate comedian Magda Szubanski's *Reckoning*…A powerful piece of writing.' *Courier-Mail*

'A brave and tender book about everything that matters most in life.' Cate Blanchett

'The writing is assured and controlled, the storytelling expert and thoughtful, the language eloquent and moving. The writing, the story, the voice—all of it is beautiful.' Christos Tsiolkas

'*Reckoning* is a riveting, overwhelmingly poignant autobiography by a woman of genius…It is an extraordinary hymn to the tragic heroism at the heart of ordinary life and the soaring moral scrutiny of womankind. Every library should have it, every school should teach it.' Peter Craven, *Australian*

'Unlike most autobiographies by famous people, *Reckoning* has substance beyond the writer's fame…Szubanski's fine memoir, written with great style, adds another layer to our history— another startling migrant story.' *Crikey*

'Powerful, exquisitely written.' *West Australian*

'With its hints of nostalgia, raw honesty, compassion, and a good amount of bravery, Szubanski's *Reckoning* reflects on the truths we hide and the realities we cannot ignore as we develop into and through our adult lives.' *The Conversation*

'Sensitive and searching, colourful and vividly composed… stylish and accomplished.' *Sydney Morning Herald*

'Nearly every memoir is described as "brave" these days but Szubanski has earned the word…An affecting story of family intimacy—soulfully and sensitively told.' *Saturday Paper*

'We all knew she was funny, but who knew she could write like this?' Benjamin Law, *Age / Sydney Morning Herald*

'An extraordinarily rare talent—somebody with first-rate emotional and comedic instincts as well as a fierce intellect which would allow her to succeed in any academic task she'd set herself… This is a book which will be good for the soul of anybody who reads it.' *Daily Review*

'A page-turner.' *New Zealand Herald*

'Untangles intergenerational trauma with intelligence and insight…[Szubanski] declares herself as a sensitive intellectual who is cursed, or blessed, depending on your point of view, with the fervent desire to understand.' *Newtown Review of Books*

'*Reckoning* isn't simply a collection of anecdotes, though—it is so much more. Sharp, beautiful, a must-read.' *Canberra Weekly*

'A moving exploration of her relationship with her Polish Resistance hero father…*Reckoning* is a quest and, in a sad but satisfying way, Magda does find what she's seeking.' *Australian Women's Weekly*

'Far more than a run-of-the-mill celebrity memoir, this is a beautifully written, heartfelt and illuminating family saga.' *New Daily*

'An inspiring memoir of a woman who faced her demons, sought treatment for depression and overcame disappointments. She is loved and admired by thousands but, more importantly, she exudes power—the power of being herself.' *Good Reading*

'Fascinating…One of our favourites.' *InDaily*

'A beautifully written book of unflinching honesty, humour and pathos.' *North & South*

Magda Szubanski is one of Australia's best known and most loved performers. *Reckoning* is her first book.

# MAGDA SZUBANSKI

## A MEMOIR

# RECKONING

TEXT PUBLISHING
MELBOURNE AUSTRALIA

textpublishing.com.au

The Text Publishing Company
Swann House, 22 William Street, Melbourne, Victoria 3000, Australia

The Text Publishing Company (UK) Ltd
130 Wood Street, London EC2V 6DL, United Kingdom

First published in 2015 by The Text Publishing Company
This edition 2016
Reprinted 2016

Typeset in 12.25pt Granjon by J & M Typesetting
Cover and book design by WH Chong

Printed in Australia by Griffin Press, an Accredited ISO AS/NZS 14001:2004 Environmental Management System Printer

National Library of Australia Cataloguing-in-Publication entry:
Creator:    Szubanski, Magda, author.
Title:      Reckoning : a memoir / by Magda Szubanski.
ISBN:       9781925355413 (paperback)
            9781922253224 (ebook)
Subjects:   Szubanski, Magda.
            Entertainers—Australia—Biography.
            Television personalities—Australia—Biography.
            Radio personalities—Australia—Biography.
            Actresses—Australia—Biography.
Dewey Number: 790.2092

Inscribed on the back of a photo of
my father, addressed to my mother.

---

*'Remembrance...is all I ask.*
*But if it be a task...*
*...forget.'*
*(L. Byron)*
*To Margaret from Peter,*
*London 4th of Febr. 1947*

# Contents

# THE STONE OF MADNESS

If you had met my father you would never, not for an instant, have thought he was an assassin. He was warmhearted, friendly, engaging, intelligent, generous, humorous, honourable, affectionate, arrogant, blunt, loyal. He was a family man. He was handsome, although he did not have heroic stature. He was five foot four. He was stylish, fashion-conscious; a dandy even. He also looked incredibly young for his age. In his seventies he took to wearing his baseball cap backwards and, believe it or not, he carried it off.

He loved tennis, he loved ballet, he loved good conversation. Out there in the Melbourne suburbs—mowing the lawn in his terry-towelling hat and his Bombay bloomers; in the lounge room doing the samba at cocktail parties; late at night playing his harmonica in the laundry—you would never have guessed that he was capable of killing in cold blood. But he was. Poor bastard.

He was born in 1924. He was a boy of fifteen when Hitler invaded his homeland and the war began, and as soon as he was able he joined the fighting. All through our growing up he would say, 'I was judge, jury, and executioner.' And I could never imagine—cannot imagine even now—what it feels like to have that responsibility, that guilt. To be a little god with a gun, and the power over life and death.

He spent the rest of his life trying to come to terms with what he had done. I grew up in the shadow of that reckoning.

In the Museo del Prado there is a painting by Hieronymous Bosch called *The Extraction of the Stone of Madness*, painted around 1494. In the fifteenth century itinerant surgeons offered relief from the scourge of insanity by performing trepanation. They would cut a hole in the patient's skull and then remove what they called the 'stone of madness'. Astonishingly, many people survived.

I swear sometimes I can feel that stone in my head. A palpable presence, an unwelcome thing that I want to squeeze out of my skull like a plum pip, using nothing but the sheer pressure of thought and concentration. If I just think hard enough...

That stone was my father's legacy to me, his keepsake. Beneath his genial surface, somewhere in the depths, I would sometimes catch a glimpse—of a smooth, bone-coloured stone. A stone made of calcified guilt and shame. I could feel it.

I can feel it still.

# DEATH OF AN ASSASSIN

'All the old warriors are dying.' The wife of young Dr Łukasz says this with a melancholy resignation as we stand outside the church waiting for the priest to arrive.

It is October 2006 and we have come to bury my father, Zbigniew Szubański. That was his name but everyone called him Peter. It doesn't mean the same thing, but Polish doesn't translate easily.

Denominationally speaking, he was a self-styled agnostic with a religious temperament. Aesthetically and constitutionally he was Catholic through and through. ('Ach, Maggie, the ritual, the solemnity, the beauty. Roman Catholicism is the only one for me.') So here we are at a Catholic church in the middle of Melbourne suburbia, one of those 1970s post–Vatican II jobs. All exposed beams and big windows that let in dazzling sunlight and views of eucalypts and the occasional honk of a semitrailer up on the highway.

The building and all the people in it are half a world—a lifetime—

away from the charnel house of Europe. It is a strange place for talk of warriors. But the wife of Dr Łukasz understands history. She knows that entire civilisations vanish, swept away like twigs in a tidal wave, taking all of their wisdom and achievement with them. She understands the protocols by which people are erased from history. She knows the horrible truth that, while suffering is universal, the world cares more about some people's suffering than others'.

My father's body lies in a coffin draped in the red-and-white Polish flag. A pirated CD of Larry Adler playing 'Clair de Lune' is warbling through a tinny PA. My father was self-taught on the harmonica and would spend hour after hour practising in the seclusion of the laundry because we didn't have a shed. Polkas, mazurkas, old Polish war songs and Larry Adler covers.

Now the older generation arrives. With walking sticks and wheel-chairs and titanium hips, these stately old Poles sail into the church like a sagging fleet of tall ships, and I feel a pang of nostalgia. They will never make them like that again: that style, that attention to detail, that level of craftsmanship.

Mrs Kobylański makes her way over and kisses my mother Margaret three times. The Poles take kissing seriously. There are the welcome kisses—warm, hearty, a minimum of three. There are kisses that know adversity—strong, hard, the sharp press of the cheekbone through the flesh. And there are kisses that are like dances—ornate, flowery vestiges of chivalry. On formal occasions the men will kiss your hand and, on very formal occasions, will also click their heels. When I took my father to the Logies he kissed the ladies' hands and they were all enchanted, even the feminist bureaucrats from the ABC. I have never seen a Pole air-kiss.

My oldest Polish friend Izabella greets me warmly—with a kiss— but remains stoic. Her father always insisted his family must never cry, even at funerals. Emotion spooked him. 'During the war people would become hysterical, get the wrong idea, make accusations. Emotions got innocent people killed.' There was to be no crying at funerals, even his.

Inside the church there are maybe two hundred of us. A surprising number, given my father was eighty-two, but he was a man who liked people and was therefore well liked. Naturally chatty, he would make friends in the unlikeliest of places—with the captain of a river boat on the Murray, or the woman conducting the gallery tour.

In the front pew my mother is bearing up, but she looks diminished, as if some of her bones have been removed.

He was selfish, he was vain, he had innumerable character flaws. You could choose to dwell on all the reasons to love him less and thereby anaesthetise the pain of missing him. But for fifty-eight years he was there. He complained, he bitched, but he was always there, and now he is gone. Torn out of her.

About two years earlier I had driven out to visit my parents. My father was in the kitchen. As I came in the front door there was a loud *screech-clunk-bang* as Mum slammed down the footrest and leapt out of her Jason recliner. She headed me off in the hallway, herding me into the bedroom and out of earshot.

'Your father's been to the specialist,' she whispered.

'And?'

'You ask him.'

'Did you speak to him?'

'Yes.'

'And?'

'Talk to your father.' She scuttled off to the dining room with her cup of tea and the newspaper to do the Codeword. Black tea, lemon. All day every day, cup after cup.

Dad was at the sink.

'Mum said you've been to the specialist.'

'Ach, Jesus.'

'So?'

'What do you want me to say?'

'What happened. Has it spread?'

A shrug. 'Well, put it this way, I probably won't be around for Christmas.'

'Two months!'

No answer.

'*What?*'

Another shrug. 'Nothing.'

'You can't say that! You can't just say *"nothing"*!'

I was a wriggling worm on a very old hook. All my life my father had been dying and all my life this was how we dealt with it.

'What do you want me to say?'

I could feel my anger starting to rise. 'I want you to tell me *exactly* what the oncologist said! Did he give a prognosis? Did he give a time line? *What?*'

'Ach!'

Now he had me: I was a silly worrying woman. As though this was my doing, as though I had made all this up and was now being ridiculous and hysterical. First he would frighten me, then he would tell me I was ridiculous for being frightened. Cat and mouse.

He needed me to worry but he couldn't bear me to worry. He wanted me to fuss over him, but only if he could control how much I would feel. How much *he* would feel.

I lost it. He had reduced me to being a thirteen-year-old again and so I fought back with the teenage girl's most powerful weapon: mocking cruelty.

'Why do you always do this?'

'Do what?'

'This! *Frightening* us with your perpetual impending death!'

He looked at me incredulously, like I was deranged—Lucille Ball to his Desi Arnaz. 'I'm not trying to frighten you! Why on earth would I frighten you? *I'm* not frightened.'

At which point Mum, her flinty Scottish accent honed to a deflating pinpoint, deadpanned from the dining room. 'Yeah, right. You're *just* as frightened as the rest of us.'

But it was another two years before I got the call, and I was living in London by then. When he stood in the driveway of their Spanish mission-style house, farewelling me, I was not to know it would be the last time. Now my mother was on the phone: terse, frightened, emphatic. 'Your father has had two falls.'

'Oh, Mum. I'll get on the next plane.'

So I did. I sat in the sky for the next twenty-four hours not knowing if, at the other end, my father would still be alive.

We landed just after midnight. I turned on my mobile and rang my brother Chris. Dad was still alive but he couldn't talk or see. He had had two strokes.

*Please, God, let him still be alive when I get there. Please, God.*

I prayed to God out of habit and because…Well, who else?

'Ach,' Dad would say, with his curious hybrid Polish–Scottish accent, 'Maggie, so many times I should have died. I have had a charmed life. I came *that* close.'

The time when machine-gun fire strafed the tram he was riding, the bullets miraculously flying either side of him. The time when he was an escaped POW riding boxcars through Germany, leaping from carriage to carriage in the pitch blackness of a tunnel. Then, years later, repeated bouts of cancer and heart attacks and a quadruple bypass. 'I escaped death so often I started to believe I was invincible.'

And now he is dead, in a coffin, dressed in the smallest suit we could find, which is still ludicrously big on his shrunken form. On his feet is a pair of shoes that Chris has lovingly prepared. My brother can be effervescent when the mood strikes, but silent as granite when it doesn't.

'I'll do them,' he said, and took the shoes into the laundry. When he returned with them they sparkled. I burst into tears and started unstacking the dishwasher so as not to embarrass him.

When I got to the hospital my father was lying on his side. He looked like ET. Small, bald, not quite human. He was so tiny he barely made a bump in the bedclothes. I went over and kissed Mum, Chris, my sister Barbara. Her kids Sarah and Simon. And then I went and kissed my father's cheek. It was warm as a freshly baked bun. I took his hand. It was like a furnace.

'That's the morphine,' the nurse explained.

He had lovely hands, my dad. Neat, well-manicured. His mouth gaped. 'Does he know I'm here?'

'Yes. Hearing is the last thing to go,' the nurse explained.

But to me he felt like he had gone, and some part of me was relieved. I could say goodbye to him now, when it seemed he had already left. To look him in the eye and say goodbye when he was fully present? Too painful.

'I never grieved for my parents,' he told me often. Some loss is just too great.

For another twelve hours we kept a vigil. And it was in those hours as I watched my father Cheyne-Stokesing to death that I realised it is as much a struggle to die as it is to live. The letting go of life is no peaceful business, and my father's body fought hard to stay. His lungs continued to suck and pull at the air, to drag scraps of oxygen through his veins.

Chris's phone rang. It was his son Michael, who was in Germany and could not get back in time. His voice was jerky with grief. He loved his Papa.

None of us had ever done this before. The nurses were kind; they told us what would happen physically. But emotionally and spiritually we were way out to sea. Is it always like this? So clumsy and banal? So bizarre and so ordinary? Billions have been down this path before us but we bumbled through as though we were the first. At one point my sister started to sing. 'Amazing Grace'. My mother joined in and eventually so did I. My brother glowered.

At about four in the morning I rang Izabella. She came straight over. Shortly after, Father Słowik arrived to administer the last rites in Polish—an insurance policy for my mother and me.

I had first suggested some months earlier the idea of visits from the Polish priest. My father scoffed. 'What the bloody hell for?'

*My god is a god of love. I don't need absolution.* I remembered his mantra. He used to run that phrase through his fingers like worry beads. He had taken the time to think about his soul and its welfare. Cut off from his family and the unit he had served in during the war, from anyone who had shared his extraordinary experience, he had been forced to make his own personal and puritanical reconciliation with his god.

Four years before his death he had written to his dear friend Ryszard Bielański, a fellow member of his unit: *You are the only person with whom I conduct polemics about subjects which could be disconcerting or worrying for other people. My correspondence with you is a certain type of confession because I write about subjects which I do not discuss or touch upon with anyone else.*

So, no priest, and no absolution.

But the things people really need to say are almost never said. An act of interpretation is an act of love. And, in any case, I couldn't bear the sight of him carrying that cross, the whole fucking horror of it, to his grave all on his own. He needed someone to help bear the load. Someone who would not misconstrue him or upset the delicate deal he had made with God. Someone who spoke his language.

So I found a priest, a Polish Jesuit. We chatted. I knew immediately he was the right guy. And for some reason when I suggested it again my father didn't scoff. There was none of the usual bravado and disdain. Slumped in his Jason recliner, he shrugged. 'OK.'

The priest came over and spoke with Dad in the den for an hour or more.

Immediately Mum got on the phone. 'The priest's been.'

'How'd it go?

'You ask.' She put down the handset.

'Peter! Magda's on the phone!'

Silence.

'Peter!'

'Yes, yes! I'm coming.' And a muttered, 'For God's sake.'

'Use the phone in the den.'

'Yes, yes. Jesus. Hello?'

'Hi, Dad. So. How did you get on?'

'Well, at least he's not an idiot.'

'Will I ask him to come again?'

A pause. 'Yes. He's quite interesting, actually. And his Polish is excellent. Not like some of those bums.'

Polish. The tongue his mother spoke. For sixty-two years my father had not heard her voice. And now, in the hospital, as the Polish priest recited the last rites, was it this or what the priest was saying that forced a tear to trickle from his eye? I don't know.

What was waiting on the other side for him? Was there a bright light? Were his parents there to greet him? Was there peace? Judgment? Forgiveness? Nothing?

*

Despite the modern setting it is an old-fashioned, solemn mass. Father Słowik is not one of those joke-cracking, MC-at-a-cabaret priests. He has a sense of gravitas. This is death—in all its glory and finality. My godless friends are deeply moved by his homily; but of course the Poles always do sadness well. Górecki's *Symphony of Sorrowful Songs* puts this sensibility to music. *'O Mamo, nie płacz, nie.' Oh Mama, don't cry.* Words carved into the wall of a cell by a young girl about to be killed. The Poles know sorrow all right.

'God is the only true biographer,' the Polish priest says, 'because only He knows what is in our souls.' Isn't that what we all hope for? To be understood, finally? Do I know my father as well as God knows him? His friend Ryszard described him as trustworthy, 'a good man to steal a horse with'. He was solid, a good burgher, a reliable citizen. The priest knows the part of my father that is now, perhaps, preparing to face judgment. The part that needs forgiveness. He has chosen a reading from Luke's gospel, the one about the Good Thief. Sin and redemption.

After the Eucharist Barbara rises and moves across to take her place beside the organist. My sister is a beautiful, delicate soul, and my father's death is a blow that strikes deep. But she is gutsy. I love my sister very much. Although we are ten years apart we have always been close. Barb loves to sing and now, in front of a packed church, at the most emotional moment of her whole life, she is going to sing 'Ave Maria'.

'Och!' My mother blurts. 'She's too sensitive for this world!' In truth, my mother thinks we are all too sensitive for this world, as though we are a family of emotionally skinless burn victims. With trembling hands my sister lifts her sheet music and nods to the organist. She stands on the precipice, her eyes wild with terror, counting the beats. Then she opens her mouth and out comes a pure, slightly tremulous mezzo-soprano voice that dips and then soars across the notes like an injured bird taking flight. We all sit there, our tissues reduced to wet snotty clumps in our hands. Then the church erupts into applause. My sister goes back to her seat, beaming. There are so many different kinds of courage.

Later at the crematorium we are all eating cakes and finger food. 'We will all miss Zbigniew.' Mrs Pieczak kisses my cheeks. 'Magda, *rozumiesz*. You *must* understand, only the *bravest of the brave* were asked to do what your father did.' She studies my face to see if I have understood. I thank her and take the plate of mini-quiches over to Mrs Dutkowski.

*Rozumiesz*. Understand. So many Polish conversations begin with this plea. Because for the most part the Polish experience has been so bizarrely awful that it beggars belief. In fact, many did not believe my father's stories from the war. They could not conceive that this dapper little man was capable of cold-blooded killing. It just seemed too… ludicrous. This is the double burden that those who are traumatised must carry. First the trauma, and then the inability of language to describe it.

Or us to hear it.

'*You must understand*,' my father would say whenever I asked him yet another dumbarse question. He wanted me to help him make sense of it, to find the right story for him. After the funeral Mum gave me a few typewritten A4 sheets. 'Your father started writing this but he couldn't go on.' His jottings were incoherent. Snatches, fragments. Like a PTSD nightmare. He couldn't sit still long enough to weave a story. Get up. Move. Go and play tennis.

My father wanted to forget history. He had lived through an awful lot of it; he had no desire to go back. But all the old warriors are dying, and their stories die with them. Someone has to bear witness, but am I the right person for the job? Do I have the stomach to gouge beneath the scabs and clean the wound? Is healing even possible?

We were tugboats in the river of history, my father and I, pulling in opposite directions. He needed to forget. I need to remember. For him, only the present moment would set him free. For me, the key lies buried in the past. The only way forward is back.

# MY MOTHER'S PEOPLE

My mother comes from an ancient Catholic clan. Her people are Lamonts, originally Irish. The clan tartan is as sombre-hued as the Scottish sky, all dark greens and bruised blues shot through with a thin, hopeful ray of white. Our people hail from the west of Scotland where the Irish coast is so close you could practically stand on one shore and blow a kiss to your sweetheart on the other. Close, but far enough away to provide sanctuary, too. The Irish Sea is furrowed with the wake of my ancestors' boats as they plied back and forth over the centuries, fleeing the wrath of the Protestant clans.

Her mother, my grandmother Meg Lamont, was one of nine brothers and sisters all of whom lived within walking distance of one another in Rosyth on the Firth of Forth, the dockyard town where the mighty Forth Bridge was built. And a mere granite stone's throw from Dunfermline, the ancient capital of Scotland and burial site of King Robert the Bruce, he of the famous 'try, try again' persistence.

I would sit for hours while my mother lullabied me in her soft Scottish accent. Tales of her Irish father Luke and of Meg and of Auntie Bessie, fierce 'Lion Aunt' and perennial spinster, who had 'worked in service' down in London. Of the great sack of money that sat on the shelf of my great-grandfather Henry Lamont's pantry among the baking soda and the treacle. And how Henry would send Auntie Bessie down to give a shilling to my gran when times were tough, even though he disapproved of my grandfather Luke, an Irishman like himself. My mother never knew why.

Of the uncles Tom, Ronald, Harry, Louis and Dan, and how one of them (Dan, she thinks) lost a foot to the diabetes. How they were all musicians and how one of them, maybe Louis, played the big fiddle in an orchestra. Of their women folk Jean Allen, and Nell McLaine, who my mother thought was full of life but whom Auntie Bessie always called 'Nell McLaine', never 'Nell', on account of the fact that she was 'no better than she should be'. Of her Irish grandfather Henry with his fine, full head of white hair that he was so proud of and washed every day of his life. Henry who helped build the Forth Bridge and who, 'Thinking back, lost a foot as well. That must have been the diabetes.' (We are ever on the alert for dietary explanations for what ails us.)

Of childish pranks and pole-vaulting across the muddy waters of the burn. Of how, in the bitter Scottish winter, she and her pals would cling together at the top of the hill in a screaming, giggling clump and slide on the black ice all the way down the street and into school. How in summer it was so hot the tar would bubble up on the street and you could burst it with your big toe. That was with Isa Leigh and her sister Emily on the way to Bluebell Woods.

She told me about gentle Jessie Isseponi, her half-Italian grandmother, who wore black bombazine with a bustle every day of her life and who never raised her voice but who, without a word, would walk up beside you, take your hand and gently lead you home when it was time to come in from play. Who would trundle along the street farting into her bustle and giggling to herself.

And Jessie's father Luigi the Italian sculptor who, for reasons unknown, was forced to flee to Scotland—during Garibaldi's time, she thinks it was—his coat lined with money, accompanied by a priest and a layman. And how Luigi did the death masks for the notorious grave robbers Burke and Hare, and how he screamed and ran out of the room when Burke's cadaver suddenly exhaled. And how it broke Luigi's heart when his beautiful sculptures were smashed in Dunfermline because he was a foreigner and a Catholic.

Picaresque tales of the rascals and scallywags and wily tricksters. The uncle who was both gamekeeper and poacher. Who stole a pheasant and, when the absentee English laird returned from his estate, rode past him in the man's own cart, doffed his cap and said, 'Morning, Squire,' and chatted with him, the laird's property under his seat all the while. Poor people but honest. Mostly.

Exploits of my grandfather Luke, with his soft Irish brogue and wicked sense of fun, his playfulness and his principles. A pious man who went to church every day but kept his own counsel. Who loathed Canon Ferrigan and said, 'I will argue with the Holy Pope himself in Rome if I know that I am right!' A wise, forgiving man who nevertheless could not forgive the Ross cousins for not being Catholic. Luke, who would joke about his shell-shocked nerves, and laugh at how he would start at cars backfiring, and how one time he found himself bolting down the street and halfway to Kircaldy before he realised that this was not the war. Luke, who always seemed to me like a minor player in a large cast of colourful characters but who in fact held the key to it all.

Vignettes of my mother herself and her sisters, Mary and Kate. The three high-cheekboned, haughty-nosed McCarthy girls who all had a look of Princess Margaret about them. Simple Scots lassies who married out and gained the curlicued names Sosnowski, Szubański and Magyar. The laughs they had together and how, one time after the war, when they were all married ladies, they were sitting in the kitchen with the laundry drying on the pulley over their heads when a huge pair of Uncle Bernard's jocks fell into Auntie Mary's lap. And without missing a beat, she looked down her nose and said, 'Just my luck…empty.' And they all roared and laughed.

And the quick-witted Edinburgh cousins. Molly and Betty and Nora Lamont, whippet-thin and razor-tongued.

Then her tone would darken as she spoke of the uncles who came back from the Great War with poisoned lungs and shattered minds. And her various beaus and the boys who went to World War II and never came back at all. And the boy, she can't remember his name, who was sweet on her and wanted to go out with her before he went off to join the air force because he was convinced he was going to die. And he did.

And of the hardship she would always say, 'It wasn't just us. We were not the only ones. And that wasn't the only thing in our lives.'

Romantic stories of the Polish officers they met in Dunfermline Glen and how her mother invited them back to the house because they were far from home and Catholic and she felt sorry for them. How polite they all were, how charming and well behaved. The time my young father, burning with the hot fervour of patriotism, sat on top of the piano in the parlour insisting that when his training was finished he would be parachuted back into Poland to keep fighting for his country's freedom. Poland, where all his family still were.

And how, after the war, when it became apparent that he would never be able to return to Poland, he stayed and married my mother. And all the Poles thought that he had married a Jew because my mother looked like Anne Frank. How when he proposed he confessed, 'I am very selfish.' And she didn't believe him. 'I thought he was joking!'

How her mother made her wedding dress and her father, trained during his years in the rehabilitation hospital, made her dainty shoes with his own hands. Those tiny pearl white shoes. A strange gift from the war. Like a diamond flung from the mouth of a volcano.

All these stories. Hours, weeks, months, years of talking around the kitchen table, weaving a tale, a spell.

# MY FATHER'S PEOPLE

Of my four grandparents I only ever met Meg, my mother's mother. I have no memories of my own so I can only see them refracted through the memories of others. I don't even know what to call them: unlike my Scottish granny, who was always 'Gran' or 'Granma', I never had endearments for Jadwiga and Mieczysław Szubański.

They were both born in Warsaw in 1894. Mieczysław was a policeman, I'm not sure what his rank was. I do know that Dad was in awe of his father's impeccable moral character—'I wish I was as good a man as he was'—and said Mieczysław left the police force because he was disgusted by the corruption. 'He thought the police were worse than the bloody crooks!' He was a keen sportsman and attained a level of some proficiency in Greco-Roman wrestling. He was exceptionally disciplined.

They had two sons called Zbigniew: the first was a little boy who died, I think from cerebral palsy. My father was born two years later.

Whether it bothered him to be named after a dead sibling I don't know. There was also a daughter, my aunt Danuta, four years older than Dad. My father always felt she was his father's favourite while he was his mother's beloved.

Jadwiga died in 1972. She was a canny businesswoman. Before the war she owned a few shops, general stores that sold a little bit of everything: perfumes, soaps, knick-knacks. She had a lot of Jewish friends. 'The Jews loved my mother. She was shrewd but fair, and so they respected her. She used to make her own bread. She would let the dough rise and then take it to the Jewish bakers who would bake it for her and flirt. They would say, *Mrs Szubańska*,' my father imitated the Jewish baker, wagging his finger cheekily, '*if you were not a goy…*'

Jadwiga liked weak milky tea—'English tea', the Poles call it in disgust. Not real tea like the bracing, metallic tanniny black brew Aunt Danuta dispensed from the samovar when we met. Jadwiga had trained as a nurse. She had a sweet tooth, which later led to diabetes. She was a kind woman. And she never got over the exile of my father.

My grandparents were both people of extraordinary courage who risked their lives during the war to offer Jewish people refuge in their home. Poland was the only occupied country where the penalty for hiding a Jew was death.

I once asked my cousin Magda, 'Where did Jadwiga's courage come from?'

'Breeding,' she said.

My family were proud Warszawians. Warsaw. War-(sore). In Polish it is pronounced Var-SHA-vah. Lovely. Like the rustle of petticoats in a Viennese waltz. But the English pronunciation, sadly, is more apt. Whenever I asked my father what Warsaw was like before the war he would say, with muffled pride, 'It was the Paris of the East.' Cafés, boulevards, monthly trips to the circus and the ballet. I always took this with a grain of salt. After all, so many places claim to be the Paris of somewhere. But as I listened more carefully, I started to realise that this was not the homesick pride of an exile—it was a plea for inclusion, to be freed from the shame of Otherness. And it was a metaphor of loss. Not just of the city and its people as they were, but also of what they had dreamed they might become. Paris. It means: we are not barbarians. The Polish and French Royal bloodlines are mingled and, while Chopin's body may reside in Père Lachaise Cemetery in Paris, his heart lies preserved in cognac in a crystal urn in Warsaw.

Still. If not for the photos it would be like my Polish family never existed. Happily, there are endless photographs. My father came from an affluent family that could afford a camera and thought itself worth documenting. (By contrast there are virtually no photos of my mother's poverty-stricken family.) These old photos are ghostly images of a vanished world. They tell the story of my Polish family's life before the war.

There are images of them in the city, all dandified in their expensive clothes and fashionable hats. There are photos of them on holiday at their country retreats. A hilarious one of my father and his sister Danuta dressed in white tunics, their hair coiffed with matching bangs. A picture of their mother Jadwiga 'slumming it' at a peasant farm, throwing out a bucket of slops and laughing heartily; the family skiing in the mountains at Zakopane, the famous resort in southern Poland; there are pictures of the whole lot of them horseriding, hiking, playing volleyball, larking about—often the whole family would go, aunts, uncles, cousins. One of my favourites has the entire family perched artily along the trunk of a dead tree that lists perilously, like the leaning tower of Pisa. They are all smiling, even though they are sitting on what must surely be an omen.

There is another of the family somewhere in the Polish countryside. It's summer. There is a bend in the river and a small boat sits close in to the sandy bank. On the boat are my grandmother and one of her sisters. Beside them is my aunt Danuta. She is slender and, even at this young age, you can see she will be a beauty. A tubby little boy grasps the tiller—my father. My grandfather stands behind, smiling broadly. They are all in their swimming costumes and apart from Danuta they are all fat. Especially the women. Like figures in a Botero painting. Fat, jolly women with large, drooping breasts and fleshy thighs and ill-fitting costumes. I love this picture.

I look like Jadwiga. Everyone always says that. The first time I met Ryszard Bielański he slapped his forehead and gasped as if he had seen a ghost. 'Aie! You look *just* like your babcha!' The physical resemblance on the Polish side of our family is preposterous. My brother and sister and I all look unmistakably like my dad. I look like my grandmother. My brother, as he ages, looks increasingly like my grandfather. In a photo of Dad and my grandfather standing in a cobbled street in Warsaw, Dad, maybe eight, is a Mini-Me replica of his father. There is no doubting our patrimony.

Mieczysław was bullnecked and barrel-chested, with brooding Slavic features. He looks like the kind of man you would not want to cross. Photos of him tend to be stern and unsmiling. In one he stands, arms akimbo, showing off a tattoo of the Polish eagle in the centre of his young, hairless chest. Such tattoos were rare for young men of his class. Later he was embarrassed by his youthful patriotic zeal and tried to have it removed.

My cousin insists he was a very sweet man. Dad never once spoke critically of his father but it was clear Mieczysław was an old-fashioned Eastern European patriarch. And I tend to blame him (perhaps unfairly) for the more challenging aspects of my father's nature. Tough. Disciplinarian. A hard man. Jadwiga, in contrast, was a soft woman, fond of sweets, pigeon plump with tender, intelligent eyes and a kind smile. I'm looking at a photo of her taken just before the war. She is standing on the ski slopes dressed in an ankle-length fur coat, stocks in her gloved hands, laughing gaily. She looks like she is preparing for a night at the theatre rather than a day of vigorous skiing. She was a fat, middle-aged, middle-class woman. In the Hollywood movies of the time she would have been cast as a jolly, dotty dowager.

It was a good life.

Hitler invaded on 1 September 1939. My grandparents were forty-five, the age when you feel your power start to wane and a sense of your mortality begins to creep in. My father was just fifteen. He was bedridden in his parents' spacious apartment, recovering from typhoid. The Bohemian crystal glasses rattled in the cabinet as he watched through his window while wave after wave of Luftwaffe aeroplanes darkened the sky.

Even so, reality had not sunk in yet. My father still beamed with boyish enthusiasm when he told me how at first it was fun to go up to the top of the building and watch the dog-fights between German and Polish planes. But the horror had begun. 'I was coming home with Father, we were caught in the entrance to our apartment block when the first bomb fell. We stood in the archway because we thought that was the safest place. Which wasn't true!' He laughed. The bomb exploded about a hundred metres from where they stood. A person was blown to bits—a piece of leg was flung through the air and landed near my father.

The Poles had the honour of being the first nation to experience Hitler's *Blitzkrieg*. Lightning war.

'What was it like to be invaded?' I asked my father.

'Well, there was panic. Many people, including close friends of the family, took their chances and fled, heading east. The roads out of Warsaw were absolutely stuffed with people. You've seen the films.'

I have. Grainy black-and-white images; great rivers of fleeing refugees. People like snails carrying all that they had on their backs. People like cattle pulling handcarts. German planes machine-gunning them as they fled.

The Polish government and administration left the city on 4 September. Even the leader of the Polish army got out. But my family did not leave Warsaw.

'We will wait and see what happens,' said my grandfather.

It is not that hard to understand why. Poland is famously a nation of geographical misfortunes: a broad, flat, defenceless plain, smack bang in the heart of Europe, a buffer between Germany and Russia. There are no mountains or oceans to protect it. For nearly a thousand years aggressive neighbours have invaded from every direction: the Mongol hordes, the Turks, the Teutonic knights, the Cossacks, the Tartars, the Russians, the Germans. Even the phlegmatic Swedes had a crack. Only for the few brief years between World War I and 1939 did the Poles know independence. They called Poles born in that period, as my father was, the Columbus Generation because they were exploring hitherto unknown territory—freedom. Ryszard spelled it out: 'We had tasted freedom and so we would fight to the death to keep it.'

My family stood their ground even as the Germans bombed it out from under them. The Panzer tanks arrived on the outskirts of Warsaw on 8 September 1939. 'They would just go along the street. Boom! Boom! Boom! House after house after house. Every house had a hole in the front. Every. Single. House.'

My family's apartment survived, but almost all of Warsaw's buildings were damaged or destroyed. The streets were filled with the corpses of people and horses. The Germans bombed the water supplies. Fires raged throughout the city. It was not long before people were starving.

My father was sent, along with the brother of one of their domestic girls who hailed from a small farm, out into the countryside to search for food. 'The side of the road, as far as the eye could see, was strewn with the dead bodies of men and horses. *Thousands* of them. The "famous" Polish cavalry,' he scoffed. 'Lying unburied. Rotting in the sun. You can't attack tanks with horses. Bloody fools! And the smell. Ye gods.'

Still my family stayed. It began to look like my grandfather had made a seriously bad decision. Then the unthinkable happened: Stalin broke his pact with the Allies and invaded from the east. All the Poles who had fled in that direction were trapped. Hundreds of thousands died or were sent to Siberia.

'Many people perished. Including some of our friends.'

There was no right decision. This was total war and no place was safe. My family stayed and fought for Poland, not knowing how long this hell might last.

And so the occupation began, one of the most brutal in Europe. Resistance increased. And my father became involved.

Unofficially at first. At the age of about fifteen he formed his own 'private army', as he used to describe it. A vagrant bunch of childhood friends roaming around doing whatever damage they could, especially killing Germans. Then, in 1943, he was recruited by his brother-in-law Andrzej to become a non-commissioned officer of the Polish execution squad, Unit 993/W Revenge Company (*Kompania Zemsta*). He was nineteen years old.

Unit 993/W was a top secret, officially mandated counterintelligence unit, directly answerable to the leader of the Polish Underground Army in Warsaw, General Bór-Komorowski. The unit was initially known by the acronym ZOM—*Zakład Oczyszczania Miasta* or City Cleaning Works. Its task was to protect the HQ of the Polish underground and assassinate agents of the Gestapo and Polish traitors. No Polish citizen, no matter their rank or place in society, was exempt from the ruthless vengeance of *Kompania Zemsta*. Including, as my father told me frankly, friends. The head of my father's unit was one of the men responsible for the 'liquidation' in 1941 of the famous actor and Gestapo agent Igo Sym, who had starred opposite Marlene Dietrich.

It sounds like a movie. It wasn't. In a city where everyone had something to be afraid of, those who aided the Nazis lived in fear of people like my father. His unit comprised both men and women. I grew up hearing some of their names—Leszek Kowalewski, Danka Hibner, Zofia Rudecka, Hanna, Stefan, Ryszard, Izabella. And of course Andrzej Zawadzki, my uncle. My father's tone was always full of affection and admiration for their comradeship and courage. Eventually there were history books with pictures of them all and I could put faces to the names. Pretty young women. Handsome young men.

They targeted collaborators who gave the names of resistance members to the Gestapo. Unit 993/W also assassinated Poles who told the Gestapo where Jews were hiding. And so the Nazi collaborators were sentenced to death by the Polish underground courts. Despite the chaos of war, due legal process was followed. The traitor would be tried in absentia in a court of law and the sentence would be carried out by my father's unit. Unit 993/W would conduct surveillance on the target. Then, when the time was right, they would run in, read them the list of crimes of which they had been found guilty, and shoot them.

The members of Unit 993/W were not snipers. In a city crawling with Gestapo they shot at close range. Close enough to see, touch, smell. My father participated in twelve such *aktions* over a period of about eighteen months.

During this time my family's apartment became a halfway house for Jews in hiding. They hid a small Jewish boy for several months. But it was not easy. From an early age I heard tales of the little Jewish boy and how they couldn't keep him quiet and how he would have tantrums and sing in Yiddish. Perhaps because of this my father had no patience for childish behaviour, and when we were unruly it would often lead by association to the little Jewish boy. 'Aie, aie, aie, my God! And that little Jewish kid used to sing! In Yiddish! We couldn't keep him quiet.'

Finally in 1944 the Poles made their last bid for freedom. The Warsaw Uprising began on 1 August 1944—my father's twentieth birthday—and the Poles never stood a chance. Of 40,000 combatants only 2500 were armed. The battle for Warsaw lasted sixty-three days. The most bitter fighting was in the *Stare Miasto*, the Old Town. That was where my father was stationed. The elegant buildings of the capital were now nothing but barricades and bomb shelters. The Soviets, who had encouraged the Poles to rise up, arrived in Warsaw but rather than joining the fight they stood on the banks of the Vistula River and watched as the Germans annihilated the city and its people with tanks and flamethrowers. An estimated 200,000 lives were lost. Polish civilians, including hospital staff and patients, were raped, tortured, burnt. Women were used as human shields in front of tanks. My father fought on until it was clear that all was lost then, along with much of the rest of the resistance, he escaped through a sewer.

The Poles' defiance enraged Hitler. He ordered that Warsaw be razed as an example to all those who would defy him. Like so many of their countrymen my family lost everything. Their home, their city, their country, their dreams of freedom. Even their dog. As my grandparents and my heavily pregnant aunt Danuta were being herded out of Warsaw an SS officer took a shine to the family pet, a little Pomeranian, and wrenched it away. Moments later, as they were shoved onto a cattle truck, they watched in disbelief as the officer drove past in his open-top sedan. There, sitting in pride of place in the passenger seat, was their little dog, being hand-fed chocolate by the Nazi.

Eventually my grandparents were resettled in Szczecin in the country's north-west, nearly six hundred kilometres from their beloved Warsaw.

My father, along with the other combatants, was caught and cattle-trucked to a POW camp. He was part of the notorious Lamsdorf Death March from which he escaped, only to be caught again and sent to two more POW camps. In 1945 he was liberated by the advancing Russians, made his way to Scotland and began training to be parachuted back into Poland when the war ended. He never saw his parents again.

I never once saw my father cry or display any emotion at all about what he had lost. Through sheer force of will all sentiment was frozen solid. But as the years wore on and his own death loomed, he would often say, in a kind of uncomprehending way, 'I never grieved for my parents. Maybe I'm weird but I never grieved for my parents.'

It was as though he could see his own lack of emotion and was bewildered by it. As though his family were woolly mammoths, caught unawares by a sudden change of events, trapped in the glacier of his unfelt feelings. My father idolised his family. He always spoke lovingly of them, especially his mother. But as death crept closer cracks began to form, the ice began to thaw. Unresolved and unexamined, feelings began to erupt. It was horrible to see.

'My father never told me he loved me.'

A single, wrenching sob burst out. He was in his eighties and about to die, but he was a little boy, too, unsure if his father really loved him.

We did our best to comfort him. My mother, who had for years been woken in the night by the screams of her own war-torn father, tried to stop the wounds from opening.

'Peter, those were different times, people didn't tell one another that kind of thing back then. Nobody did.'

They *were* different times. So different they are hard to conjure. My father's boyhood was smashed apart by the war. The idyllic Poland of his childhood ceased to exist. It was now a country synonymous with Nazi death camps. Auschwitz. Treblinka. Nearly one in five Polish citizens slaughtered. Almost the entire Jewish population of over three million had been annihilated, including my father's beloved childhood friend, Wacek Goldfarb.

What is it like to be a boy at a time when your 'home' *is* the war, where the enemy is among you, when there is no relief, no dream of peace or safety?

'You always have a choice,' my father used to say. Why did some people collaborate while others didn't? Was it weakness? Greed? Fear? Why did my grandparents risk their lives and those of their children to try to save the lives of Jewish strangers? Why did my father choose to become an instrument of revenge?

And what would I do?

Growing up, as I learned more about what my father and his family had done, this question haunted me. Was I like them? Was I like him?

My mother wants me to stop talking about my father. 'Stop calling him an assassin.'

But I remind her how I would ask, 'What did you do in the war?' And he would laugh, self-mockingly. 'I was an assassin.'

# I AM BORN

I was born in Liverpool, England, on 12 April 1961, sixteen years after the war ended and 'the same day that Yuri Gagarin went up into space'. In family parlance that phrase became synonymous with my birth so that, in my psyche, my entrance into the world and Yuri's exit from it are fused as one event. Yuri was the first human being to see our planet from the outside, a dazzlingly beautiful blue bauble hanging in the black infinity of space. Like a Christmas decoration. And somewhere on that planet was me.

I was born starving. My mother suffered terribly from toxaemia during pregnancy. This meant that in utero I was being poisoned and there was not sufficient nutrition passing through the placenta. So as my brain and nervous system were forming they were receiving information that there was not enough food for me. I was born two weeks early, weighing a measly 2.5 kilos, and I suspect my body has been trying to make up for it ever since. But I was lucky. At least I lived.

I am the youngest of three children but whenever I say this, my mother reminds me that actually I am the youngest of four. The toxaemia killed my older brother John while he was still inside my mother and he was stillborn. It was brutal and traumatic. My mother was left for hours in blood-soaked sheets. That night, unable to bear it, my father escaped to the pictures.

My father's first attempt to create new life had resulted in death. At the age of twenty-five he had lost family, country—everything—and now there he was with his first-born lying dead in a tiny white casket on his knees.

'When I saw that little casket,' he told me years later, 'bloody hell, Maggie. Bloody hell. And I had to carry it on my knees in the back of the car to the church. Jesus.' My father possessed an indomitable optimism but even he must have been shaken by this blow. My mother never forgot John but she did not dwell on the sadness. Typical of her generation, my mother does not individualise her grief. 'We weren't the only ones. You just had to get on with it.' Still, she will always say, 'You are the youngest of four.'

Soon after, my sister and brother arrived in quick succession two years apart; then I arrived eight years later. My mother insists I was not a mistake. 'You were a joy!'

I idolised Barb and Chris. They were as remote and magical as the gods on Mount Olympus. They possessed rare skills and could be entrusted with doing the dishes. I was always too young and my motor skills were too gross to be fully included. I would be given token jobs, or none, until gradually my practicality atrophied.

Being so much younger meant I was neither fish nor fowl nor good red herring, as my mother would say. I never had to share my toys, but I also rarely had new ones. I didn't resent the hand-me-downs. Quite the contrary. They were like a badge of belonging for a child uncertain of her place in the scheme of things. I was lonely. As my sister and brother grew older the years between us stretched further apart. I used to plead with my parents to give me a little brother or sister. I became obsessed with dolls that looked like babies.

But the moment had passed. 'Och, *wheesht* and be away with you,' my mother would laugh as she dragged hard on her Piccadilly cork-tipped cigarette. In the space that a sibling might have occupied, my imagination grew. I always had hobbies and projects and plans. Fantasy became my friend.

My parents were thirty-six when they had me, comparatively old for those days. It may account for their rather laissez-faire attitude to parenting. Like a self-saucing pudding, I was pretty much put on set-and-forget. And I was a cheery child. 'Never any problem,' Mum says. Bright, perky, sociable. A quick study. But there was something else that my mother detected in me. 'This one's for the world,' she said. She always said she knew I would be famous.

I ask her why.

'No idea. I just felt it.' She didn't do a single thing to make it happen. She just saw it coming. When I pleaded to be on *Brian and the Juniors* she stomped on my ambition. 'No, that's only for special children.' Her Catholic ambivalence about anything that makes you stand out is something I share. That said, I was a born show-off. At the age of six I sat in front of the television and splayed my ponytail across the screen to get the family's attention. I did a striptease tossing my singlet around the room like Gypsy Rose Lee. I devised plays and press-ganged the neighbourhood kids into performing them.

But along with the cheeriness there was also a discordant strain of anxiety. 'Och! Don't be so bloody touchy!' My mother was always saying I was jumpy. Sounds upset me. I couldn't stand to have anything on my skin that wasn't pure cotton. My comforter was an old cotton t-shirt, always freshly washed, which I called my 'keen' because I couldn't pronounce 'clean'. I would fall into dark moods. I cannot remember a time when I was not fretting over unnamed fears. I had a fierce perfectionist streak and things had to be just so. I devised strange little counting rituals, tallying rapidly on my fingers every syllable as someone spoke, and I would stop only when I had reached a multiple of four. If my hands were busy I would count with my teeth. I would clear my throat repeatedly; until I had heard that sound I could never be certain that I had a voice. I would obsessively fold and refold pieces of paper, napkins, hankies. I would fastidiously tear lolly wrappers into neat piles or tight spirals. I still do.

The sixties was an era of surfaces: laminates, formicas, veneers, lacquers. Shiny finishes that looked exactly like what they were not. Appearances were everything. Of *course* it was all about surfaces. Bandaids plastered over the Holocaust and Hiroshima. We eschewed Mother Nature's crappy homegrown efforts, certain we could do a much better job ourselves. And so there were plastics, polymers and man-made fabrics. It was an age of fakery decorated with astroturf and aluminium Christmas trees.

My father was a true man of the sixties, a modern man. He was a textile technologist and he worked first in man-made textiles and later in fabric finishes. Nylon, rayon, polyester. 'Intelligent fibres' that have an IQ higher than a two-year-old and are made of substances that will outlast humanity.

And that is what brought my family to Australia. Nylon, invented by Wallace Carothers in 1935. Stockings and knickers. My father was flown out by ICI as part of a team to introduce quality control, of which there apparently was none in this country before their arrival. He ran the laboratory at Fibremakers and became a member of the Standards Association, the independent body responsible for maintaining a universal standard of quality in all areas of manufacturing.

He was the perfect man for the job since his own level of personal fastidiousness hovered just this side of OCD. Your plate would be whisked away, washed, dried and back in the cupboard before you had actually finished eating. If you looked into his wardrobe you would find all of his shirts colour-coded and arranged neatly from dark to light, subdivided into long and short sleeves. Sometimes the apple falls very far from the tree. I am the complete opposite, a subcontinent of chaotic mess. I have no idea how he tolerated me, but he did. Cleaning up other people's mess was his thing.

After the war my father wanted to become an Englishman. With no roots to bind him, he was a Displaced Person, one of the great mass of homeless, stateless refugees that drifted across the globe.

He did not want to go back to Poland, he wanted to stay in the UK. He loved British people. During the war, when he had to pick his code name for his counterintelligence unit, he chose Clive, after Clive of India. He learned English at school and the POW camps made him fluent, but with an American accent. When the Russians liberated Luckenwalde camp it was a couple of American pilots who got him across to the American lines, thereby saving his life. Had he gone with the Russians he believed he would have been killed. He said, 'The Russians were bloody panicking.' And drew his finger across his throat. 'They had seen too much freedom.'

From there he made his way to the UK. He was thrilled. The fact was, my father could not shed his Polishness fast enough: 'I went to Britain to become British, not to become some sort of British–Pole, or Polish–Brit. I didn't really have much to do with the Polish community.' His reinvention had begun.

Luckily for him he was smart. After the war he was accepted into the Polish School of Medicine at Edinburgh University. A plaque explains that the school was established by the Scots as a gesture of solidarity 'in the dark days of 1941 when Polish universities were destroyed and Polish professors died in concentration camps'. For about three years he studied medicine at Edinburgh University.

Exiled Polish fighter pilots had been decisive in the defence of the UK during the Battle of Britain. But the debt of gratitude soon watered down into mild appreciation followed ultimately by impatience. Now the Poles were competing for jobs and it was time for them to go home. In 1949 the Polish School of Medicine had its funding cut off and the school was closed. Three years into his degree, my father found himself standing in the busted-up ruins of the only thing he had left—his cherished dream of being a doctor. He was heartbroken. But not bitter. One of the remarkable things about my father was that he had no bitterness in him.

He picked himself up and started again. He went to Bradford and studied textile chemistry. There are pictures of him in class, all five foot four of him, monstered by a great towering loom, diligently studying his profession. I have his notebooks from that time and they are full of mathematical formulas and diagrams of chemical molecules. He was a meticulous student who learned quickly. The pages are orderly and neat. He was also required to produce sketches of women's fashion. These were executed, by contrast, in a blur of messy edges and squiggles. They show a good deal of artistic flair.

He took a job as a textile technologist in Dewsbury and then Plymouth. When, in 1960, my father moved again for work, it was to another great maritime city—and so I was born in Liverpool. We lived in Great Crosby. Other Liverpudlians have said to me, 'Thah's not Liverpewl! Thah's dead posh thur!'

Our house was nothing fancy but at least we owned it. It was a compact, prewar, two-storey, stuccoed number pretty much like every other house in the area—a benign neighbourhood where I was free to venture about on my tricycle. I befriended the old man across the street. He was in an old wicker wheelchair and had a large greenhouse.

He used to give me sweet cherry tomatoes as a treat, holding them out in the palm of his fingerless gloves.

My mother had already taught me to read and write. I remember the tiny blackboard on an easel that she set up in the dining room so I could write while she baked in the kitchen. And the thrill of realising that the clumsy squiggles I could make on the board corresponded to thoughts and words.

We lived a typically British life with big bonfires and fireworks on Guy Fawkes Day, chestnuts in December and games of tennis late into the lingering twilight of the northern summer. My days were spent playing pirates or conkers with the Dinwoodie boys next door, exploring anything that could be explored. One day Chris and Barb and I found something strange in the attic, with huge eyes and a long, rubbery snout. My brother worked out what it was—a gasmask left over from the war.

My fondest memories from that time are of my grandmother. I adored Gran and she adored me. We were crazy about one another. To this day, whenever I see a head of snowy white hair my heartstrings tighten a little. She was the essence of grandmotherliness: wire-rimmed glasses, soft crepey skin, ample mono-bosom and long hair which she would plait and then wind around and around her head in a bun. She always wore three cardigans at once, and on windy washing days her bloomers ballooned on the line like the sails on a fat Whitby collier.

Before she came to live with us we would go every summer to stay with her in Dunfermline. I remember the smell of polish on her old wooden floorboards, the cheeriness of quilts, the trickiness of stairs. The car winding round the shoulders of strong hills under heavy skies. Bursts of bright yellow sun. A roadside wee stop next to fields of purple heather.

When she moved down to us in Liverpool she and I shared a room and she was my best friend. Gran was known to have 'the healing hands', soft and cool but thrumming with life. She was an excellent baker and those cool hands were the perfect temperature for making tricky Scottish shortbreads, gingerbreads and apple pies. In my mind she is always coated with a faint dusting of flour. When you were sick she would lay her hands on your forehead. Headaches and tummy aches vanished under their soothing touch. My mum inherited the baking and the soothing and the healing hands.

But mothers are not the same as grandmothers. Gran was my playmate, my best friend and my co-conspirator. One time when I was about three I wet my pants. As she helped me out of my soaking knickers I asked nervously, 'Do we have to tell Mummy?'

'Och, hen, no no no. No need to tell yer mother. This is oor wee secret.' She was pure love with the thorn of parental anxiety removed.

And she was fun. Liverpool proper was just a bus ride away and once a week Gran would take me into town. The bus drivers would play and joke with us. One of them chucked me under the chin: 'Do you want to be my girlfriend?' We always sat up top in the front seat, sightseeing through the big glass goldfish-bowl window that was perpetually spittled with Liverpudlian drizzle.

To my little eyes the city of Liverpool was the most exciting place in the world. It was pure showbiz. The wet streets caught and refracted the glow of the neon signs. The low cloud, which could have made everything dismal, turned it into a film set, containing and intensifying the light. It was Petula Clark's 'Downtown'.

I had no inkling that everything was about to change. But my mother may have. Years before, she had been to see a gypsy fortune-teller for a laugh. The gypsy woman had told her that she would move far away. That she would live on top of a hill next door to a red-headed man. And then she intimated that something bad would happen to my father. My mother scoffed. Of course she did. But years later she would have cause to remember the words of that old gypsy woman.

As part of the postwar 'populate or perish' imperative, the Australian government had begun a vigorous sales campaign to entice people to leave the old world and come to the new one Down Under. We kept a poster from this campaign on our dining-room wall in Australia for years. A cartoon image of a bronzed surfer standing on a golden beach with his long board, waving. A big speech bubble trumpeting, *Come to Sunny Australia!*

But my first encounter with beach culture was actually in Britain. North of Liverpool there is a patch of coast every bit as wild and beautiful and treacherous as Heathcliff himself. Our favourite was Formby Beach. The approach to it was through a rambling forest of pines. As you crested the dune your first glimpse of the Irish Sea was through a fringe of Christmas trees. Every year we would clamber into the Wolseley and go to Formby to find our Christmas tree. Dad would tie it to the roof and we would take it home and decorate its spindly needles with tiny wax candles and miniature musical instruments made from chocolate wrapped in gold or silver paper. Cellos and violins and little-drummer-boy drums. The fire would be lit and the smell of peaty smoke and pine filled the room. On the tiny record player we would play *Peer Gynt* and *The Nutcracker Suite* and I would watch adoringly as my sister and her ballet friends jetéd around the tree, while clean, white snow banked up outside the window. In the morning all the messiness of life would be covered with a blanket of white neatness. That was Christmas. After we came to Australia those rituals gradually shrivelled in the heat. The pine tree was replaced with an aluminium one.

Anyway, the Australian posters worked. Hundreds of thousands of Brits responded, and we were among them. But we were not ten-pound Poms, the British migrants who came over in droves on an assisted passage. We did not come over on a boat. We never stayed in any of the notorious migrant hostels. We came on a plane, and we had a company house. And we had no other family with us.

So what made us leave? There was no glaringly obvious need for us to come to Australia and in fact I always believed that we came for a trial period of two years. (My mother informs me no, we always intended to stay. For the term of our natural lives.)

And why Australia? My father gave one simple reason: the weather. He was a dedicated Anglophile who came from the frigid east, but still he *hated* the way Britain does cold. It is a cold that, as my mother says, 'creeps deep into the very marrow of your bones'. The Scots have a fabulous word for it—'dreech'. The *ch* is pronounced like you are clearing phlegm from your throat which, if you lived in Scotland, you probably would be.

Poland can get crazy cold. But it is a dry, invigorating cold. In 1996 I was in Warsaw on a press junket and the temperature was a chilly minus eight degrees Celsius. I foolishly went for a walk hatless and came back with a skull-cracking brain-freeze headache. 'Imagine,' I thought, 'fighting for your life against the Nazis in this weather.'

'That's nothing!' my father said over the phone from Australia. 'The first winter of the war was one of the worst for years. Minus thirty-two. I used to wrap little pieces of shredded newspaper around my toes and fingers. They all used to laugh at me but I was the only one who didn't get frostbite.'

The other possible candidates were the United States, Canada and South Africa. Canada was too cold, obviously. Mum didn't want to go to America. And South Africa? I once asked my father about this.

'There was a chappy, worked at Littlewoods, and he had been in South Africa in the fifties. And he told me not to go to South Africa.

He said, "Mate, with a history like yours you will end up fighting for the wrong side!"'

I was horrified.

'What do you mean? Fighting for the Afrikaners?'

'Don't be stupid. The blacks.'

'I'm confused. Aren't the blacks the right side?'

'Not to this chappy. He didn't particularly like blacks. He left because he couldn't stomach it. He didn't like blacks but he still couldn't stomach it.'

'And why did he say that to you?'

'Because he knew what I did during the war with the Jews. He thought I wouldn't be able to help myself. I would end up fighting for the underdog.'

'And would you?'

'Ha! Probably.'

Something in my father needed to get as far away from blood-stained Europe as possible. Once here he refused to look back.

There was no precedent for this. My father's family were stayers. As far as we know we have been in Poland for centuries. Szubański possibly comes from the Polish word *szuba,* the name of a fur-lined coat, which has led to speculation that our ancestors were furriers. In any event my father was the first of his family to leave for a long time. And once he got to Australia he never wanted to go anywhere again. Not even for a holiday.

The men in my mother's family are the migratory birds. Made exiles by war and intrigue and poverty, they have wandered the globe while the women have, more or less, been the ever-fixéd marks. And so it was that when we left, my Gran stayed behind. I am frantically searching my stupid head for a memory of saying goodbye to her but I can't find it. Which is breaking my heart. She meant so much to me, it violates all sense of rightness not to be able to remember. I can recall so many useless things—the plots of films, the star signs of acquaintances, the lyrics of pop songs. But this moment of losing someone I loved is completely gone.

In December 1965 we packed up all that was us, went to Liverpool station and got on the train for London. My memories are of fog at Liverpool station—of course—and delicious chops at a Chinese restaurant in Wales. En route we stayed at the very posh Harrogate Hotel, where your toast arrived in an elegant silver toast rack and the cool yellow butter pats curled in on themselves like seashells. I developed a fascination for the antique lifts; I loved their ornate wrought-iron doors. I nearly wore them out riding up and down and that was how I met old Mrs Wilson.

Mrs Wilson was a wealthy, rather eccentric elderly woman who lived permanently in the hotel. Her son had been to Australia and she felt it her duty to bestow upon my mother the benefit of his experience. She looked at me full of tender concern and said, 'Whatever you do, *don't* let your children mix with the natives. And for heaven's sake, *don't* let them pick up one of those *dread*ful Australian accents!'

When we were in London about to fly away forever my father received news from Poland that his father had died. Although I was not quite five I understood that something terrible had happened. There were frantic conversations. He couldn't go back to Poland. At best they would never let him out again. And so his mother would have to bury his father without him.

My father and his father had fallen out before he left Poland. I never found out why. The last time they saw one another was after the uprising had failed and my father was being taken off to a POW camp. And now he was being wrenched away again. We had a plane to catch, a new life to begin. There was no time to grieve.

But in another sense time did stand still. My father had a watch Mieczysław had given him, the only memento he had of his father.

And that watch stopped at ten to two: the exact time my grandfather died. We kept moving but the watch stopped permanently: on its face the moment of my grandfather's passing marked forever.

In the 1960s air travel was glamorous. We flew Boeing and Pan Am and the aeroplanes had bars. Air hostesses with trim figures and make-up as thick as the earth's crust brought me endless glasses of Coca-Cola. I was made a member of the Pan Am Club and given a 'set of wings' badge and a pretendy captain's cap. I loved that cap. I wore it for the entire flight. The excitement of flying has never left me.

Our route took us from London to New York. Late one night Chris and Barb and I heard a strange sound outside the door of our hotel room. Someone was trying to open the door. We screamed out and my mother bolted awake and tried to rouse my father. He refused to go and see what was wrong. So with her heart pounding in her chest Mum opened the door to discover a man holding a gun with a silencer. He looked at her and left.

'It was so strange,' she has since said. 'I don't know why your father wouldn't do anything. I mean, he was not a coward.' It was as though his ability to respond to the warning signs of danger had worn out.

Later we strolled through the man-made canyons of Manhattan, gazing at the department store windows. Then, back on board Pan Am, we traversed the continent, flying over the actual Grand Canyon. From a distance of thirty thousand feet all traces of human activity were erased, leaving nothing but the wonder and majesty of nature. Sprawling beneath us was the American frontier, the gateway to new beginnings. We stopped over in Honolulu and stayed at a groovy circular hotel opposite Waikiki Beach. There is a photo of me paddling in the water. This was the first time I had ever swum in the Pacific. I didn't like it. The sandy seabed was covered in spiky things that prickled.

On 23 December 1965 we arrived in Australia. We had flown from a white Christmas smack bang into the blast furnace of an

Aussie summer. My father had dragged us halfway around the globe seeking the life-giving rays of the sun, and boy did we get 'em. When the plane landed at Essendon Airport, the doors opened and 105 degrees Fahrenheit of dry, choking heat roared up off the melting tarmac and into the cabin like a fireball, sucking the air out of our lungs. It was…incomprehensible. My five-year-old self did not have any way of understanding what was happening. I just knew that it was unbearable.

Harry Vincent was at the airport to welcome us. He was my father's work colleague and he had made the same trip from the UK only a short while prior. As we climbed into the back of Harry's EH Holden station wagon, our soft English fingers recoiled from the burning doorhandles.

'Better get used to that,' said Harry.

And so began our first expedition on this island continent: twenty-five roasting kilometres inland to our motel in Ringwood. My legs were soon stuck, quite painfully, to the vinyl seat. I didn't know what to do with myself, how to get relief. Another thing perplexed me, something very weird about Harry. Something I had never, in my whole little life, seen before. I peered over the bench seat for a closer look. 'What *is* that?' I piped up, pointing to Harry's back.

'Shhh!' my mother scolded, yanking my arm.

The whole back of Harry Vincent's short-sleeved three-tone shirt was soaking with sweat. Absolutely saturated. I gasped in awe and horror.

Playing in the heat was a whole new adventure. We kids spent the entire day in the motel pool, the heat already making us Australian. We would stay in the water until we were almost hypothermic and then lie shivering on the hot concrete edge.

When we were finally installed in our weatherboard company home in Bayswater—five kilometres further inland—we were troubled by a strange, non-directional, high-pitched screeching. It sounded electrical in nature and vaguely ominous. While my father and brother checked the fuse box I was sent next door to ask the neighbours. The door opened and a flat, faded little girl stared at me blankly through the flywire screen. She thought I was an idiot. I dutifully delivered her reply to my parents in the same nasal drawl it had been conveyed to me. 'Cicadas.'

For my father Australia was love at first sight. The moment we landed he knew he had done the right thing. The blast-furnace heat invigorated him. Only mad dogs and my father would go out in the midday Australian sun. He wouldn't just go out in it…he would *mow the lawn in it*. We had a big, bumpy, untamed backyard and when the mercury hit 103 degrees Fahrenheit he'd be out there dragging the lawnmower across every inch of it. Wearing Bombay bloomers and a terry-towelling hat, singing Polish songs over the din of the mower.

My mother has a different sense-impression of her arrival.

'Och, the smell,' she says, 'that beautiful smell of all the eucalypts. You saw it first, as the plane came into land, a great perfumed cloud of it hanging over the whole country. As soon as you got off the plane you could smell it. Gorgeous! I knew then I was going to love it here.'

The truth is she didn't immediately love it. None of us did, except Dad.

I felt apprehensive. As we drove along the highway the gumtrees that populated the un-kerbed median strip did not look like the mighty elms and oaks of England. They looked like beggars, their bark hanging from their limbs like tattered rags. They held no promise of adventure. Robin Hood and his Merry Men could never have camouflaged their green hats and tights in dull grey leaves like these. Like the early settlers, I found my five-year-old eyes straining to transform the Aussie bush into a familiar form. It refused to comply with my chocolate-box vision, remaining stubbornly scrappy and scabby. I had no myths or legends with which to populate this landscape. Sounds, sights, smells: everything was different. My shocked senses groped through the cognitive fog, straining to find patterns, fragments they could piece together. Over the months and years, a bank of sensory experiences accumulated. Repetition created a comforting palimpsest of familiarity and a harsh beauty revealed itself. A new life began to emerge.

But the chance of a new life does not come for free and although it was a few years before life presented its invoice, the price was high. One day I found my mother in her bedroom, crying.

'Grandma died,' she sobbed.

I had not seen my mother cry before, not like that. I wasn't sure how to respond. Perplexed and frightened, I smirked. 'You're crying!'

'Well, what do you expect?' she snapped. 'My mother just died!'

So I ran away. I ran to the bottom of the garden, to the bit of land where the fence ended and no one knew if it was ours or the neighbour's or the council's. And in that jurisdictional no-man's-land my confused feelings overwhelmed me and I began to sob too.

Tommy Taylor appeared. I didn't like Tommy. He was mean and he scared me. He put clothes pegs on my cat's paws and laughed about it.

'Why are you crying?'

'My grandma died.'

'Oh.'

Thankfully he had no interest and he left. So there I was, on a suburban nature strip at the bottom of the world, sobbing for my Gran. Spinning untethered through the vacuum of space. Like Yuri.

*

Mum and I are sitting in the Jason recliners in the TV room, she in hers, me in what used to be Dad's. We are talking about Dad and death and if there is an afterlife. 'Who knows?' she says. 'But when my mother was dying your uncle Dominic said to her, "Ma, when you go give us a sign from the other side." She loved birds. So she said, "Birds. I will send birds." There were two swallows that lived in the roof outside your grandmother's window. And the day she died they flew away and never came back.'

# MEDICINE MEN

By 1966 we had been in Australia for a year and the Szubański's were well on the way to becoming Aussies. Still, culturally we were British. Even though we spoke the language, all our references, all of our knowledge of custom and practice, was British or European. We knew nothing of local lore or wisdom or parochial efficiencies. We had no connections. We didn't know the names of streets, towns, birds, trees, famous people. We knew nothing of weather patterns and warning signs. Of the dangers—bushfires, floods, heatstroke, poison berries and sharks. Or sensible precautions—shaking out your shoes in case of spiders; making loud noise in long grass in case of snakes; lifting the toilet seat to check for redbacks. The myriad survival tips that get passed down passed us by. Everything was jarringly and excitingly new.

It took us years to learn how to holiday—that on this island-continent travel is measured not in distance but in hours. That you can travel for three thousand kilometres without seeing the sea or the border of another country. That Sunday drives were potentially life-threatening expeditions on which a carelessly tossed cigarette butt could unleash the fires of Gehenna. My parents tried to grapple with this new reality. My father would get ideas into his head. Ideas like 'beating the heat' and 'feathering the brakes'. Which is how we came to be yanked from our beds at two in the morning and bundled into the pre-packed Holden. 'Come on. We need to get on the road. We need to beat the heat.' We were terrified of the heat. My sister and brother and I would try to recover our lost sleep in the back seat as Dad herky-jerked the car to a stop at every set of lights, pumping the pedal in the belief that this would prolong the life of the brake pads.

We holidayed as if we were still in England. We drove for eight tedious hours along the utterly featureless Calder Highway to Mildura. We took a ride on a paddleboat and the captain let me steer, which was great fun. But after that we couldn't think of anything else to do so we drove straight back home again. Another time we went for a long and windy Sunday drive around the Dandenong Ranges, stopping constantly for my carsick friend Izabella to vomit. We got all the way round and it looked like Izabella's ordeal might finally be over when Dad took a wrong turn and we did the whole circuit again.

'Well,' Dad tried to put a positive spin on things, 'at least you have seen the Dandenongs.'

'Yes,' Izabella groaned. 'Twice.'

There was the time Mum and Dad and I drove to Lakes Entrance and they decided to pick up a hitchhiker—a young man who claimed to be a soldier on his way back to barracks in Puckapunyal—only to regret the decision moments later. Mum was adamant. 'She cannot sit in the back with him!' she whispered furiously when we stopped for petrol. So I was made to sit on the console between the front bucket seats for three uncomfortable hours. Clueless.

But there was one British road-trip tradition that still worked. We sang. My father had a fine Volga-boatmen kind of baritone, my mother a rich and pleasant alto. My brother and sister and I would sing harmonies. Every time we were all in the car together there would be a joyous cacophony of voices. It wasn't some kind of regimented Von Trapp Family awfulness—it was spontaneous, riotous fun. We all still do it. We did it just yesterday on the way to the Chinese restaurant for my niece's birthday.

As part of his contract, the firm my father worked for had given us a house, an old plain weatherboard in Bayswater, about thirty kilometres east of the city. But Dad wanted something new, so we bought a block of land in North Croydon, about half an hour away on the same thirty-kilometre radius, and began to build a brick-veneer house on it. Our house was next door to the Vincents', Harry with his gingery hair and Maureen with her glamorous, Ann-Margaret shade of red. I remember the excitement of visiting the block, teetering on top of a steep hill. Of seeing our new home emerge from nothing. All around, the landscape was bristling with the skeletons of such new homes. One of our favourite pastimes was to use the raw planks as a jungle gym.

Croydon was an outrider suburb, the wild east. All bush, farmlands and orchards. It had been settled in about 1840. Before that, it would have been forested with eucalypts. The early pioneers had scraped as much of it clean as they could. Long before we arrived teams of bullocks dragged heavy chains across the land, clearing away the dense bush. And of course it wasn't just the bush they got rid of. By the time we got there the original inhabitants, the Wurundjeri people, were long gone. All that remained now were place names that hinted at their existence—Wonga Park, Mooroolbark, Maroondah, Yarra River. In fact they were so spectacularly absent that I never even saw an Indigenous person until I was about nine. I went to a birthday party and the family had a little adopted girl, who I now realise must have been one of the Stolen Generation. I felt awkward around her, not knowing what to say or do. It was many more years before I even met another Aboriginal person. At school I never learned a single thing about Indigenous history. I was never told of the brave and gallant Simon Wonga, after whom Wonga Park was named. Or his cousin William Barak, one of the first Aboriginal artists and a great statesman of the Kulin nation, called King of the Yarra. Barak was born just down the road from our school at Brushy Creek. It was all within a stone's throw, and we were taught none of it.

Whenever we watched cowboy and Indian films, my father would shake his head and mutter, 'Poor bloody Indians.' I was too little to understand. He knew what it felt like to be an Indian. The cruel irony was that here he was, on Aboriginal land—in a sense, an Indian dispossessing another Indian.

Not everything was new. There were pockets of oldness. The Flynns had lived on our street the longest and, unlike the clinky brick-veneer houses we all lived in, their old weatherboard house had an outside dunny—the nightsoil man still came to empty their loo. The house was a haven for redbacks and big fat huntsman spiders. One day Mrs Flynn found a two-metre brown snake coiled up in a kitchen cupboard. Mr Flynn chopped it in half with a shovel, sending the head and tail slithering off in opposite directions.

Their house would have witnessed an awful lot in its day. Ours was brand new and had seen nothing. It was a modest little place with three small bedrooms and thin walls that gave little privacy. The lounge room was separated off with the mandatory frosted-glass sliding doors and the whole place was carpeted throughout with a bilious blue nylon job-lot Dad got cheap from work. The outside was decorated with what looked like quirky, misshapen statuettes but were in fact hardened piles of dross from the extrusion process at the lab. My parents thought this was an ingenious repurposing. Every stick of furniture was new except for the beds, so it was like living in a model home. I felt very groovy.

The land around Croydon had little softness in it. Beneath the grey sagging gum trees the ground was hardscrabble, the grass sharp as burnt matchsticks. Even so, on Saturday mornings the dawn chorus of lawnmowers would start. The low, rumbling hum would be punctuated with the sound of blades crunching on granite and the zing of blinding stone chips flying through the air. A cloud of two-stroke fumes hung over the houses, wafted down the chimneys and into the kitchen and finally settled on your Weet-Bix.

In the distance the rolling hills were rarely green. Mostly they were sundried beyond brown or even yellow. Dried to white or burned black. Far away, on the other side of the highway, long-dead gum trees stood waist deep in the bony grass, their arms outstretched, their twiggy fingers splayed.

But across the valley, on the rise of the opposite hill, was a field of emerald green. Our house was at the top of the hill and our veranda was built high up on top of the garage, like a lookout. I would sit cross-legged on the hard concrete, picking at the bubbles of paint in the corners of the white iron safety railings while I gazed out through the bars and across the valley and dreamed of lying in that lush, gentle grass. The green, green grass of home.

One day when I was about eight the Pommie kids next door and I decided to walk to that field. I got up early and packed my schoolbag with a plastic bottle of frozen orange cordial and a leftover sandwich from my lunch box. We assembled on the nature strip to determine our route and then set off down the steep hill full of intrepid confidence. But once we had crossed Maroondah Highway there were no roads or signposts to guide us to our Shangri La. Overwhelmed by the nearness of things, we soon lost our way. Our resolve stalled in the baking heat. Like the early explorers we had not planned well and did not have adequate provisions. We had furious debates about which way to go. Finally we settled on what we thought was the right path and our high spirits returned. For hours we trudged across pocked, rocky paddocks. We trekked along fire-breaks and across cow-shit meadows and shinnied across the slimy water pipe that spanned the stagnant creek. We braved bees and bulls and barbed-wire fences. Finally we arrived at what must have been our field. There were no other candidates. Our hearts sank. Close up, the field was not much greener or softer than on our side. It had the same sharp stones. The same bull-ant nests. We sat for a small while and then went home, having learned the hard way about the false promise of greener grass.

What the landscape lacked in comfort it made up for in space. Our block was a good deal larger than the standard quarter acre. It was irregular and sloped steeply upwards, with unpredictable dips and bumps and no foliage. It was bare and a bastard to mow. My father was forever trying to tame this lumpen block, buttressing it with rock gardens and rock walls garlanded with pigface, courtesy of my mother. Great truckloads of volcanic rocks would arrive periodically and my father would set about arranging them. A rented cement mixer would churn into action and we would be marshalled into shovelling spadefuls of sand and gravel into the porridgy grey maelstrom. He always gave us the shitty, boring jobs. He was not a natural handyman and from my bedroom I could hear the hiss of muttered curses as he blackened yet another finger under a twenty-kilo igneous ornamental feature. I admired his application to something he clearly loathed. Whatever he started he always finished. 'Once your father took something on,' Mum said, 'he would spear the backside out of it.'

Behind the house, way up the top of the back garden, was a huge, unkempt wall of quince bushes and blackberries that loomed forward like a frozen wave in a Japanese woodblock print. This marked the end of civilisation. Behind that everything ran wild with bushland and chicken farms and foxes. There were ramshackle orchards, their trees garlanded with crisp red apples and gaudy lemons like the sleeves of Peter Allen's Rio costume.

In the height of summer the winds blew down from the centre of the continent where they gathered up the dry desert heat before unleashing it on us. The heat was unrelenting and everything felt combustible. Your fingers throbbed and swelled with your own broiling blood and you feared that if you brushed them against the tinder-dry flakes of a paperbark tree the bush would burst into flame. Deadly brown snakes twined themselves through the hot, singing grass; their shed skins lay in the long grass like used prophylactics.

Up behind our back fence was the mythological bush, where the wild things were. It was vast. It didn't care if you lived or died. Our cricket balls disappeared into it, never to be seen again. It was not far from here that Frederick McCubbin had found the inspiration for his famous painting *Lost*, in which a girl stands alone, crying in the bush. This painting embodies the fear that stalked the early settlers—being lost in the vertiginous, agoraphobic immensity of it all. *Picnic at Hanging Rock* without end.

But for me, the freedom of space and open air loosened my limbs and filled my soul with possibilities. I became a frontierswoman. I was Daniel Boone. With a marauding posse of the neighbourhood kids I would be up until all hours playing hide and seek, running through the bush and from house to house. In the eerie black night we would terrify one another and run screaming across Old Man Chandler's place, clambering over fences, getting the seat of our pants caught, skinning our knees. Pretending not to hear our parents who stood at the back door yelling for us to come home.

The roads were unmade and there were no kerbs. Packs of gum trees loitered about the streets like old hobos. The dirt was pale grey and talcum soft under your bare feet. I remember one night running up to the top of the hill and there, at the end of the silver dirt road, perfectly framed between the trees, was the biggest, fattest full moon I have ever seen. It was pale, watery gold and completely filled the frame. And I ran towards it believing, with all the conviction that an eight-year-old heart can carry, that I could touch that moon.

My parents were happy to let me run wild. Both of them had enjoyed outdoorsy childhoods, full of play. But it was necessary, at some point, to civilise me. So at the beginning of 1966 my formal education began.

'It is a sin to waste the God-given gift of a good brain,' my father would say. Probably because by the end of the war that was all he was left with—his own wits. He wasn't sure if he believed in God but, like most migrants, there was one thing he put all his faith in—education. The ranks of the second generation are full of doctors and lawyers and professionals.

His own education had been conducted surreptitiously, under the tyrannical thumb of the Nazis. He and his sister Danuta were obsessed with their studies. Before the war, schools in Warsaw were ranked by number. Dad's was number three, a strict school where the boys would be made to eat their meals with a book tucked under each arm to prevent any wing-nutting of elbows. But the Nazis forbade all education. The only schools they allowed to remain open were the trade schools, in which Poles could learn to be useful slave labour.

Then the Nazi regime set about exterminating the Polish intellectual class. Tens of thousands of professors, teachers, academics, writers, artists and actors were slaughtered. Even so, an elaborate network of secret underground schools and universities soon sprouted like irrepressible weeds. My father and my aunt would sneak into the homes of their former professors and teachers—the ones who hadn't been executed. Somehow Dad completed a classical education, complete with Latin and Greek and the histories of Herodotus, in these 'floating schools'. He learned physics and chemistry but, as he said, 'It was all theoretical. We couldn't do any experiments.'

He and Danuta were fiercely competitive. She and my father would devise their own academic athletics which my aunt always won. So when the war ended he was like a contender who has missed the chance to prove himself in the big fight. His competitive streak sought an outlet.

It didn't matter what his children did, what hobby or game or pastime, my father would be right there beside us doing it better. Whether it was drawing, playing a musical instrument, ice-skating, playing tennis, swimming or bike riding, he would join in. And be just that little bit, or even a lot, better. He couldn't help himself. His need to be best at everything was palpable. He would start out trying to teach us but his greater need took over and we became a means to an end, caught up in his never-ending struggle to prove himself. We always ended up abandoning whatever it was we were doing. Eventually we became wily. We chose activities we knew he couldn't possibly be good at. There weren't many.

Once I was playing with my plasticine, making the usual childish, blobby figures. My father sat beside me and began to show me how to mould the squidgy mess. Then, using nothing but a hairpin and the miniature plastic scalpel from my doctor's kit, he fashioned a tiny sculpture: the head of an old Aboriginal man—a bit like something by William Ricketts, whose forest carvings we had seen in the Dandenongs. It was really quite fabulous. Yet again I felt lesser. Like an inferior version of him.

But for some reason he had decided I was smarter than he was. There is a photo of me when I was about two, sitting on my high chair. I have a beaming round face and my eyes are sparkling. I look alive to the world and its possibilities. On the back my father wrote, 'Intelligence personified.' And from that moment, without ever knowing he was doing it, he took all of his crushed dreams of another life, and placed them about my frail little neck.

From the outset it was taken for granted that I would go to university. The story goes that after my first primary school report card my brother turned to my sister and said gloomily, 'Well, that's the end of us.' As happens in every family, we each carved out—or were allotted—our own turf. Barb was the arty beauty, Chris was the mechanic and I was the intellectual. My father was particularly hard on his only son. Chris fought back by becoming brilliant at all the things my father couldn't do. He excelled at practical tasks and mechanics. He was always pulling apart and rebuilding transistor radios and motorbikes and later, when he could afford them, cars. Cars are my brother's weakness. To this day the entrails of dissected cars still spill out over the front lawn outside the house. He wanted to be a racing car driver. My father talked him out of it.

My sister was going through an awkward phase when I started school. Her beauty had not yet fully blossomed and she was pimply. Worse than that—she had failed at maths. My father barely spoke to her anymore. Should I misstep, this was the fate that awaited me.

But for now, all of the family's educational hopes rested on me.

North Croydon State School was nestled at the bottom of the hill. It had started life as an isolated little one-room bush school. It was beautiful. You entered through a creaky old timber archway that gave on to a long and dusty path, so that by the time you reached class your shoes were always dirty. The 'old' part of the school was a white weatherboard structure. The playground and the scrappy edges of the balding footy oval were still thick with gum trees. Gradually the tidal surge of suburbia had swollen up around the school and more classrooms were added. A black asphalt playground spread across the grass and up to the entrance. And eventually a raft of boxy demountables was plonked out the back.

I couldn't wait to get to school. I had an unwavering sense of vocation. Whenever anyone asked what I wanted to be when I grew up my reply was instant. 'A doctor.' Actually not just a doctor. A surgeon. My conviction had the power of a calling. My father certainly never encouraged me, even though his own medical career had been thwarted. In my fervid imagination I dreamed of Bunsen burners and beakers and bubbling flasks. Most exciting of all—microscope slides! I packed up my little satchel and, with my head full of dreams, strode down the hill with my mother.

School was one of the most crushing disappointments of my life. Nothing could ever have lived up to my fantasy of what school should be like. I wanted it to be like it was in the movies and on TV, with uniforms and hockey sticks and boarders. Instead, it was a drab slog of rote-learning things my mother had already taught me. All done in our own boring civvies.

Grade two was where I met my first true sadist. Our teacher Mr Oldman was a music-loving, cardigan-wearing tyrant. He wore prim ties and took far too much pleasure in giving the strap. Girls didn't get the strap. We got the ruler. He would stroll along the aisle between the desks like a prison warden. And then, without warning, he would pounce like a crazed cat and give a sharp, painful whack across the knuckles for some trivial and often imaginary transgression. We were seven years old. We instinctively loathed him.

Then Mr Peterson arrived. As much as we hated Mr Oldman we loved Mr Peterson. He lit up my grade-three world. He would sit up on the desk like a tubby Socrates, pouring into us a great passion for learning. My soul vibrated in unison with his enthusiasm. I wrote tomes for him, screeds. A thirty-two-page epic called 'Journey to the Jurassic Age', based on Arthur Conan Doyle's *The Lost World*. I talked screeds, too. One day in class I was holding forth, rather epically, in response to a question, when Mr Peterson interrupted me. 'Get to the point, Magda!' he chuckled. My cheeks burned with shame. I told my parents, and my garrulousness became a family joke. I still don't know when to shut up.

And then, in grade one or two, disaster struck in the middle of a spelling competition. The word was 'eight'. I knew how to spell it but my mind went blank. Sue Dahn got the prize. I didn't sleep all that night. I lay awake fretting obsessively. Maybe I wasn't smart enough to go to university? Until that point being clever was who I was, it was the way I got my father's approval. Now I dreaded that his love was in jeopardy. And I was left with the gnawing fear that perhaps I wasn't as smart as I wanted or needed to be.

Soon after we moved to North Croydon my father got out of bed one morning and mentioned to my mother, for the umpteenth time, the funny lump on the back of his left thigh. Her nagging him to get it checked hadn't worked. Nagging and denial—the dance of marital intimacy. So this time my mother cast her beady eye over it and pronounced, like the Pythia on her tripod, 'That's cancer.'

And it was. He was only forty-two.

The surgeon told my parents Dad had a tumour 'the size of a man's fist' in his thigh. Melons, grapefruits, golf balls, marbles, peas, fists: the units by which the lay person measures cancer. With sarcoma, size matters. Soft-tissue sarcoma is rare and, back then, it was usually fatal. Combination chemotherapy, the most common and effective cancer treatment used today, had just been discovered in 1965 and was still in its infancy. The only treatment offered to my father was surgery. He stood before a panel of thirty surgeons who gave him two options: amputate the leg at the hip, or die.

Only one surgeon, a man named Frank Hurley, thought it was possible to save the leg *and* my father's life. My father chose the long odds. He decided that losing his leg, not being able to play tennis or any other sport, was a fate worse than death.

The day we took my father to hospital my mother made me wear my best dress. The atmosphere in the house was scary. My mother was angry and my sister was crying. Mum, packing Dad's suitcase, picked up his shoes. She looked at the left one and said, 'We might not need this one,' and she started crying.

Six-year-old me wanted to go out and play. 'All right,' Mum said, 'but don't you dare get dirty. Promise me.' I promised her and I meant it. 'I won't get dirty, Mum.' I was running, laughing when my little toe caught the corner of a rock and a chunk of skin flapped off. It really hurt. I wanted to cry, but I didn't. I was good at not crying. Even when I ran headfirst into the monkey bars and got a bump the size of an egg I didn't cry. And now there was blood on my dress. I tried to hide it, but Mum saw and slapped my leg. My mother had never slapped me before. But it was not the slap that hurt. It was the look in her eye. The mother who loved me and laughed with me and taught me to read had been replaced by someone angry who didn't like me. And that did make me cry. But this just made her more cross.

The surgeon carefully excised the tumour. And then we waited. Days. Months. Years. Five is the magic number in terms of cancer survival. Against our will we were all gamblers in a crapshoot with lousy odds. With each passing yearly milestone our hopes that my father would escape cancer's prickly tentacles were higher. But five years is an eternity for a child. My father would not be safe until I was eleven.

The pressure on my mother must have been unbearable. She was in a strange country with three kids and a husband who might die. We lived miles away from any decent public transport, and she couldn't even drive. The only acquaintances we had were the Vincents next door.

So there we were, at the far end of the world, living on top of a hill next to two redheads. And my father had cancer. Not that anyone in their right mind pays any heed to gypsy fortune-tellers.

No one told me something bad was happening but I knew. I sensed it like a dog. The frayed nerves, the short tempers. Anxiety with an edge so sharp you could cut yourself on it. I began to feel that I was a nuisance because people were always annoyed with me. My child's mind knew no boundaries. If there was something wrong, terribly wrong, then there was only one person to blame. Me.

My confused knowing about my father's illness found a bizarre way to express itself. One day I went to a school fete and, because my dad was in hospital, I decided to buy him a present to cheer him up. There were lots of stalls with lots of crappity knick-knacks to choose from, and I deliberated a long while. Then, with care and precision, I made my choice. Someone, we think it was my sister, tried to talk me out of the present but I was adamant. *This* was just the thing!

I rushed home very pleased with both myself and my gift. I couldn't wait to show my father. He opened the wrapper and I waited for him to beam and thank me. The atmosphere became strained and, to my disappointment and bafflement, the present was quickly spirited away. Years later when I found the present again in a cupboard, I realised why. It was a hand-carved, one-legged sailor—Peg Leg Pete. My mother told me later she thought it was hilarious and she and my father 'roared and laughed'. We still have Peg Leg Pete. He stands crookedly on a shelf in the den next to my father's ashes.

Besides Frank Hurley, the surgeon, Dad had another curious ally, an eccentric Dutchman named Gerald. Gerald was old and he lived out bush but he had skin as flawless as an airbrushed supermodel. I'm not sure how my father met him, but they struck up some sort of offbeat European friendship. When my father told Gerald about the cancer he said, 'Do as I tell you and I will get you through this.'

Gerald had been a prisoner of war in the Japanese camps in what was formerly Dutch Indonesia. He was a herbalist who had learned the ways from his mother who had learned them from her mother and so on. He attributed his survival of the camps to this knowledge. He would fossick around the perimeters of the compound, gathering seeds and weeds. He tried to persuade the other prisoners to eat his gatherings but they refused. Gerald was one of the few who survived. No wonder my father had faith in him.

Gerald was like a crazy prophet for the gods of kelp, vitamin C and lecithin. He fulminated against Frankenstein-ish food additives and hazardous chemicals and the evils of ice-cream.

'Little girl,' he sneered in his guttural Dutch accent one day when he sprang me eating an ice-cream. 'Do you know vot dey put in de ice-cream to keep it icy?' he asked.

'No.'

'Enti-freeze. Same as you put in de engine of de motor car. Vood you eat something det is in de engine of de motor car?'

I could never look at a tub of ice-cream in the same innocent way again. It was no longer a treat that tasted yummy. It could kill you. For the rest of my life, food was either poison or panacea. Frequently both.

Every morning my father dutifully ate a foul-tasting concoction prescribed by Gerald. It was a combination of molasses, yoghurt, yeast, wheatgerm and God knows what else. And we were all included in the plan. Every morning my mother filled my tiny six-year-old palm with upwards of ten vitamin tablets. She tried to incorporate this new regime into her plain cooking. Porridge and Weet-Bix always came with a topping of wheatgerm and lecithin. Into each bowl of Scottish vegetable and barley soup went a fat tablespoon of brewer's yeast.

'Just stir it in and you can't even taste it.'

It tasted foul. It tasted like punishment. It is only now that I can see it for what it really was—love.

But there were some things even the food could not mend. Like a seismic fault line, my father's illness was beneath and below everything. We would never again be standing on solid ground.

# LIFE LESSONS

When I was six Mum decided it was time to go to work. My father's illness stirred deep echoes of trauma from the years of hearing her own father's screams in the night. She was frightened my father would die and so she sought distraction.

I was grief-stricken, facing the prospect of losing my mother as well as my father, and I clung to her, weeping inconsolably, despite both parents' attempts to reason with me. Necessity prevailed. My father's life hung in the balance and my mother needed an income. She had not worked outside of the home for years, so she started with what she knew. She got a job on a fruit-and-vegetable stall at the market.

In those days Croydon had a fabulous livestock market, right across from the railway station. My mother loved to go there and chat with the stallholders while she was buying her groceries. On Market Mondays the reassuringly fruity smell of animal dung would drift across the carpark and into Main Street. As you went to the hairdresser or the chemist or the newsagent you would catch a whiff of the earthy odour of cattle and horses, pigs and poultry.

Eventually I got used to my mum working at the market. It even became fun. I would go down to visit her. The concrete floors were wet and slippery with rotten lettuce. It was a huge open shed, cavernous, with high ceilings that rang with laughter and the strange banter of the women who worked there. It was a joyous place, and my mother made friends among the other women.

As I recall this, another memory floats up and rests just beneath the cloudy surface. Movement and colour. Shapes. And then it rises, clean and clear. My mother also bought her groceries at the market and, as one of the women—my mother's favourite—reached over to place our purchase onto the metal scales, I saw something on the soft skin of her forearm.

'Why do you have a number on your arm?' I asked.

She looked at my mother who tried to shoosh me. But the woman smiled. She was asking my mother's permission for something. The women were watching us.

'She should know. May I tell her?'

My mother apprehensively agreed.

The woman leaned down to me. She had a kind face. 'Do you really want to know?'

'Yes.'

She said, gently, 'Magda. It is my number. A very evil man put this number on me.'

'Why?'

'Because he wanted to kill me.'

'Why?'

'Because I am a Jew.'

I didn't really understand what a Jew was. Or why anyone would want to kill such a nice lady. Was she related to the Little Jewish Boy Dad was always going on about?

'I am telling you this, Magda, because it must never happen again.'

I nodded. I felt bad that this had happened to the nice woman. And I agreed it should never happen again. And I remember now—as I looked up, the other women all held out their arms and showed me their numbers.

After a while my mother left the market and got a job on the assembly line at the Black and Decker power tool factory across the road from my school. She was working mostly for pin money, as they used to say. But I think the job gave her not only a sense of agency but also some female company. Most of the women working at the factory were English migrants. The accents, the cultural references, the sense of humour were all reassuringly familiar.

Mum's shift knocked off at three so every afternoon she would come to pick me up from school. We would either walk home up the hill together or sometimes one of the factory women would drive us in her overcrowded VW beetle. As always seems to happen near my mum, snappy one-liners zinged around the car. It was great fun. And often, out of guilt I suspect, Mum would buy me lollies from the milk bar. Despite Gerald's dire warnings. We would laugh all the way up the hill as I related the day's events and conversations, and she would try to teach me to be as witty as she was. Then we would cook dinner together, sometimes singing the recipes in the style of mock opera. I loved this time with her.

I am not the funny one in the family. My mother is. On her side of the family there exists a kind of matrilineal hegemony of hilarious, droll, sarcastic, devastatingly funny women. A mercurial, sometimes cruel, humour that crackles across the family firmament like lightning. Dangerous, exhilarating.

Just as a sculptor might work in steel or clay my mother's sisters and cousins worked expertly in the medium of the Scottish accent. Scottish is dry. It is sharp, hard and haughty. Sarcasm is easy in Scottish. The voice can drip with disdain without even trying. In the hands of experts it can also be playful, inclusive, cheeky, irreverent and warm. My mother is an expert, and my father never got the better of her. None of us did.

But when I was about seven something magic happened. I made my mother laugh. I can't remember exactly what we each said, but it turned into one of those giddy moments when you are riffing back and forth and ended with me saying a line that became a catchphrase between us: 'Throw the mud and run.' My mother threw her head back and roared with laughter. There was not a trace of condescension. I knew I had earned that laugh. I knew that this was a rite of passage, and that I had inched closer to being a human. And humour was the life line. It had got her people through famines and clearances and clan wars. Humour. The life force.

Mornings were a different story. Mum's shift started early and Dad, Barb and Chris were already out of the house, so at the age of eight I was left to lock up. I fretted and obsessed over this task, locking and relocking the back door to make sure it was done. The responsibility weighed on me. I was an almost morbidly earnest little girl. Mum always says, 'You were no bother. We never had to worry about you,' but this same self-sufficiency was what guaranteed my isolation. Being *able* to be left alone meant I *was* left alone. It also left me with a sense of being slightly feral, like Mowgli: not quite properly socialised. That stuff had to be knocked into me years later through a succession of shared households and relationships.

But there was an upside. At the age of eight, I owned the morning. I could eat what I liked. I could watch whatever TV show I wanted. I felt absolute power surge through me like some tyrannical Sun King.

Other than locking the door I didn't do one single thing I was meant to. It was electrifying, if not, ultimately, in my best interests.

Meanwhile at school there was only one real lesson to learn—'Fit in'. Croydon in the early sixties was more whitebread than a loaf of Sunicrust. The inner city was changing as waves of southern Europeans arrived, but Croydon was like a time capsule. I was one of the few European kids in my entire school; certainly the only one without an Anglo-sounding first name. By the time I was in fourth grade the school was full of English kids. There were Mancunians and Londoners and Lancastrians and Geordies. I listened to their accents, learning how to imitate them. But as we were not ten-pound Poms I hadn't lived with them in the migrant hostels and so we had little in common.

I was an outsider even among the outsiders. I developed an almost pathological desire to be normal. But there were obstacles.

One day Mrs Hardy asked me to talk about England and I launched into a description of Liverpool with special reference to the ferry on the Mersey. She pulled me up mid-sentence. 'We don't say "ferry" here,' she sneered, 'we say "faihree".' The other kids all laughed and for the first time in my tiny life I experienced the humiliation of exclusion from the herd. It was made clear that I was different. I was mortified but also spooked. With a jolt I realised that fitting in might be beyond my control. My mother was livid when I told her.

Like Eliza Doolittle, I knew that learning to speak 'like the natives' was the way to gain acceptance. But still, for a long time the Aussie accent felt like a second language to me, as if I was wearing the skin of another animal. Tiny traces of Englishness lingered on until well into my twenties. This forced adaptive skill turned out to be a boon. I suspect that changing your accent early in life trains your ear forever after to be receptive. Accents are frequently the key that lets me find my way into a character.

I hated my name, too. It was probably the weirdest name ever heard in Croydon until that point. I thought it was ugly. I spoke no Polish and was stuck with a name I could barely even pronounce myself until I was about ten. My father was no help. Temperamentally and ideologically pro-assimilation, he never spoke Polish at home. He didn't forbid it. He just withered it with disdain. 'What do you want to learn Polish for? It's a useless language.' But some deep atavistic urge in me longed to know about my roots the same way an adopted kid wants to know her biological parents. I felt scattered and I needed to join up the dots of myself.

So when I was eight or nine I found a battered copy of *Teach Yourself Polish* in the den. If my father wouldn't teach me I would teach myself. And I set about doing just that.

I was like a weekend rambler tackling Everest. Polish is acknowledged as one of the most difficult languages on earth, a tangle of consonants in search of a vowel. And the grammar is a chamber of horrors. I barely knew the rules of the English language. I would bang my head up against the wall of this impregnable word fortress for hours on end until, defeated, there was nothing else for it but to ask my father for help. Like Oliver Twist I would take my pathetic little book over to him.

'How do you pronounce this?' I pointed at the word. It was the Polish word for 'three'—*trzy*.

He sighed. '*Trzhi.*'

I dutifully repeated, '*Trzhi.*'

'No, *TRZhi.*'

'*Trzhi.*'

'No no no! *Trzhi.*'

This went on forever. Until I gave up and my father could go back to his spy novel in peace. Which I suspect may have been the whole idea in the first place. I felt like I was trying to hit a moving target—my father's standards of perfection. If I could not pronounce the word perfectly then in my father's mind there was no point even trying.

While I was racing backwards towards my Polishness, my father was rushing in the other direction, assimilating at a rate of knots. As soon as he could he took out Australian citizenship. There was, however, something that forever set him apart.

His shorts.

European men wear shorts that defy belief. Grown men in little-boy shorts. They are called *spodenki,* which means 'little pants', and seem to be a fashion favourite in central Europe. I can barely even bring myself to describe them. My father's were the same shade on the colour chart as my brother-in-law's Leyland P76: Peel Me a Grape Purple. My father would strut along the main street in Croydon wearing his purple *spodenki*. Whistling.

My brother and sister and I couldn't get far enough away. We pleaded with him. 'You *cannot wear* shorts like that!'

'What are you talking about? Nothing wrong with them! They are perfectly good shorts.'

For someone who professed to care so much about the virtues of assimilating, he simply did not give a toss what anyone thought of him. We would wince at the things he would say to other people. He would look at us with incredulity. 'What? It's the truth! She *does* have bandy legs!' He thought he owed it to you to be honest. His morality demanded it. And of course he turned the blowtorch of his truth most severely on himself. Perhaps it was as a reaction to his uncompromising candour that I became such a careful bridge builder. Such a people pleaser.

If my father was not going to help me, I would have to find another way to get to my Polishness. It was not going to be easy. There are not a lot of famous Polish role models. Chopin. Copernicus. Joseph Conrad. After the letter 'C' they thin out. Then one day I stumbled across a biography of Marie Curie on one of the shelves in the den. I felt like Robinson Crusoe when he found Man Friday. Not only was she Polish, her original name sounded quite a bit like mine. She was born Maria Skłodowska. She was Warszawian, the daughter of a professor. And she was in a medicine-related field. Curie studied like it was an extreme sport. She studied until she fainted. She martyred herself to study. She became my hero. In her I found a woman of science who was as tragically romantic as any poet. Her dedication, her pitiless demands of herself, her tenacity. Her self-sacrifice. I wanted to be exactly like her. There was just one problem—I hated actual study.

At school I was bored out of my mind. Lessons about Malayan rubber plantations and the history of the sheep industry were sucking the life out of me. I fretted that I was learning nothing about medicine. Like my idol Marie, I threw myself into my own private medical studies. I couldn't get my hands on any actual dead bodies, but one day my brother came home with a jar of sheeps eyes he had scrounged from one of the local farms. We laid down sheets of newspaper on the kitchen bench and sliced one open with a razor blade. We pulled out the lens, marvelling at the magnifying effect it had on the newsprint.

Beyond that we didn't know what to do with the things. So Chris stashed them and we completely forgot about them until, months later, my mother asked what the hell that stench was emanating from my brother's room. No one entered my brother's room without permission, but my mother stormed in and found the jar of reeking sheeps eyes under his bed.

But one day my curiosity about all things medical would get me into trouble.

We are a book-loving family. We don't care if they are good or bad, we just love reading. Next to Mum's bed is a big stack of Rosamunde Pilcher, Maeve Binchy, Georgette Heyer, Jeffrey Archer, Bryce Courtenay and some Mills and Boons. Dad devoured non-fiction and loved a good thriller. There would always be John Le Carré spy novels scattered about the house, a thick pair of glasses and the stumpy twig remnants of an apple or pear (my father would devour the fruit top to bottom leaving nothing but the stalk) resting on the open pages.

When I was little I thought my father read these books for fun, as a bit of escapism. It never occurred to me that he could have been a character in one of these tales of espionage and intrigue. Or that from those spy stories he was crafting a world view, an identity and a redemption mythology.

Of all the books in our house there were two I was forbidden to read or even look at. In the den, along with the *Encyclopaedia Britannica* and the books on textile chemistry, was Dad's old anatomy book. It had a cracked black spine and gold embossed lettering. Stamped inside it was the insignia of Edinburgh University and written in his distinctively European hand was my father's name. Now all that remained of his precious dream of being a doctor was this battered book.

If I was going to be a doctor I would have to read that anatomy book. So one day I took it down from the top shelf and opened it. Instantly I found myself in medical geek nirvana. I shut myself in the den for hours, pretending to do homework, entranced by the cross-section line drawings of human anatomy. I had no patience for school, and yet I had limitless patience for this. I rote-learned the name of every bone in the human body. I was familiar with most of the organs and had a basic grasp of some of the autonomic systems. I particularly relished all of the stuff about how to cut up dead bodies. I was in love with autopsies. I had a tiny plastic doctor kit with a stethoscope and a miniature scalpel. I memorised in ghoulish detail the procedure for dissecting a cadaver. When my parents eventually discovered what I was doing, they decided it was probably worse to discourage my curiosity than to let me see anatomically correct pictures of the human body. They relaxed their policy and allowed me to study the book. By the time I was eight it had become my party trick. When my parents had friends over I would recite the names of all the bones and then re-enact a dissection.

Can you imagine? Seriously.

It was from reading one of these books that I learned the healing powers of vitamin C. My mother had some gum problems and I told her to take more vitamin C. Her gums improved. I felt like a miracle worker. The idea that I could learn how to heal people filled me with a profound sense of joy and purpose. Perhaps if my father's cancer returned I could save him?

There was another book in the den I was strictly forbidden to look at. It was hidden away behind a sliding door at the bottom of the teak veneer cabinet. But I had seen glimpses of it. Someone had sent it from Poland soon after the war and miraculously it had survived the gauntlet of the Polish postal service, the censors and corrupt border guards to reach my father. It was a large coffee-table book about the Warsaw Uprising called *Dni Powstania* (Days of Uprising). Occasionally this book would be brought out when guests were over because there were pictures of my father in it. One shows him, fresh-faced in a double-breasted suit and open-necked shirt. He is standing in line in the Evangelical Cemetery with about twenty or so other young men, surrounded by large stone monuments to the dead. His friend Ryszard is standing a few men along to the right. He told me that this was their battalion (*Pięść*—The Fist) and that this is the very moment when their commanders announced the beginning of the Warsaw Uprising. He and his city are about to begin the fight of their lives. In a 'bone yard', as Dad called it. It would be a cruddy piece of symbolism if not for the fact that it is true.

It was rare for my parents to bring out this book. My father only showed it to people who were genuinely curious. Whenever the book was brought out I would hover by the frosted-glass sliding doors of the lounge room, hoping to be allowed a proper look, but my parents were firm. The book would be swaddled back in its brown paper wrapping and tucked safely away at the back of the bottom drawer.

Which made it irresistible.

Perhaps emboldened by my success with the anatomy book, I determined to conquer this one as well. One day when no one else was home I slid open the drawer and pulled it out. It was as heavy as a house brick. I peeled back the brown paper. On the cover was a grainy black-and-white image of people with machine guns peering from two windows of a partially destroyed building. In all of the nearly 320 pages of that book there is barely a single intact building.

I couldn't understand the Polish words but that didn't matter because it was mostly pictures anyway. Pictures of bombed-out buildings and people scurrying for cover, their shoulders hunched, their heads ducked as they try to dodge a sniper's bullet. There were little kids running crouched over along the edge of a building, Sten guns in their tiny hands; people digging trenches and constructing barricades; men and women in black berets joking, laughing, sharing cigarettes. Red Cross trucks; a nurse tending a patient. A pretty blonde resistance fighter holding a Tommy gun.

I knew this was where my father had grown up but it was barely recognisable as a city at all. Mostly it was just piles and piles of rubble. It was like another world, some kind of sepulchral wonderland. The gutted city had the same savage and strangely compelling beauty as the Book of Revelations. Or Donatello's gaunt and harrowed statue of Mary Magdalene.

And yet in those pictures there was a palpable sense of camaraderie that contrasted with my own lonely existence. I felt a deep envy of the drama, the action. Everyone was pulling together for a greater cause. And it was undeniably glamorous. I no longer wanted to be a doctor. I wanted to be a fighter.

But there were other perplexing images that, at first, I could not understand. A long line of people standing under the narrow eaves of a building, passing bricks to one another and gazing with terrified faces at some unseen horror in the sky. Another man standing in the street, transfixed. By what, I had no idea. In another a man was pulling down from a window what I know now to be a swastika flag. There was a picture of a fat unexploded bomb that looked like a metallic beached dugong. In another, a window was filled with flames. I examined it closely. Was there a gun in the middle of the flames, and a person, engulfed by fire, pointing it at some unseen enemy?

And then I came upon a picture that plunged like a depth charge into the fear centre of my little brain. It took me quite some time to figure out what it was.

In my father's anatomy book I had seen many line drawings of bodies. I had never seen a photograph of a real dead body. A murdered body. Lying face down was something that looked like an old bundle of torn clothing. But there seemed to be a hand attached to it. And another hand, unconnected, a few inches away. What appeared to be a head was lying face down and had a hole the size of a fifty-cent piece in the back of it. But it was the body I couldn't understand. It wasn't there. It was like what was left of the Wicked Witch after she melted—it had disintegrated, leaving behind only fragments of itself. Then came more images: a man being dragged by his arms from under a pile of dirt, and he has no face. A body crumpled unnaturally in the street. I knew they were dead. These were nothing like the neat diagrams I had practised dissecting.

I shuddered. But I couldn't stop looking. Then, suddenly, I felt frightened. I slammed the book shut; I put it back and closed the drawer. I didn't tell my parents.

The book became a strange and solemn ritual. I would force myself to go into the den, slide the door of the cabinet across, open the book and look at the pictures of the dead bodies. At first I would just skip past the terrifying pages. But each time I made myself look for slightly longer until it didn't scare me at all. My heartbeat slowed down. I felt in control.

Understanding continued to elude me, however, and eventually my driving need to comprehend forced me to confess to my father.

'Ach! What are you doing looking at that book?'

'I don't understand what that picture is.'

I showed him. He shrugged, with his familiar edge of annoyance at my ignorance.

'A dead body.'

'I know, but it doesn't look like a person,' I ventured.

'Because it has begun to decompose. It has rotted.'

I knew what rotted meant. It was what happened to vegetables and meat.

He stared at me. 'What are you scared of? Don't be silly! It's just a picture.'

The rebuke made me feel ashamed of my stupidity and weakness.

He wrapped the book in its brown paper. 'That will teach you to go looking where you are not supposed to.'

One day soon after this my mother was cooking chips in the kitchen. The phone rang and by the time she got back the oil was ablaze. She grabbed the pan and threw it out the back door but, as she did, the boiling oil splashed back onto her hand, giving her a nasty third-degree burn. When she came home from the hospital her hand was swathed in an impressive bandage. My father was in charge of changing the dressing on the wound. I was practically salivating. This was just about the most exciting thing that had ever happened in my life. This was my big chance. An actual injury! I was desperate to see but my father shooed me away.

'Come on, out you go.'

'I *have* to see this.'

'Maggie, don't be silly. You are too young.'

'Please, please, please!' I used every bit of pester power in my arsenal. 'If I'm going to be a doctor I have to see!'

'All right,' he sighed. 'But I warned you.'

My eyes were wide with excitement as he peeled back the layers of bandages. I wasn't prepared for the smell. The smell of my mother's burnt flesh, cooking. I felt sick and woozy. I wanted to run away. But I felt now, after making such a fuss, that I had to see it through. I didn't want them to know I was scared. So I forced myself to look with the same detachment as my father. My mother's skin frightened me. It was transformed. It was messy.

My father's demeanour remained professional, capable, reassuring. He loved any opportunity to use his medical knowledge. I watched him and I learned. The lesson was this: numb yourself to what would naturally sicken and sadden. Crying is not an option.

It was an early hit of intergenerational novocaine to the heart: my sentimental education in the art of clinical dissociation had begun.

# FEELING DIFFERENT

The absence of sibling distraction in my childhood left me time for projects. I wrote little books and plays and drew cartoons. At school I wrote, directed and acted in plays. In grade five I started a school newspaper which I would painstakingly Gestetner during recess. But nothing was ever as good as television. I especially loved *Get Smart* and *Lost in Space* and *Daniel Boone*. I thought *Gilligan's Island* was stupid and improbable, as was *I Dream of Jeannie*. But of course towering above all of them was *The Brady Bunch*. It wasn't just a TV show. It was a survival manual.

Being the youngest child by a long way was something like being an only child, with all of the attendant freedom but none of the fussing over. There was also the dull ache of perpetually being left out, a feeling that has never quite left me. (Perhaps it explains Sharon Strzelecki's uncertain, provisional status as perpetual 'second best friend'.) My isolation also meant I had no points of comparison; no way of knowing if what I felt was normal or weird. There were only two things that gave me a sense of perspective—*The Brady Bunch* and the moon.

Nothing ever fazed the Bradys. Every crisis and calamity was met with equanimity and good humour. They managed to sail on through moral challenges such as high-school election vote-rigging and sibling rivalry. Even Jan's braces barely ruffled their feathers. The Bradys were a handrail on the vertiginous slopes of my own family life. They became my ersatz family. They were what real families were like: families with ordinary names whose dads didn't have cancer.

I wanted to be Marcia Brady. I convinced myself that I looked like her and I did, a little. I wore my hair like hers. The fact that our names both began with an 'M' I took to be encouraging. There was a strange intensity to my feelings for her that I couldn't quite figure out. I wasn't sure if I wanted to *be* her or…something. I could feel an intense electricity in my body at the thought of her but it was diffuse; it had no shape. I just wanted to be close to her. Very close. But Marcia Brady was more remote than the moon.

Much more remote than the moon actually, because the Americans were about to land on it. My moon. The moon at the top of my hill. I gazed as it hung there, full and fat and far away. If it could be reached then anything was possible. The moon drew me towards it the same way it dragged the heavy oceans. I loved its fragility. Its delicate luminosity. The way it shone its light tenderly and modestly. I longed to touch it, to be an astronaut held in the embrace of its gentle gravity.

I also loved the paraphernalia of space flight—the switches on the roof of the cabin, the insect spindliness of the lunar module, the space suits, the back packs. I was glued to all TV shows about exploration: *Lost in Space, Thunderbirds, Stingray*. I actually had a crush on Scott, one of the Thunderbirds puppets. I collected every single newspaper article that I could find about Apollo 11 and its crew until I had stuffed several great big crackling scrapbooks. My life was an endless round of scissors, paper and Clag.

Finally, in July 1969, it happened. In an old bush school in a corner of an ancient continent, my classmates and I were all herded into the sick room, converted into a makeshift TV room, to watch a space-age miracle. Mr Arblaster fiddled with the antenna. And then grainy black-and-white images spluttered onto the screen.

I cried. I thought it was the most beautiful thing I had ever seen. Like an anchorwoman with Asperger's I spewed out facts, telling the other kids all of the wonderful stuff I had learnt about the moon. Until someone told me to be quiet. Mr Arblaster, I think. When Neil Armstrong climbed down from the bottom rung and placed his foot on the moon my heart exploded like a firework.

As much as I loved the moon I hated dolls. I hated frills. I hated ballet. I was a tomboy. And something about this made my mother nervous. I wanted a boys haircut, boys jeans, a boys bike and a toolbox. I never got any of them. I don't know if this was because my mother detected signs of my incipient lesbianism, but she certainly set about a not-so-subtle program of de-tomboying me. Anyway, whether my mother knew or not, *I* knew. There was a dark side to my Marcia madness. I knew that I liked her in a way that was different from the other kids. I didn't just want to be her friend. I wanted to kiss her. I had kissed a couple of kids in the neighbourhood, both boys and girls. Mostly girls. And, without being told, I knew this was not 'normal'. Somehow I knew that I posed what researchers call a 'social identity threat' to myself. I redoubled my efforts to Marcia Bradify myself, to squeeze my weird, Polish-Scottish-Gay square peg into the Brady round hole. So to speak. But the crushes on actresses just would not stop. Marcia was quickly followed by Laurie Partridge. (I also had a thing for Keith, but that was because he was pretty like a girl.)

Once again this sense of my own difference rattled me. I turned into my own hyper-vigilant thought police. TV was my normaliser. Its nowhere-land was where my true schooling took place, the place I looked to for answers about my own strange feelings. I plunged into its cool, bland platitudes. It was my sanctuary, the only place I truly felt I belonged.

My father loved movies. As a kid in Warsaw, he used to go to the movies with his best friend Wacek Goldfarb, whose rich uncle owned a bunch of cinemas, so Wacek and my father could get in for free. *Captain Blood* with Errol Flynn was a favourite. As were the Mickey Rooney films of the thirties. As we sat together late in his life watching a re-run of *Babe: Pig in the City* he beamed with incredulity. 'Ach, Maggie, if someone had told me back then that one day my kid would be in a movie with Mickey Rooney! Aie!' He trailed off, unable to express the incalculably enormous odds against this ever happening.

Dad also loved to watch war movies, but he found them preposterous. He would scoff, providing a cynic's running commentary: 'Jesus! Ridiculous! You did that, you'd be dead!' 'The Germans weren't idiots!' 'Hah! That geezer never held a gun in his life!' And, 'Don't stand there talking. Finish the bastard off!' John Wayne's mincing, pigeon-toed walk nearly always got a special mention. 'Surprising such a big man would have such a sissy walk.'

The only actor he had any respect for was Audie Murphy, a returned war hero who became something of a movie star in the fifties. 'He knows. He was there. He was a brave man.'

These films were mostly about American—sometimes British, rarely French—soldiers. And of course Germans. I never once saw a Pole, and so I formed the view that my father had fought in a kind of secondary, peripheral war. And consequently one where seriously bad things didn't happen. Despite the forbidden book in the den and the grisly images it contained, I double-thought my way into the conviction that only the Americans had really been at war.

But there was often an American Pole named Kowalski (*kowal* means 'Smith', Dad informed me) and frequently a German named Grüber. And Dad would always say, 'Ah, Grüber!' and I would ask him why he sounded affectionate about a German, but he would never tell me.

I loved watching war movies with my dad. But then one day when I was about nine the family was sitting in the lounge room watching TV when a different kind of film came on. It was a documentary about the Holocaust. I understood that this was the same war, but these were not actors. These were not even soldiers. These were families. Old people. Little kids.

This was what the nice woman at the market with the number on her arm was talking about.

I watched as the images got worse. Suddenly TV was not a hidey hole—it was a conduit to hell. As I saw those images of Jewish children pleading for their lives, of gaunt eyes staring from behind barbed wire, of piles of bodies being bulldozed into pits, I understood that this had really happened.

And then my father said, 'That is our street, where we used to live. Before it was rezoned as part of the ghetto.'

My father had not been on the periphery of the war. He had been right in the centre of it. Warsaw. This unspeakable, terrifying horror was Warsaw. His Paris of the East. My nine-year-old mind struggled to understand the relationship between the Hollywood war movies my father loved and this vile horror we were watching now. Were they the same war? Was this the war my father was talking about when he called himself the 'original war lover'? How could he say that?

I began to panic. My heart was a thumping lump of meat in my throat, choking me. I couldn't get air past it. I felt myself drowning in a swirl of black emotions. The only lifeline I had was my father. So I looked to him for—I don't know. Reassurance? Validation? Comfort?

But I could see no reflection of what I was feeling. Where I was a roiling mess of hot feeling he was a mask. To him the Holocaust was nothing out of the ordinary. It was an everyday occurrence.

In that instant I felt a great chasm open up between me and my father. His lack of feeling seemed monstrous. I knew instinctively that my response was the right one. I couldn't understand. Did he not care about what was happening to the Jews? I could sense his discomfort with my feelings. Then an unmistakable emotion flickered across the mask of his face. Contempt. It looked to me like contempt for my fear.

He shrugged. 'There was nothing you could do.' He seemed cross.

In that instant I vowed never to show fear again. And I realised that not even my father—my symbol of strength and courage, protector of hearth and home—not even my own father could save the Jews from being bulldozed into a pit. I could not dissociate myself from these abused bodies. Those sickeningly elastic forms that twisted in ways no living body ever could, they were a warning.

At school the next day I tried to tell the other kids about the Jews. No one knew or cared. I felt ridiculous. Some time later we were playing a game of softball. It was my turn to go up to bat. The other kids on my team started up the chant: 'Slogger it! Slogger it!' I wrapped my little fists around the skinny end of the bat. I decided to dedicate my swing to the Jews. I took my helpless rage and cast it into that bat. As the ball came spinning towards me I cursed under my breath, 'Fucking Nazis, fucking Nazis!' I swung the bat as hard as I could and I felt it instantly—I had the sweet spot. The ball sailed far out of the playground for a home run. The other kids looked dazed. They couldn't understand why I was laughing and crying.

# THE END OF THE WORLD

From a young age I knew I was going to hell. I even had a date.

Soon after my home run, the redheaded Vincent kids next door, who had recently converted to become Jehovah's Witnesses, told me the calculations had been done. The end of the world was scheduled to happen in 1972, when I would be eleven. And because I was a Catholic idolater there was no hope for me. When Armageddon arrived I would be horribly ripped apart like an expendable extra in a horror movie.

In England we had been regular churchgoers. Not that we were God-botherers. My father was agnostic. My mother's Catholicism was as much informed by Celtic mysticism and superstition as dogma. And clannishness. But when we moved to the southern hemisphere our religious attendance, along with many other civilised customs, fell by the wayside.

I wasn't happy about it. By the age of three I was already ravished by the beauty of the Latin Mass and would recite sizeable chunks of it. My full name is Magdalene Mary Therese Szubański, and a more Catholic name you could not find. It's surprising I'm not a nun. It's easy to imagine: *Sister Magdalene Mary! An emissary from the Vatican has arrived and you are being sent to the Congo.*

But the Church and I got off to a bad start due to my habit of heckling the priest, as my mother reminded me recently. 'You were only about three and he was going on and on and shouting and getting a bit hellfire and brimstone. You couldn't understand what he was saying but you didn't like his tone so you yelled out, "SHUP-UP!"'

I can't remember the incident but 'shup-up' has been a family catchcry ever since.

'Gee. What happened?'

'Silence. Absolute silence. So the priest started up again. And you piped up, "SHUP-UP!" again.'

'Really?'

'Yes. Two or three times.'

'What did the priest do?'

'He said, "Apparently I have a heckler."'

'What did you do?'

'Laughed.'

I went to a godless state primary school so there was little opportunity for further dissent. My first real introduction to Bible studies was via the Vincents, who had been Catholic like us until Harry decided that they should all become Jehovah's Witnesses.

The Vincent house was covered in plastic. Maureen had been the older sister to seven brothers in a poor, working-class family from a rough part of Manchester. She valued her possessions, and all major traffic areas had sheets of hard plastic laid down to prevent wear and tear. Harry was loads of fun. They had a Clark above-ground pool in their back garden and he would play with us for hours, tossing us in the air and dunking us. We would shriek with fear and exhilaration, screaming for more.

And now he tried to convert us to the Jehovahs. He proselytised a pure religion, one that returned to the original teachings of Jesus. Dad was curious. And perhaps there was some lingering part of his agnostic soul that hoped to lay down his burden at the feet of a gentle God.

So we went to Bible studies in the Vincents' lounge room. I remember my father and mother sitting on the couch—I think it may have had a plastic cover as well—listening while Harry tried to explain that the Bible is scientifically accurate. My father instantly decided it was nonsense and never went back.

But I continued and would even go with the Vincents to the Kingdom Hall. I would flick through copies of *The Watchtower* like it was *Dolly* magazine. As we tooled around the neighbourhood, playing cricket or going down to Croydon municipal pool or to the cinema to watch Jerry Lewis films and roll our Jaffas down the polished wooden aisles, the Vincent kids would tell me stories from the Bible. They informed me that they were no longer permitted to have blood transfusions. This I really struggled with. It went against my medical training.

Now my vocabulary was enriched. Words like apocalypse, resurrection, idolater. Armageddon. The Vincent kids especially loved talking about Armageddon.

'What will happen?' I asked apprehensively.

'There will be a big war and Jehovah will destroy the whole world,' Jodie replied. 'And all the people who are not Witnesses will be ripped apart.'

I quivered. Jodie was four years older than me and she wanted to become a 'pioneer' when she grew up—which is to say a door-to-door missionary, selling her version of God.

'What about me and my family?'

'You won't be saved.'

'Why?'

'Because you are Catholic idolaters.'

'What does that mean?'

'That you worship idols.'

'But what does that mean?'

'I don't know. Anyway, afterwards everyone will be brought back to life in the Resurrection.'

'Everyone?'

'Only the 144,000 who are going to Heaven and the other Witnesses here on Earth.'

'What about people who died in the olden days? What about Daniel Boone?'

'All people who died in the olden days will be resurrected.'

I liked the idea of living in the same world as Daniel Boone. Part of me thought this was silly. But another part of me started to think about converting. (I have had a bit of a survivalist streak in me ever since. I mean, I'm not a Doomsday Prepper. But I did buy Tamiflu.)

I started counting. Throughout 1972 I kept an eye on the calendar, waiting for the day I would perish horribly.

It was at about this time that I started to form my obsession with the saints, especially Saint Bernadette of Lourdes and Saint Teresa of Avila. In other words, the pretty ones. I watched *The Nun's Story* starring Audrey Hepburn. Ingrid Bergman in *The Bells of Saint Mary's*.

My God was not a god of love. He was a pre–Vatican II god of fear and damnation. Despite my early protestations the Church got to me, and I drank deeply from the poisoned chalice of old-time Catholicism. I examined my conscience with excoriating vigour. I obsessed over my many imperfections and tried to live up to the example of the saints. I prayed for sainthood—which is to say, I prayed to be beyond reproach. This is probably why, when the notion of going to convent school came up, I was at first tantalised. It seemed like a potential fast-track.

The Kobylańskis were the first Polish family we ever met in Australia. I was eight. Chris was seeking advice about an apprenticeship from a dental technician, Adam Kobylański, who was four years younger than my father. Adam's father had been an industrialist, a newspaper publisher and a senator in Warsaw before the war. In 1943 Adam's parents and sister were arrested by the Gestapo and sent to Auschwitz. They survived. After the war Adam migrated to Australia. He and his wife Alina had three kids, and the middle one, Izabella, was my age. We became friends.

The Kobylańskis lived in Canterbury, an older, more established suburb than Croydon. The houses were large, heavy, dark and double brick. They weren't going anywhere. Unlike our brick veneer, which felt like it might take off in a strong gust. When it came time, Izabella was going to be sent to a convent school in neighbouring Camberwell. I could sense that my parents were thinking of this as an option for me.

The Kobylańskis were a family of sweet tooths. It was in their home that I was first introduced to Polish cuisine—pierogi and cabbage rolls and dill and cheesecakes and poppyseed cakes and glazed fruits. But I had no sweet tooth as a child so I didn't especially like the culinary arts of my motherland.

Izabella spoke Polish. Her father was much stricter than mine. She was not allowed to have posters on her walls. Adam Kobylański looked like Prince Rainier of Monaco, a distinguished middle-aged man with a pencil moustache. But the thing I remember most about him was his laugh. The Kobylańskis' house was often full of family, friends and refugees. They would sit and talk for hours in Polish and Adam would tell jokes. I couldn't understand a word, but it didn't matter—he had funny bones. It was all in his delivery. He rarely made it through a story without crying from laughter, stopping to remove his glasses and wipe tears from his eyes. I would laugh and weep with him, never really knowing why. I longed to speak Polish so that I could be in on the joke.

But they would also talk about the war. From time to time they would stop to translate for my mother. Of course all the kids would be banished from the room but Izabella and I would hang around the door, eavesdropping. And she would interpret for me—words, phrases, fragments. Stories. Of smuggling guns, of hiding from the Germans, of nearly getting caught.

Other than the Kobylańskis my world was a sea of Anglo-Celts. I was maturing with few signposts to help me grapple with the darker part of my heritage. But as puberty was approaching so was Polish culture—in Panavision.

# MAGDA AND MAGDA

When I was little Poland seemed to me like a magical fairytale kingdom. One that no one else had ever heard of or particularly wanted to visit. It was full of counts and countesses and castles and heraldry. And then one day this faraway magical world came to life on the screen of a dingy 'foreign' movie theatre somewhere in the inner city. My father announced, 'We are going to see a film with your cousin Magda in it.'

In the 1960s my cousin Magda Zawadzka was the hot young ingenue of Polish cinema. Golden-haired, with huge green eyes and long spidery lashes, she was a curvier version of Twiggy. Throughout my early years Aunt Danuta would send us press clippings about her daughter via the corrupt and unpredictable Soviet bloc mail. I couldn't understand a single word but the pictures were enough: Marcia Brady was finished. I had a new role model.

The film was called *Colonel Wołodyjowski*. It was based on a novel

called *Fire in the Steppe* by the Nobel Prize–winning author Henryk
Sienkiewicz. It is now considered to be a classic, like a kind of Polish
*Ben Hur* or *Taras Bulba*. It's about the Poles and the invading Turks
and my cousin played the lead female character, Basia Wołodyjowski.
Basia is a much-adored figure in Polish literature, a feisty Polish
warrior princess—only more realistic than that sounds—who rides
into danger for the love of her man. It's a really great role.

I think I was twelve or so when I saw the movie. I know I was
still at a very self-conscious age, mainly because I remember fiddling
anxiously with the zipper of my knee-length black vinyl boots when
I didn't know where to look. Or maybe that was during the sex scene
in *Ryan's Daughter*.

As we drove through the grey and dismal streets of inner Melbourne
I imagined sparkling minarets and scimitars and golden steppes
stretching as far as the eye could see.

We herded into the cinema and the projector flickered on. I vividly
remember the opening sequence—for some time the camera held on a
panoramic shot of a wide, grassy steppe, completely empty and silent
except for the high-pitched hum of insects. And then the sound of
hooves in the distance, growing louder and louder like an approaching
storm. Until, over the distant horizon, a legion of horsemen came
thundering past the camera, feathers flying, brandishing their curved
swords. This was exactly what I hoped Poland would be like. I could
feel the blurry lines of my identity becoming sharper, like a Polaroid
photo.

Shortly after this my cousin appeared. It is a strange thing to see
on the screen someone you know, whose name you share. I'm pretty
sure it went to my head. In all sorts of unfortunate ways.

In her first major scene she is sword-fighting and it quickly becomes
apparent that she is playing a tomboy. (This is not code, by the way.
My cousin is possibly the most heterosexual woman I have ever met

in my life.) The thought that someone I already worshipped, who shared my name and my cultural heritage, whom I was *related* to, for God's sake, could also be a tomboy like me, added high-octane fuel to my obsession. I decided then and there—I was not a Scottish–Pole or a Polish–Scot. I was Polish.

*Colonel Wołodyjowski* is pretty much an exercise in nation building for a nation that barely existed. It's about the gallant, foolhardy, romantic, brave, proud Poles. If you want to really understand old Poland you have to understand the noble class, or *szlachta*. Prior to the eighteenth century the Polish-Lithuanian Commonwealth was one of the mightiest nations in Europe. Its elite class was unlike that of any other country, in as much as the Poles doled out noble titles like show bags. Perhaps around fifteen per cent of Poles are deemed nobility, with the rule of thumb being if your name ends in 'ski' then you are from the nobility. This in itself tells you something about Polish character. Everyone is special. Unless you were a serf. Other than that, class was fluid and you could rise through the ranks. So it was, at least to some extent, a meritocracy.

Anyway, the fun thing is that the Polish *szlachta* classes were fabulous. They were like the P-Diddys of Poland, the Kanye Wests and Kim Kardashians of central Europe, preferring show to substance. They were extravagant, ostentatious. They pimped their rides. Their horses were festooned with jewels and gems and on high days and holy days the horses' coats would be bedazzled and dyed deep crimson with Polish cochineal made from the small native insect.

My cousin's character in *Colonel Wołodyjowski*, thundering across the steppe on her horse while firing a pistol at her rapining pursuers, was just the silver nitrate embodiment of the same spirit that burned so fiercely in our grandmother—an overweight middle-aged lady who slept with a folded-up Polish flag under her head and a pistol in her pocket, ready to kill any German who threatened her life or her country or her loved ones. Polish women are every bit as *fatale* as they are *femme*. Polish girls are required to be hot, but also handy with a spanner. A tractor licence is an asset.

I was seeing, in the impressionable years of adolescence, the ideal of Polish womanhood in the person of my cousin and namesake Magda Zawadzka. A holy trinity of Madonna, shiksa and Joan of Arc. Cousin Magda told me later that she did many of her own stunts and once feared she would drown when her horse crashed through the ice of a frozen river and she was about to be sucked into the fast-flowing waters beneath.

Even though the Poles vanquish the Turks and help save Christendom the film ends with the two main characters sacrificing themselves for the greater good. I was both seduced and traumatised. I longed to fight. Or act. I wasn't really sure which. Mostly fight, I think. Until the film revealed one of the most gruesome scenes I wish I had never witnessed. Tugay Bey, the traitorous Tartar who is in love with my cousin's character and turns bad when she spurns him, is dragged by horses and impaled through his anus onto a massive, sharply honed wooden post. It is a revenge killing for an equally bloody deed off-screen. His hands are bound with straw and set on fire. I fiddled with the zip on my boots.

Many years later I remarked to my cousin Magda, 'Phew! That's a pretty brutal film!' She regarded me coolly through lowered eyelids and purred, 'Ourrr history is brrrutal.' Polish women are sexy even when they are talking about impaling traitors up the anus.

Afterwards, in the foyer, someone casually remarked, 'Your Magda looks like her cousin.'

My father appraised me. 'No. Not really. Magda Zawadzka's jaw is more…determined.'

I pounced on the remark. 'What does that mean?'

'More…I don't know…determined.'

Was I *not* determined? Was I weak? I started to jut my jaw forward in what I guessed was a determined style. And my cousin became a totem of impossible heroism. Would I pass the test when the time came? I fervently believed that I would give my life to the glorious Polish cause if called upon. Of course Dad didn't know about those fantasies. But there was a reason he tried to curb my enthusiasm for the world of *Colonel Wołodyjowski*. He had grown up surrounded by stories of Polish nationalism and courage. And self-sacrifice. And violent death dressed up to look glorious. He was enormously proud of my cousin, but he considered the Polish romantic tradition to be little more than brainwashing. He loathed all forms of nationalism, and he mistrusted causes. He knew all too well what they demanded.

I didn't. I wanted to be a marching girl. I longed to parade in serried ranks. I was a sucker for a cause, a born flag-waver. And there was not a thing my father could do about it.

# LEON URIS

The film deepened my identification with my Polish side but it shed no light on the shadows of what my father had done during the war. My mind kept circling back to the Holocaust. Maybe a year or so after watching *Colonel Wołodyjowski* I embarked on my Leon Uris phase and read *Exodus* and *Miła 18*. As I opened the pages of these books I was scared but my heart was wide open, full of sympathy for the Jewish people. I knew that my family had hidden Jewish people. I knew we were on the same side, the good side. In some way I identified with the Jews. I wanted to stand shoulder to shoulder with them. To take up arms with them and destroy Hitler. I had seen the film and wanted to go to Israel with Ari and Karen from *Exodus* and be a child of light.

And then I read Leon Uris's description of the Poles.

It was not just Germans who hated the Jews—it was Poles as well. Betraying them, selling them, profiteering and collaborating in their destruction. During the Jews' brave but doomed ghetto uprising in

1943—their final defiant act before their extermination—the Poles, according to Uris, turned their backs. Refused to give them guns and ammunition. While the ghetto was annihilated the Poles went about their lives, indifferent and unaffected. I was astonished. How could the Poles do this? The brave Poles. The gallant Poles.

It was as if someone had plunged a red-hot iron into my sympathetic nervous system. Pain shot through my whole body. I lay on my bed trembling. The Poles were not just the good people. We were also the bad people. We had not helped the Jews. Had my father hurt the Jews?

One day I could contain it no longer. I went to my father holding the book, angry with him for not being a good person. He was ironing a shirt. Whenever you wanted a shirt ironed my father was the man for the job. Every crinkle would be removed, every crease made immaculate.

'Is this true?'

'What are you talking about?'

'This!'

Dad looked at the book.

'Ach, Jesus.'

'Is this true? Is that what the Poles did?'

'Some Poles, Magda. Some. Not all.'

And that's when I said to him, 'The Poles were as bad as the Germans.'

He put the iron down. 'What are you talking about?'

'The Poles were as bad as the Germans.'

He stared at me. 'Magda, Leon Uris wasn't bloody there. How would he *know*?'

'Is it true?'

'Yes, some of it. There were many brave Jews. But that is only one side.'

'What do you mean? Is this what happened?'

He waved me away. I was too young for this conversation. But I was already in it, whether I wanted to be or not. 'Tell me! Were the Poles as bad as the Germans?'

'Some, Magda, some. You always have a choice. Some people did the right thing.'

'But why didn't you help the Jews? Why didn't you give them guns?'

My father looked like I had slapped him. He composed himself. 'Leon Uris wasn't there. He doesn't know what it was like for us. You must understand, Magda. We. Had. Nothing. *Nothing!* It wasn't that we wouldn't give guns to the Jews. We *had* no bloody guns!'

'But did the Poles *do* that?'

'Ach, Jesus. Just forget about it.'

Like a thief, shame crept into my soul and took up residence there. Although I couldn't name the feeling then, it was as Jean Genet said: *Crimes of which a people is ashamed constitute its real history. The same is true of man.* I absorbed things entirely and allowed them to sink into the centre of my being, to become my identity. I was a half-Polish girl with a Polish name on an island in the Pacific. The Poles' shame became my shame, fused to my soul. And I decided that I did not have what it took to be truly good.

# FIGHT, FLIGHT, FREEZE

It's 1972. I am 5-2 up in the third set. Heat radiates off the en-tous-cas court. I hold the ball in my sweaty hand, its peachy fuzz prickling my fingers. There is red dust on the tip of my Dunlop Volley, stained from repeatedly dragging my toe as I reach up to serve. Just the way Dad told me. My serve is in especially good form at the moment and has bagged me several aces. Hard, flat, mighty. I have found my groove. I look at my opponent across the net. She is a kid like me. Maybe eleven or twelve. She is sweating and she can't do a thing right. She is so small at the other end of the court. I see her parents watching. I see the look on her face. I know the feeling well. Humiliation.

I know what I am supposed to do. But I can't do it. I cannot bring myself to finish her off. As I bounce the ball, trying to gather myself to serve, I am overcome with pity for my opponent. Deep, heaving waves of pity. As I toss the ball to serve, my eyes are blinded with tears, my cheeks bright red with grief. And I double-fault. That's OK.

Let her catch up. Let her have a few points. Allow her some dignity.

I lose the next game. And then the next. And now her confidence is coming back while mine is ebbing away. Oozing out of me like blood from a slit wrist. I can feel the reversal. Now I am the victim. Like the weakest impala at the watering hole, I'm a goner. And I can do nothing to stop it.

Game. Set. Match. It's over. I lose.

I have become that most despised of tennis pariahs—I am a choker.

I ask my father's advice. He sighs, reluctant to tell me the truth—as he sees it.

'The problem is you are getting too heavy. You aren't fast enough on the court.'

I don't know why I am getting too heavy. My hips are getting bigger and so are my breasts. They get in the way of my ground shots. But I don't know what to do about it. I can't seem to stop it.

'If you just lose half a stone you'll be fine.'

'What should I do?'

'Don't eat. Starve yourself.'

'But what if I get hungry?'

'Ignore it. Have a piece of fruit. If you just lose half a stone you will be fine.'

When my father came out of the POW camp he was rake-thin. Prewar photos of him reveal a little Billy Bunter, puffy and plain as a boiled bagel. Standing next to him, his sister is a svelte beauty. When he emerged from the stalag it was like a butterfly emerging from a tubby cocoon. Gaunt and handsome with angular cheekbones, he resembled Dirk Bogarde. And it must have seemed to him that finally he had escaped the family curse. His fat mother, his inelegantly solid father. He had escaped the genetic fate that awaited him. Now he was waiting to see if I would do the same.

It's true what my mother says. I did have 'a belting good figure'. I was only eleven, but already there was evidence of womanly curves, of the breasts and slender waist that denote my natural hourglass shape. At such a young age my body, my 'womanliness', was beginning to betray me. My weight was getting in the way of my tennis. So I began starving myself. Never to the point of anorexia, I hasten to add. But I have been playing Russian roulette with hunger ever since.

Every family has one big thing, one defining metaphor, that shapes it. One arena where every battle is fought, every character is formed. Ours was tennis.

My father was obsessed with tennis. And whatever dark energy it was that fuelled this obsession made him relentless. Nothing, not Jehovah himself, would come between him and tennis. If you wanted to be with my father you would have to share his obsession. Age did not weary it. Right up until two days before he died he was still glued to the television, watching tennis.

In Poland before the war my father played all kinds of sport— ice-hockey, soccer, swimming, skating. In winter, with the Vistula beginning to freeze over, he would dive into its frigid waters to compete in swimming contests with his friends as great chunks of ice floated past their shivering bodies. In summer there was volleyball.

And after the war? After the war my father just could not sit still. 'Och, for god's sake, that fella just cannae sit still! He's aye fidgetin'!' my Scottish granny bemoaned. During mass, reading a book, watching television, eating dinner. Fidgeting, adjusting, moving. He was like a Futurist sculpture, a blur of slight but perpetual motion. It was like that when he drew a sketch or wrote a letter. His hand would fidget and hover over the page, twitching for what felt like an eternity.

After the war tennis was his game. My father taught himself to play. Of course he chose tennis, that most English of games after cricket. He would sit for hours, poring over textbooks and magazines, painstakingly absorbing and instructing himself in the latest methods.

My father gave me my first tennis racquet when I was about six. It was a hand-me-down wooden-framed Slazenger. I could barely get my hand around the worn leather grip. We were at St Edmond's, the local Catholic parish club, and I wasn't really even in the game. I was crouched in the tramlines at the side of the court when I sensed the ball heading towards me. Instinctively I stuck my racquet up and fluked a perfect volley, right in the sweet spot.

That sweet spot is a slice of heaven, a glimpse of perfection. It is the spot around the middle of the racquet where impact achieves maximum speed and minimum jarring. All of the forces of physics— torque, vibration, energy—align. And you can feel it. It is percussive; your ear registers instantly when you have hit the sweet spot. *Puck*. Nothing gives you so much of a sense of the divinity of the sweet spot as experiencing its opposite—the dead spot at the top of the racquet where the ball gives all its energy to the racquet but the racquet gives nothing back. And the ball falls dead at your feet. Just like the impala at the watering hole.

The sweet spot became my drug. My life twined itself around tennis until it was impossible to tell which was the parasite and which was the host. Every weekend all weekend and two to three nights a week it was tennis. All of my friends were from the tennis club. We played at Croydon and Montrose and Kilsyth. Every school holiday was spent playing tournaments. Every Easter break a great caravan of families would drive for several hours up the Calder Highway to play in country tournaments in towns like Cohuna and Echuca and Kerang and Swan Hill, some with populations of only a thousand or so. The Easter tournaments remain a great source of civic pride in these towns. In the midst of the wizened, arid Sunraysia District an oasis of beautiful, bright green lawn tennis courts would appear.

At the age of eleven and twelve we kids would play several sets of tennis a day in the broiling heat. Valiant little gladiators in frilly knickers and bobble socks, we would smack the ball back and forth, our sinewy adolescent arms growing strong and assured. We were already trained to ignore our screaming muscles and burning lungs.

In our small amounts of time off we would wander down to the nearby river. Once we found a tin dinghy and used a plank to shove off from the eroded muddy banks and into the brown waters of a thin tributary of the Murray River, where we drifted silently. And maybe, I can't be sure, the faint ripples of the paddle-steamers gently rocked our vessel in their wake. Or maybe I am being fanciful.

My father would take us to the Australian Open at Kooyong. Every year, for every single day of the tournament, we would pack up an esky of food, fill the thermos with tea, drive into town, put on our terry-towelling hats and sit for hours on the peeling forest-green wooden benches, baking in the merciless midsummer sun. And when we weren't watching matches we were watching the players out on the practice court, studying their form. My father would point out with admiration their prowess, their skill, their sportsmanship.

I loved Kooyong. It was built on the sturdy bones of tradition but new blood surged through its veins. If Wimbledon was the ancient seat of Britain's tennis empire, Kooyong was the rebel stronghold, the place where the descendants of convicts trained to defeat their former overlords. Australia could never hope to win against Britain in the culture wars because the deck was stacked. Literature, art, theatre—their value is determined subjectively. But in the sporting arena there is no room for opinion. The ball is either in or out.

The sixties and seventies were still the glory days of Aussie tennis—Lew Hoad, Rocket Rod Laver, Margaret Court, Ken Rosewall. Between matches we would go down into the cool of the undercroft and buy cups of Peters ice-cream with flat wooden spoons. There you could rub shoulders with your heroes, the giants of tennis:

Chrissie Evert, Martina Navratilova, Jimmy Connors.

I still have autographs and instamatic photos of Guillermo Vilas and John Newcombe. And Di Fromholtz. *Lots* of Di Fromholtz. When the snaps came back from the chemist my mother cast her eye over them. I held my breath. I felt like a fugitive in a science-fiction film being scanned by a lie detector. She looked at the photos then at me. 'Why are there so many of Di Fromholtz?'

I blushed and stammered. I hadn't realised that my obsession was showing. 'Her backhand. She has the best backhand in women's tennis.'

My topspin backhand was my best shot so this was plausible. My mother skewered me with That Look. She said nothing and handed the photos back.

My mother didn't share our tennis obsession and so she became a tennis widow. She had tried early on but my father, either through competitiveness or scorn, made it plain she wasn't welcome. So every Saturday morning my father and I would head off to Croydon Tennis Club in the Triumph 2000 sports car. That bloody Triumph. For a brief moment my brother had owned a second-hand Triumph Herald, which he stripped back and painted gunmetal grey. It had a slightly sticky gearstick which came to a grizzly end one day when my father found Chris lying dead drunk at the bottom of the driveway after a night of partying, the recalcitrant gearstick still in his clenched fist. The car was found some time later in a ditch, the engine running, the wheels still spinning.

The Triumph 2000 was an impractical car but my father loved it. It was designed by the Italian Giovanni Michelotti and had gorgeous wooden panelling and leather seats. When he saw it in the showroom it was love at first sight. Later that night, when my parents were debating the purchase, he sat on the edge of his chair, his hands clasped between his knees, and said, 'I love that car, Margaret. I know it's not practical but…I love that car.' We got the car.

The drive to the club was always fraught for me. I wanted to go and play tennis with my friends but I knew that my mother would be left behind all weekend, stuck in the house at the top of the hill with no car and not much of a bus service. Even worse, on those drives my father would complain to me about my mother. I understood. They were going through a rough patch. But I also resented him for it. Deeply. So, much as I too loved the new car, I also dreaded it.

I had a coach at the club but my father decided to give me extra lessons on the side. Coaching was in his blood. My grandfather, Mieczysław, had been a referee of Greco-Roman wrestling. Dad seemed to recall he was associated with the Olympics. When he travelled around the country to scout for new talent and judge matches Dad would tag along behind him like 'the stench behind an army', as he put it.

Mieczysław was a harsh taskmaster. Stern; iron discipline. After the war, when the communists forced him and my grandmother to 'resettle' into a minuscule one-room flat in the newly reclaimed Szczecin in north-west Poland, every morning without fail he would move the beds, the chairs, the tables, pushing them out of the way so he could perform his calisthenic rituals. And then replace them.

It was from this arrested and idealised adolescent memory of his father that my father's own standards of excellence were born, like Pallas Athena out of the head of Zeus. There was always something strangely Leni Riefenstahl-ish about my father's veneration of sporting prowess. I recoiled from it instantly and forcefully: the moment I became proficient at a sport I began to feel like a Nazi and would stop. Especially swimming, where there is so much time to think. In the middle of a lap I would stop, get out, go to the showers, change, go home and not come back. It has made sustaining any kind of fitness regime well nigh impossible.

Professionally committed to the idea of independent, verifiable standards, my father loved quality but he loathed all forms of toadying with the same vehemence that Jesus reserved for the Pharisees and the traders in the temple. He refused to curry favour, to flatter, to compromise or grease the wheels in any way. He was unbribable.

Probably because of his objective, disinterested nature, my father was appointed to the selection committee at the tennis club. Everyone knows that your game improves when you play against players better than yourself. Some parents would jockey fiercely to get their child into the best possible spot. There were heated arguments. My father remained above it all, impervious to pleas and threats. In fact, in order to quash any perception of favouritism, he demoted me. My mother was ropable.

Interestingly, his Olympic standards were genderless. He brought me up to believe that I could be as good as any man. At anything. He was that uniquely Polish oxymoron: a feminist male chauvinist. (Polish men are all rampant patriarchs living in a matriarchal society.) Accordingly, Dad was adamant that to play tennis properly you had to play 'like a man'. Because that was the most efficient, streamlined, 'orthodox' way to play.

The British player Virginia Wade embodied his ideal. Not only was she a champion, she was also a doctor. Wade oozed English chilly aplomb and, best of all, she served 'like a man'. She arched her back, she leapt into the air, she bent her elbow. She did not allow femininity to get in the way of getting it right. Serving uses the same action as throwing a ball. I already threw like a boy. So to teach me to serve like one my father gave me an old broken racquet and sent me off to throw it around the backyard for hours at a time.

He was fascinated by the women's power game which was emerging in the seventies. All of the women he grew up with—his mother, the women in his unit, his sister—could handle a gun. They were feminine, but they still knew how to shoot properly. A tennis racquet was no different from a gun. In my father's book, not to do something correctly for fear of being seen as unfeminine was idiotic. He was gender-blind before the phrase existed. He thought it was a criminal waste to deprive the world of half the population's talent. So I was to play to the best of my ability: like a man. But it wasn't just power he admired. 'You have to be clever. You look at all the great players, they know how to read the game, how to anticipate their opponents.'

On the court there is nowhere to hide. You are relying on no one but yourself. Your deficits cannot be hidden in the scrum of the team. Too little confidence, too much confidence, fear, arrogance, injury. The job of your opponent is to find your weakness and exploit it.

Of course my father chose tennis. And not just for its pukka Englishness. The language of tennis is the language of killing. When backed into a corner, when lesser players fold under the pressure, great players bring out their best shots. Genius shots. Impossible shots.

Killer shots.

My father was my coach but he didn't teach me to play how he played. He taught me to play how he *wished* he played. He wanted me to go for the odds-defying winners that are the hallmark of the truly great. He wanted me to play like a champion. His own game, however, was no reflection of his Olympic ideals. It was effective and efficient. It was the game of a saboteur.

As a method of coaching my father would often play me. He never once let me win. He would do whatever it took to beat me. Gamesmanship, pity plays, craftiness. He would drop the racquet and rub his leg, evoking the spectre of his cancer. He employed a campaign of misinformation, advising me to do something and then turning it against me. It didn't matter that I was nine years old or a girl or his daughter. He fought dirty. He showed no mercy. What would be the point? What useful lesson would I learn if he let me win? That would be patronising. It would be dishonest.

When I started to lose my nerve and put on some weight he stepped up his attack. He made a point of running me all over the court until my cheeks were puce with exertion. He would keep up this game of cat-and-mouse for some time. Then he would 'finish me off'. The deathblow wouldn't be a zinging forehand or an un-gettable smash, one of the big shots that he loved to see others play. My father would finish me off with a drop shot. A ridiculous, humiliating drop shot. Ignoble but effective. And when he had beaten me he would mock me.

I adored my father. But as I grew older I hated him for this with an absolute rage. Impotent fury beyond fury, in those moments *I* could have killed *him*.

He beat me because he wanted to teach me a lesson. He beat me to teach me how to keep fighting against an opponent even when there is no hope of winning. But mostly he beat me because he needed to. He needed to discharge the pent-up killer energy inside him. So periodically he would perform a ritual bloodletting, and I was the sacrifice. He had lost everything—the war, his family, his country. He needed to win at something.

Afterwards, he was invigorated, enlivened. He would puff up like a little bantam. He was testing me, finding the limits of my character. I knew even then that my father had learnt many useful lessons from the war—how to survive, how to outwit—but not how to be merciful.

'You have no killer instinct,' he told me. 'You don't have what it takes. You can't finish off your opponents.' He said this as though he had no personal stake in it, as though I was not his daughter, as if he was an employer having, regretfully, to dismiss an underachieving worker. 'I don't say this to hurt you. It's just the truth. You haven't got it.' I was eleven. He defined how far my dreams would take me. 'You will never be Evonne Goolagong. You could be a good A-grade player. You're good, but you'll never be great.'

That was it. The mixed message of expectation and inadequacy was crystal clear. I would never be Evonne Goolagong, but I was still expected to train like I might. As my brother says, he trained us *not* to win. He trained us to be good also-rans. There was always, supposedly, an obstacle to our greatness. We were too short. We weren't pigeon-toed. (Splayed feet are not nimble on the court. I tried to cultivate a pigeon toe.)

In spite of all this I still quietly hoped I might be a champion. And in the summer of 1972 I received what I believed to be a sign. I was photographed for the newspaper. Twice. The first picture was on the front page of the *Sun*. It was during the Victorian Schoolboys and Schoolgirls Championship. The tournament was played at Kooyong, which meant all of us kids got a chance to play on the hallowed courts.

This front page was my first brush with fame. It is a great action shot. I am mid-lunge, hitting a backhand volley. My technique is perfect: arm rigid, eye on the ball, left arm counter-balancing perfectly. My tongue is poking out for added concentration. There was only one problem. It was all a lie. It was not a match at all. A friend and I were hitting on an outside court when a photographer came up and asked if he could take pictures of us practising. And the ball was not a winner. It clipped the top of my racquet and went sailing out of court. The caption, by the way, was *I'll lick 'em all*.

Kooyong was also where I made a lifelong friend. In order to get to the outside courts we would be loaded onto the back of a ute and driven out, and on one such trip I struck up a conversation with the girl next to me. She was funny and sweet and soon we were mucking around and giggling like idiots. That girl was Marg Downey.

My second brush with fame was in the local rag, also during a tournament. The shot is of me sitting on Dad's lap as he points out some detail in the distance. All posed, all faked. I felt like a fraud. Deep down I knew my father was right: I didn't have what it took.

But there was someone who did.

Mandy Plunkett.

Mandy Plunkett was everything my father deplored in a tennis player. She was powerful but not elegant. She was a scrapper, a slugger, a battler. Worst of all she was 'unorthodox'. Her stance was wide open. By the look of her she had no right to win. But she did. In truth she was a natural athlete, and soon she was smashing me off the court.

'I will say one thing for her. That kid has killer instinct,' my father informed me as I zipped my racquet back into its cover after yet another mortifying defeat.

That was when I knew that my mind was not like my father's. I had no mental toughness. My mind was the enemy betraying me from within. And to say I lost my confidence does not begin to describe what happened. I couldn't hit a ball over the net. I would be convulsed with shakes. No one wanted to partner with me. Even my backhand deserted me. Everyone could see I was unravelling. 'What on earth is wrong with Magda?' one of the other parents asked.

My father pulled a face. 'I don't know.'

It was a complete humiliation, repeated with routine horror. Week after week I would go out there and disintegrate. But still I kept playing. What else could I do? I pretended I didn't care. I pretended I wasn't really trying. At tournaments my father would prowl theatrically up and back like a lion behind the court, while *on* the court I was yet again self-destructing. He would slap his forehead melodramatically when I missed a shot, muttering, '*Aie*, aie, *aie*, aie, aie!'

The girlfriend of the coach took pity on me. She took me aside and tried to teach me consistency, how to simply keep the ball in play. Her name was Sally. She may have no idea how grateful I still am for that act of kindness. My father encouraged me to learn from her, but I could see the hurt on his face and I couldn't do it. I couldn't betray him. I thanked Sally but I never went back. Even though I was only twelve I understood. And because I understood I forgave him. He simply couldn't stop himself.

It must have been a Saturday when the incident with Trevor Hanson occurred because the whole club was there. It was a hot day and I wanted a drink from the clubhouse drink machine. For some reason my parents didn't believe in pocket money so every time I wanted something it meant a major round of negotiations. I went over to Dad, who was sitting at a table chatting during afternoon tea.

'Excuse me, Dad,' I began. 'Can I have twenty cents for a drink, please?'

'You don't need it.'

My cheeks flushed. 'But I'm thirsty.'

'Have some water.'

'I don't want water. I want a soft drink.' The other kids were standing there with their bottles of Hoy's.

He looked at me. 'The last thing you need is a soft drink.'

Fury boiled up inside me. 'Forget it!' I stormed off.

'Aren't you getting a drink?' one of the other kids asked.

'I'm not thirsty.'

There was a match the other kids wanted to watch so we went and sat at the back of the court. Trevor Hanson was playing. Trevor was a leering creep. I really didn't like him and watching him play wasn't my idea of a great time, but I didn't know what else to do with myself so I joined them. Trevor was an OK player. But that day he was losing, and he wasn't happy. He fluffed an easy shot. He turned, looked at me, took a spare ball from his pocket and whacked it at me with all of his strength. It hit me full force in the shoulder.

I shot up to my feet. 'You bastard! You fucking creepy bastard! I'm gonna tell my dad on you!' It was the only threat I had. I ran to the back of the court where my father was by now playing. 'Dad!'

He ignored me.

'*Dad!*' I stood at the back of the court, tears stinging my eyes.

He reluctantly interrupted his game and came to the back of the court, laughing. 'Maggie. Calm down.'

'I won't calm down! Don't tell me to calm down!'

'What happened?'

'Trevor Hanson deliberately smashed a ball at me!'

'Well, what do you expect me to do?'

'I want you to tell him off!'

'Maggie,' he chuckled, 'people get hit sometimes. It's part of the game. Calm down.'

I twisted my fingers through the cyclone fence at the back of the court and shook and throttled it, tears of fury streaming down my face. I started screaming. By now everyone was watching. 'You tell him off! You stick up for me and you fucking tell him off!'

'Magda. Come on. Stop it.'

'You tell him! You tell him off! *You fucking tell him off!*'

The other club members couldn't believe what they were seeing. I was such a well-mannered girl. The one without any guile, as someone once said. I had turned into a howling banshee. My rage frightened even me. I fell to the ground bawling. 'Why won't you stick up for me! Why won't you ever stick up for me?'

'Maggie…'

He moved towards me. All I wanted now was to get away from him. But there was nowhere to go. Croydon. The middle of nowhere. I had no money; I couldn't even catch a bus. I was overwhelmed by my own helplessness. Then I saw it. My only option. The Triumph 2000.

I ran to the carpark and climbed into the only sanctuary I could find. I locked the doors and sat there crying and raging. I locked my father out of his own beloved car.

I don't know how long I sat there. Long enough for my father to finish a couple of sets. Finally, I saw him heading up the grass verge towards the carpark. I was still diamond-hard with fury.

'Maggie. Come on, love. Open the door.'

I ignored him.

He tapped on the window. 'I'm sorry, love. Come on, open the door.'

'Go away! Fucking go away!'

He went off for half an hour or so. When he came back I was still furious. 'Maggie.' He reached into his pocket and pulled out a twenty-cent coin.

'Go. *Away!*'

He started to wave the coin across the window like a mesmerist. 'Ooh, Maggie, don't you want the twenty cents? Come on hen, I'm sorry.'

He was sorry. Despite myself I laughed. And I opened the door.

The next day my mother flew down the road in a hot fury to Trevor Hanson's house and stood in the front garden demanding the boy come out and apologise. Eventually he did, nearly in tears, and I was completely mortified.

That was the year my father gave me a gun. A rifle. A point two-two. I would fire practice shots into the sloping hill of our big backyard. I loved target practice.

One day Dad took me rabbit hunting, just the two of us. In the unsuitably low-slung Triumph we drove to a pine forest on the edge of Lake Eildon. Brittle pine needles smothered the forest floor. Nothing lived there except rabbits. The forest was crawling with them, all of them riddled with myxomatosis, which meant they were blind, dying and in pain. It was a kindness to kill them.

My father and I trudged across the slippery pine needles for a few kilometres until we reached a good vantage point on a hill.

'Look. There.' My father pointed. Movement. Signs of bouncing, furry, fluffy life. I raised my rifle and in the crosshairs, far away, a rabbit was leaping about, never suspecting that these were its last moments. I felt no fellow feeling. No pity. It was a pest that needed to be shot. I was excited, and happy to be doing the right thing. As my father had taught me, I took a deep breath and then exhaled half of it. That way I would have enough air in my lungs that my chest would remain steady as I took aim. I was going to be like him: a hunter. A woodsman. A killer.

The rabbit stopped going about its life for just a second. It seemed to be making a decision. Slowly, as I had been told, I squeezed the trigger. 'Don't jerk. Squeeze.' But I was a kid and the rifle was big. I jerked. The bullet zinged through the air and the rabbit skittered away. 'Did I get it? Did I get it?' I squealed. I wanted to be a good shot.

'No. You only wounded it. You have to finish it off. Come on.'

I froze. I did not want to go near the wounded rabbit. Suddenly it was not a game anymore.

'Magda, come on.'

My sense of myself collapsed inwards. I did not know who I was or who I wanted to be. Was I his daughter? Was I capable of being his daughter? I could not move.

'Magda. Don't be silly.'

The look on my face must have been awful. He softened, as best he could. There was a job to be done.

'Maggie. You can't just leave it like that. That would be cruel.'

We trudged for an eternity across the burrow-pocked grassland. There was the rabbit. It lay dying, painfully and slowly. Its little head turned and it looked into my eyes. I saw what I had done and I burst into tears. The rabbit was a living thing and I had just killed it. It wasn't vermin, a plague-riddled pest. It was a bunny rabbit. A furry little Peter Rabbit. Bugs Bunny. Thumper. It was a creature that wanted to live. By now I was shaking and crying uncontrollably.

It was growing dark, and my father was losing patience. 'Come on. You have to finish it off.'

I raised my rifle and stood over the bunny, taking aim. The bunny was looking at me. I had to make a choice. 'I can't! I can't do it!'

'Ach, Jesus!'

My father pulled me aside. 'Look the other way.'

I turned my face. There was a loud crack. I knew it was done. I looked round just in time to see the rabbit's head sink to the ground.

We sat in the car in silence. On the long road home the low-slung Triumph hit a bump and the muffler fell off and had to be tied back on with a wire coathanger. My father never took me hunting again. And he got rid of the Triumph.

# SHARPIES

Everything that mattered happened in 1973. And everything else happened in 1974. David Bowie released *Pin Ups*; my mother got her drivers licence; I started secondary school. And I hit puberty. Or rather it hit me—with all the delicacy of a freight train. I woke up one morning and I was a different person. There was a brief moment of pert blossoms and then *boom!* Boobs. Big ones. I felt like a cartoon character. I was henceforth known as 'the one with the big tits'.

I wasn't the only thing that was changing. Civilisation was on its way to the outer suburbs. Which is to say, the roads were being made. Each home had to pay over a thousand dollars for the patch of dirt in front of their house to be levelled out and coated in bitumen. Road crews arrived. Bulldozers and graders trampled and gouged the talcum-soft dirt. Surveyors arrived with spirit levels. The soft fuzzy edges of the road were straightened out and hard concrete kerbs were put in. I hated kerbs. Kerbs signalled the beginning of the end. We were not country anymore. We were suburbia. Everyone thought this was a good thing, an emblem of progress. Everyone except me. The silvery road to my pale yellow moon was covered in tar and cement.

Roads meant cars. They lay sprawled like mangy camp dogs across driveways, nature strips and front lawns. Highway lanes reproduced themselves in multiples of two. Black bitumen carparks oozed across the landscape like oil spills. And all the way along the Maroondah Highway, on either side, there was an infinity of car yards, their cheery bunting waving in the breeze like the flags of all nations.

I loved some of it. It was modern. Ringwood with its ten-pin bowling and ice rink and car yards was crazy-paved enough for me to be able to pretend I was in a *Brady Bunch* episode. But in fact I was living in a wasteland. It was all squat boxes that did a job and nothing more, Bauhaus's bastard child. No surface decoration, no playful embellishments, no fanciful curves or ornamental follies. Just bald tin sheds, flat-faced shops, pre-fab concrete boxes. Fish and chip shops, auto-repair joints, electronics resale outlets, unisex hair salons, white-goods warehouses. Croydon in 1973 had become a desolate, violent outpost.

It was this wasteland that gave birth to the sharpie gangs of Melbourne. Back then a sharpie was not a felt-tip pen. A sharpie was a locally grown version of a skinhead. Their dress code was stricter than a naval uniform. Tight clothes, block-toed shoes. The haircut was a cross between a mullet and a skinhead, and in those days shaved heads were scary. They conveyed a message of primaeval menace. They were the badge of the sociopath.

The weirdest thing of all was sharpie dancing. I have no idea where it came from. It was animalistic and sexually provocative—the nuns forbade it at school dances. The shoulders were hunched and the arms pistoned up and down in front of your chest as if you were trying to punch yourself in the chin. The head, jaw stuck out, jutted back and forth like a lithium-induced tic. The knees were bent, and flapped in and out like wings going nowhere. Years later I created a character called Michelle Grogan who parodied that dancing with her silent partner Ferret.

I knew of the notorious sharpie gangs. Everyone did. They were the Mongol hordes of the suburban train lines. Tales circulated of their unprovoked cruelty, the reign of terror they imposed. And public transport became the locus of fear, the means by which they created and maintained their empire. Many of the gangs associated themselves with a particular train station. There were the Croydie Boys, the Ringwood Sharps, the Mentone Sharps, the Jordie Boys. Ringwood railway station was the epicentre in our region, a place synonymous with fear and loathing. My brother Chris had told me how he and a few friends had once come upon a gang of a dozen sharpies beating up one defenceless guy. He was lying on the ground as the leader of the gang jumped up and down on his stomach. As soon as my brother and his friends got close the sharpies scattered like roaches. Chris and his mates piled the poor guy into a car and took him to hospital, where he was treated for a broken pelvis.

Sharpie violence was a peculiarly Australian form of violence. It was apolitical and ahistorical. It had no objective. It was not a working-class movement that sought better conditions for itself. Nor was it self-consciously iconoclastic like British punk. Its creed was pure, simple, mindless violence.

Our home life was as desolate as the suburban wasteland that surrounded it. Five years after Dad got cancer he was given the all clear. No announcement was made. He just stopped going for check-ups. But the impact of his illness had atomised my family in slow motion. We each floated off and shrank into our own tiny universe, determined by our interests, talents and obsessions.

For Chris it was cars. In his late teens Chris decided to build his own Clubman sports car from scratch. It arrived in parts and through sheer force of personal power and technical skill my brother commandeered the garage. The family Kingswood, which had replaced the Triumph, was relegated to the bottom of the drive. All weekend every weekend Chris would rev the million-horsepower engine, its deafening roar fuelled by his bottomless rage at my father. Occasionally Dad would hover near, awestruck and intimidated by my brother's mechanical virtuosity. Sometimes Chris allowed my father to hand him a spanner. Sometimes I would even venture down but he had no interest in a little brat like me—as the increased volume of the throttle testified.

For my father, of course, it continued to be tennis. More and more, his weekends were spent at the tennis club until eventually it became all weekend, every weekend.

My mother slept. Every day, for hours and hours, we didn't know why. She slept so heavily that not even the roar of Chris's sports car could rouse her. She slept like she was, as she put it, dead to the world, and began to suffer from vague debilitating nerve ailments, like the non-specific 'neurasthenia' that had kept her father in hospital for years after the war, what we would now call anxiety and depression. No one knew what to do. Certainly not my father.

My mother was shipwrecked and foundering on his adamantine shores. He was not kind about her weakness. It spoke too loudly to his own gentle heart, lying dormant inside the armour of the assassin, sure to break if ever fully awakened.

Drowning in menopausal hormones and despair, my mother began to worry that he was having an affair. There were bitter arguments. The paper-thin walls of brick veneer homes keep no secrets. Alone in the realm of my adolescent bedroom, all I could hear was oaths and curses. Soon my father began to use me as a kind of chaperone, a witness to his innocence. He wasn't having an affair. His desire wasn't for other women. It was for sport, the least problematic relationship of his life.

And now my father stopped speaking to my sister. Ever since she announced that she was leaving home to 'go flatting' he had sent her to the Polish equivalent of Coventry: Siberia. A lonely place, and cold. I was eleven. My sister was twenty-one.

I adored Barb and my father's treatment of her upset me. My sister was from the Age of Aquarius—which is in fact her star sign. She was like a rare woodland creature; grass and flowers sprang up where she walked. She was my oasis of sanity, the one I turned to when I had awkward questions about school or boys or sex. With the age difference it was like having a young groovy mum. She was the one who gave me 'the talk'. And now she was leaving home. She had a job in the city, as a secretary.

Before she left, when she was doing her stenography course, I'd pleaded with her to teach me shorthand. I used to stare at the indecipherable squiggles in her steno and shorthand notebook. I loved the idea of a secret language. I would fall asleep to the clacketty tap of the typewriter keys as she practised, getting her speed up to 130 words per minute. Chris helped her load up a trailer of her things. *Jonathan Livingston Seagull* was crammed into an old waxed cardboard fruit box alongside Hermann Hesse and Solzhenitzyn's *The Gulag Archipelago*. Milk crates were filled with vinyl records, their sleeves splashed with psychedelic, acid-inspired cover art. Her groovy clothes were in her suitcase. And she drove away.

I went a few times to visit her at her flat in South Yarra. I had rarely ventured this close to the city before. I loved the ornate Victorian buildings with their tessellated verandas and wrought-iron balconies. The mock-Tudor shops on Toorak Road reminded me of England. Barb bought a motorbike and every week she would ride the thirty kilometres from town to visit us. But the tyranny of distance prevailed, and her visits grew less and less frequent. I felt terribly alone.

But soon I had other, more pressing worries. I was being sent away to a convent.

All of my best friends from school and tennis were going to Croydon High, so I desperately wanted to go too. Both my brother and sister had been there. But at that time Croydon High had a scary reputation. Sharpie culture had infiltrated. There were rumours that a student had been viciously attacked in the high-school grounds. A gang of girls had pinned her down and the leader had scraped a metal tail-comb across the girl's cheek because she was 'too pretty'.

I still wanted to go there but my report card sealed my fate. My grades were too good. My sixth-grade teacher pulled my father aside at a parent-teacher meeting and told him bluntly, 'Get her out of here.'

My father informed me on the way to tennis that I was enrolled to sit the entrance exam at Siena Convent—the same school Izabella was at. 'I would have given anything to have the opportunities you have, Magda. You are lucky, you are smarter than me. It is a sin to waste the God-given gift of a good brain.'

I wanted to protest but I sat in stony silence for the rest of the journey, crushed by his reasonableness.

Siena Convent was miles away. I would have to leave home with Dad at 6.30 a.m., get a lift to the station then catch two trains and a tram, or walk for half an hour, in order to beat the bell at 8.30. I would not get back to Croydon station until 5 p.m. and then I would have to wait until Dad picked me up on the way home from work. There was only one other girl who lived as far out as me and she was in sixth form. This meant that except for limited tennis practice there could be no socialising on weeknights. School friends would not be able to come over and hang in any casual way. Like a major expedition, everything had to be prearranged weeks in advance so they could sleep over. I was not a boarder, but not like a normal day-girl either.

This was banishment. There was no other word for it. First, though, I would have to pass the entrance exam.

The school was on Riversdale Road, on top of the hill. Opposite stood St Dominic's Church, its large, blue-grey neo-Gothic spire looming over middle-class Camberwell. As we drove up I realised it was a different world. I knew this was a great opportunity. And I knew that part of me wanted this. But there were powerful reasons not to want it, too.

A nun fluttered silently along the row of battered wooden desks and set the exam paper face down in front of me. This piece of paper would determine my life. All I had to do was fail, and I would be free to follow my heart to Croydon High. I looked around at the other girls, their heads bent diligently over their papers. I picked up my pen. I started to write. At the end of the exam I handed in my work. And then we waited for the results.

I passed my entrance exam and was accepted to Siena. My dalliance with the idea of failing was brief: I knew my father was right. But I felt crushed by the feeling that I was just an extension of him, there to live his unlived dreams. More than that. I was there to live Poland's unlived dreams. There was the illusion of freedom, but it was just that. Scores had to be settled, the ledger balanced. Wrong, terrible wrong, had to be righted. My life and achievements were not mine alone.

Uniforms were compulsory at Siena. I was secretly thrilled, even though it was an appalling colour—rust brown and forest green. Siena was not one of Melbourne's grander convent schools. The rather cramped grounds were nothing like the sprawling, botanical showpieces of Genazzano or Star of the Sea. The front was bordered by a wrought-iron fence. All was presided over by the cream brick convent built, according to my old year book, in 1939 and 'designed by the architect, Mr Agabiti, in the Italian style'.

Many of the girls already knew one another from Catholic primary school. I knew no one except Izabella. But I soon made some new friends—Sharon Pesavento and Nikki Worth. There were lots of girls at Siena with names as weird as mine. There were Italian girls and Dutch girls and of course the Irish. There were even Jewish girls. Compared to North Croydon Primary, Siena was a veritable melting pot.

I hated to admit it but I enjoyed convent school. I was talkative and earnest, a goody-two shoes. Those qualities got me elected in year seven to the Student Representative Council. I was the golden girl. It was as if I had rolled off a factory conveyor belt perfectly formed into exactly what I was supposed to be.

Then one day Mum awoke from her slumbers and announced that she was going to get her drivers licence. She was no longer content to be trapped at the top of a lonely hill, waiting for my father to drive her into Croydon at his convenience. She would damn well drive herself. She would go where she liked, when she liked.

Like dominoes, other changes followed rapidly. She got new teeth. She read my sister's copy of *The Female Eunuch* and the second wave of feminism churned the waters around us. Mum announced that she had found a job. She would be working away from home as a live-in nanny—a kind of Mrs Doubtfire. For up to six weeks at a time my mother would leave and I would be home alone with my monosyllabic brother and tennis-obsessed father. My competence, my biddable reliability, had once again doomed me to self-sufficiency.

My parents were self-absorbed in the same way a drowning man is. They made sure that I was all right and then tried to save themselves. It was painful and I was angry with them. But this quickly cooled and hardened into indifference. They toyed with the idea of getting a built-in pool, I suspect to mollify me. I told them not to bother.

We managed reasonably well without my mother. My father was clean and efficient. Cooking was basic. Truth be told I was relieved she was away. In the hormonal storm front created by my puberty and her menopause, there was little peace between us.

My parents were going through a difficult phase. I wanted them to separate. When they were bickering I would sneer, 'Why don't you just get a divorce?' But despite everything, despite my efforts, they stayed together. There was a deep and invisible love that existed between them that I could neither see nor understand. Do children ever really understand their parents' marriage? Their love was not showy or cutesy or demonstrative—it was inexorable, like the push of the continental plates towards one another.

We would go and visit my mother at her job. She kept house for a family of six in Ivanhoe, half an hour's drive away. I felt a certain pride tinged with envy as I saw how prized my mother was by these strangers. They loved her accent, it made her strictness and sharpness charming. She was a 'character'. They loved her sense of humour. They loved her loyalty. She was an excellent cleaner. Her own mother was slovenly (like me) and 'always left everything at her arse'. Obsessive cleanliness was one area in which Mum and Dad were completely compatible. I frequently endured the humiliation of leaving a shop or a restaurant because the place was not clean enough.

My mother may have attained her freedom, but I hadn't. I was still stuck at the top of the hill with no way to get out. The focus of my adolescent universe had moved from my family to my friends. They all hung out at Iceland Skating Rink, Eastland Shopping Centre, Ringwood Bowling Lanes and Arndale. I didn't even have a bike. I was like a Chekhovian character, languishing far from the action: Croydon proper was my Moscow. It was about five kilometres from our house as the crow flies and buses were rare. With Mum away I needed Dad to drive me to see my friends. So I had to book a time with him to take me into Croydon. But then, at the appointed hour, without fail, I would hear coming from up the top of the back garden that familiar *zwang* followed by the nasal whine of a two-stroke engine. The lawn mower.

I felt like a prisoner in an isolation unit, deprived of my rare visitation rights. My blood boiling with adolescent hormones and injustice I charged out the back door and up the hill.

'What are you doing!' I screamed at my father over the din of the Victa.

'What does it look like?' he yelled back.

'You told me you would take me into town. You promised!' I shrieked.

The trace of a memory darted like a tiny minnow through my mind, so fast I could barely catch it. I had slighted him: weeks, maybe a month ago. I couldn't even recall exactly what it was. But he could. He waited until I was most vulnerable, and then he struck. Mercilessly.

'And I will,' he muttered as he pushed the mower along. 'When I have finished mowing the lawn you can go and see your friends.'

I hated that lawn. I wanted to smash its smug face in. It wasn't even a lawn. It was a vast, stupid, piebald weed patch. I couldn't wait for Fitzcarraldo to conquer it.

So I did what I always did: I walked. I trudged through the searing heat to visit my friends, taking shortcuts across housing estates and through backyards. To slake my thirst in the scalding heat I would drink from the taps at the bottom of people's gardens. Patrick Avenue was the quickest route but every spring a mother magpie made her nest there, and as you walked past she would swoop low and try to pluck out your eyes.

There was a reason I was so desperate to get into Croydon. I needed to buy a record. I had scored some hand-me-down records from Barb and Chris, some Sizzling Hits compilations. But this was going to be my first self-determined purchase. And I knew exactly what I wanted. I wanted 'Sorrow', the single from Bowie's *Pin Ups*. It was a cover of a sixties song by The Merseys. I had heard Bowie's version on the radio and its haunting sadness had resonated with my own lonely melancholy. I knew nothing of Bowie, of his experiments with drugs and sexuality and music, the boldness of his vision. I just loved that song. With its adult themes of loss and unrequited love, it spoke to me. My own yearnings were vague even to me, the person who was having them. Desire has never been as clear-cut for me as it is for some; I am like one of Dante's uncommitted, doomed to follow a nameless banner for eternity. But I had a powerful need to own that record.

I wanted it for Kerry. Just like the song, Kerry had long blonde hair and eyes of piercing blue. I had several best friends at that time but she was my *first* best friend. Her father and mine played pennant in the same team at the tennis club and that's how we became friends. She was in the same year as me at school, but she went to Croydon High. Kerry and I were not arty. We were sporty. We spent most of our time kicking around the local golf course, fishing stray balls out of the brown dam and selling them back to the club. But from the moment I played *Pin Ups* for her we were obsessed with that album. We would sit in her bedroom for hours playing it over and over. We knew all of the words to every song. But there was also something about the cover art with its androgynous images of Bowie and Twiggy that mesmerised me. It felt dangerous and decadent. It spoke to me like a language I had learnt long ago and since forgotten.

It was Kerry who first suggested that we kiss. It was supposed to be a way of 'practising for boys' and 'making them jealous'. It was all the rage at Croydon High apparently. I was nervous and a little reluctant. But I wanted to do it, and by now I was old enough to understand what it really meant. So we began. Kerry told me what to do and how to do it. It wasn't very sexy or romantic; it was more instructional, like an air hostess demonstrating the safety procedures. But to me it was electrifying. It was not long before I realised that I looked forward to the 'practice' with Kerry much more than the real thing with boys. But I could sense that our kissing sessions never meant the same thing to Kerry as they did to me. So while they gave me an exquisite joy it was, indeed, tinged with sorrow.

I was in a hopeless position. I both wanted and didn't want Kerry to know how I felt about her. I wanted to kiss her, again and often, but I was afraid she would think I was that most reviled and despised thing: a lezzo. My tender feelings were like a jammed signal, unable to escape my furiously beating heart. I was paralysed, like a hysterical mute, wanting to tell her but desperate to hide my true nature. So it was that the moment of my gay adolescence was delayed at take-off and has, I fear, been stuck on the runway ever since.

As my feelings for Kerry were intensifying I knew I was losing her. I felt a searing isolation: like a girl who has fallen overboard and is watching the ocean liner, packed with merrymakers, steam away from her towards the limitless horizon. When Kerry got a new best friend at Croydon High and moved up in the social hierarchy, I could feel the shift. But what did I want to happen anyway? The idea of having a crush on another girl was terrifying. I could find no explanation except that there was something very wrong with me. I was sick, weird, creepy. What was my cleverness worth if I couldn't figure out and stop this one thing? I saw my life stretching out before me—long and loveless.

It wasn't just that, though. At the end of my first year at Siena I was made a dux (there were a few of us as that was deemed more egalitarian) and was named outstanding member of the SRC. But beneath my success I doubted myself terribly. I felt like a fraud. It was tennis all over again. I was a choker; I sensed there were other clever girls, perhaps cleverer than me. Having achieved such heights,

I could only go down. In the end, the prospect of failure seemed a welcome relief.

Without my conscious awareness rebellious forces were gathering beneath my biddable exterior. I longed to be busted out of the prison of my false self, to be cracked open and emerge real, without pretence, without artifice. It wasn't just sexuality. It was everything.

It was wrecking-ball time. I began to tear myself down. The catalyst was, of course, Kerry. Now that she was in the cool gang at Croydon High she decided that I would have to be 'made over'. And in my stupid, smitten heart I hoped that if I changed, maybe she would feel the same way about me as I felt about her.

So in that summer of 1973 Kerry became my Henry Higgins and set about turning a convent-school dux into the belle of the sharpie ball. She decided I was to make my grand entrance at the Australian Open at Kooyong just after Christmas. The sharpie thing had percolated up through society by then. Even middle-class Kooyong was not immune. There was a lot of work to be done. I would have to learn how to walk, talk and dress. I had to make the toughest girls at school befriend me. And then the biggest challenge of all. I had to gain acceptance into the local sharpie gang.

Just as I had a school uniform, I now had to acquire a sharpie uniform. And its dress code was far stricter than any rule ever imposed by the nuns. The sharpie uniform is perhaps the most unlikely fashion statement you will ever see, a Frankenstein's monster of baby-doll plucked eyebrows, skinhead-meets-mullet hair, 1970s fat ties and just a hint of bovver boy. Clothes worn too tight and too small.

Kerry had prepared a shopping list:

- bluebird earrings
- three-inch Mary Jane corkie platform shoes
- treads (shoes made using recycled tyres for the sole with suede thonging for the upper)

- Lee canvas jeans
- beachcombers
- short white bobby socks
- ribbed tights
- a short, flared, preferably panelled skirt
- satin baggies
- a striped Golden Breed t-shirt or a KrestKnit polo shirt
- a tight coral necklace from the surf shop
- a Conti brand striped cardigan
- blue metallic eye shadow from a small pot or a crayon

Somehow all of this stuff had to be got. And remember, this was a no-job, no-pocket-money economy. So I had to be smart about it. First things first: I had to get my ears pierced, to which I knew Mum would never agree. One day when she was back home for a stint we went shopping. I started with the direct approach and received the expected response—'Don't be ridiculous.' So I disappeared and reappeared some minutes later with pierced ears and the chemist's girl tagging along behind me, asking for twelve dollars in payment. My mother was cross for about an instant before she decided it was funny.

Kerry and I headed off to the landlocked surf shop off Main Street in Croydon. They had treads, but only a few pairs were left in the wicker basket so I ended up with a hideous yellow and maroon pair. The rest of it went smoothly and before too long I had my entire sharpie uniform. Only one thing was missing—a Conti. This smart striped cardigan, worn high and tight, was the centrepiece of the ensemble, the definitive wardrobe item of the sharpie. But none was available, not in Croydon anyway. We had to settle for a plain cardie, rolled up at the bottom until it sat under my boobs. I never did get a Conti. I think it was a sign.

But something in me faltered when it came to the hair. It wasn't vanity, although it should have been. I just sensed that if I went all the way—close crop, peroxided fringe and rear tails—there would be no turning back. I would not be playing at being a bad girl—I would be one. The nuns had banned the use of peroxide, and I seized with relief on this excuse.

With any performance there is a key: some little thing that opens the door and lets you into the character. The key to my sharpie role was the shoulders. They had to be hunched round as far as you could get them. There was something defiantly thuggish in those rounded shoulders, something that refuted evolution. Assuming this posture plugged me into just the kind of atavistic malevolence that was required. So I took my beautiful posture, my ramrod Polish spine…and I bent it. I twisted it into shape. (To this day I am paying for that affectation with chiropractor bills and buckets of ibuprofen.)

Now Kerry turned her attention to the way I spoke. It had to be flat, nasal and no-nonsense. Vocabulary mattered. 'Grouse' meant awesome, and the thumbs-up sign did *not* mean good luck but 'up yer bum'. Hot boys were 'spunks' and when you had a crush you were 'rapt' in them. Kissing was 'pashing'. But there was one all-purpose phrase that would guarantee me instant entrée into all good sharpie society. And that expression was 'shit, eh?' It could be used as a question or an exclamation. Or just a simple indication that you were listening during a long-winded story.

Kerry had a plan. I had to hang around the Siena tough girls saying 'shit, eh?' and hunching. During recess I spotted the school tough girls in the undercroft and slouched over. I hung around on the periphery, muttering 'shit, eh?' as instructed, and almost immediately I was asked if I wanted to have lunch with them. It was disappointingly simple but my transformation was complete.

I could now dress, speak and hunch like an expert. I was ready to make my grand entrance at Kooyong. Kerry decided I should wear my Lee canvas jeans with beachcombers and a tight cardie, and she carefully selected the audience for my gala performance.

Lizzie T was a tennis girl, a bit of a Toorak snob who had been my doubles partner for a while until I lost my nerve and she dumped me. When my father came to pick me up from her house one time her braying twit of an older brother called out, 'Mister Whatsisname is here,' while he kept my father standing at the door.

Kerry gave me very specific instructions. 'Walk past her. Don't say anything. Just see what she does.'

I slouched past Lizzie in the undercroft at the tennis centre. She didn't recognise me. We followed her up to the players' concourse.

'OK, this time, say "Hi, Lizzie" but don't stop and talk. Just keep walking. Ignore her.'

'OK.'

I slouched towards Lizzie and muttered, 'Hi, Lizzie,' as I passed.

'*Magda?* Is that you?'

'Yeah.' And I kept on walking while she stood open-mouthed. She was dumbstruck. Staggered. That night she rang and asked if I wanted to play doubles with her.

Kerry was elated. I felt an unfamiliar surge of power and confidence: I was a tough chick. Or at least I looked like one. The broken part of me, the choker, felt vindicated. And I dared to hope that maybe now Kerry might feel the same about me.

By now I was in year eight at Siena. My life was divided—I was a convent-school good girl during the week and a neophyte Croydon sharpie on the weekends. I was never recruited into the sharpie gang. I kind of drifted into the edges of it when Tracy, one of the girls I played tennis with, started dating a guy called Steve, who was in the gang.

Soon all of my tennis-club friends were hanging out at Steve's place and playing pool with the sharpie boys. We would cram into Joe the Wog's yellow Gemini and hoon down to the river. There the girls would sit on the muddy banks while the boys swam and bombed and dunked. We would spend our weekends playing pool except for Saturday nights, which were reserved for throwing empty beer bottles at the trains. I never did that myself. I was never a fully fledged member. Not even close. I was always an afterthought, a tag-along squished in the back seat. I was the 'convent-school sharpie' so I was tolerated but that was about it.

Every age has its booze, its defining drink. The jazz era had gin. The eighties had pina coladas. The *Sex and the City* generation had the cosmopolitan. And the elixir of my youth was Marsala and Coke, a sickly sweet brew. I was gaining weight and to cover my shyness I started drinking. I had no idea how to drink responsibly, so I drank it like a soft drink. I drank it until, like a Bernini fountain, I spewed up frothing purple plumes that arced majestically across Steve's lounge room. I was that girl—the uncool one who can't hold her booze.

Shane was the leader of the Croydon gang. He was lean and wiry and not that big. His face was pointy, like a hungry fox. He was handsome in a stringy, busted-tooth way. A bit like a blonde Bon Scott only less wrecked, and covered in tattoos.

From my perspective on the periphery it was hard to understand what gave Shane so much power over the others. He was not the biggest or even the most violent of the gang. But he was revered, even by baby-faced Tiny, the explosive man mountain with the slightly doughy upholstery. I couldn't understand it. Until one day Tiny gave me a clue. I must have said something that questioned Shane's intelligence in some way because Tiny sprang to his defence. 'Ya know, Shane is really smart.'

'Shit, eh?'

'He is. He reads the paper. Every day.'

'What? The *Trading Post*?'

'Nup. The *Age*.'

I was dumbfounded. A sharpie reading a *broadsheet*? What possible reason could there be? It wasn't that I thought Tiny was lying. I was intrigued.

Soon after this I was tagging along when Tiny announced he had to swing by Shane's joint. He lived in a weatherboard house not far from Croydon station. It was sparsely furnished with shredded sagging couches and herniated chairs bulging foam rubber.

As soon as I entered the lounge room I saw it. There, sprawled majestically across the coffee table next to the empties and overflowing ashtrays, was definitive proof of Shane's intelligence—a copy of the *Age*.

I have never forgotten the look on Tiny's face as he spoke of Shane's intelligence. He was awestruck, like a pilgrim before his patron saint. Shining with the humble recognition that he would never be capable of such feats. In that moment Tiny was seeing something bigger than himself. He saw the limits of his own life. And he didn't envy Shane for his intelligence, he respected him. He was proud that one of his own tribe was clever.


Despite my longstanding crush on Kerry—which I don't think she ever twigged to—or perhaps because of it, each weekend I would set out with her to trudge several kilometres along the train tracks, the stones like hot coals beneath our beachcombers. We were headed for Eastland shopping centre in Ringwood, where there was good hunting to be had. Once there, we planned to scour every level of retail for boys. The train tracks were the shortest, most direct route, but also the most dangerous. There is some acoustic anomaly which means you cannot hear trains behind you. I know because a boy I knew lost his legs that way.

At Eastland I would spot what I thought was a spunk, and Kerry wouldn't even bother to conceal her contempt. The boys I liked were good-looking in a clean-cut Brady Bunch way. Of course. They would never do. It was Kerry who showed me the error of my ways and introduced me to the allure of bad boys.

When I actually found one, it was not at Eastland but via my family, of all things. Every little while, former members of the *AK*, the Polish Home Army, would meet to reminisce and the kids would come along. Dad could only tolerate so much reminiscing, and none of the other Poles had had the same experience he'd had. But they were as close as he would ever get.

Dorota and Bogdan were one of the more colourful couples. Bogdan was suave and wore cravats and was just the wrong side of sleazy. One day, when a girl named Hanka and I were in the kitchen during one of these reunions, Bogdan slithered in and stood in the doorway, resting his slightly-too-broad hips on the doorjamb while he sipped on his martini, asking us about boys—a common way for middle-aged men to try to flirt with young girls at parties. We were thirteen, and we weren't really offended; we thought he was ridiculous. Just then Hanka's mother swung into the room like a big bell. She was a grand, theatrical character and the rumour was that she was a gypsy princess, daughter of the great Kwiek himself, chief of the Kalderash Roms and king of all the gypsies, who presided over the gathering of the tribes in Poland before the war and whose coronation in 1937, amidst great pomp and ceremony, was performed by the archbishop of Warsaw himself. She denied it but I like to think it's true.

'Is zis old man bozerink you?'

'Yuck, he's flirting with us,' Hanka groaned.

Bogdan quietly slipped out. Hanka's mother regarded her daughter with a tipsy gypsy eye and declared, 'Vel, dahlinks, at least vee know he isn't a poofcher!' and swayed back out of the room.

Everyone drank in those days. What's more, everyone drank and drove. (Except my parents who, as Celtic and Slavic teetotallers, were statistical freaks.) Dorota and Bogdan drank more than anyone.

Dorota was a straight-talking 'peasant' and Mum and I really liked her. You knew where you stood. Not for her the braggadocio of shared war exploits. She would stare at whoever was annoying her, close one bleary eye in order to halve her double vision, and say, 'Vie don't you shut bloody up!'

I don't know what demons tormented Dorota and Bogdan. Their son Sasha was two years older than me and he was nearly as pretty as Leif Garrett. But he also had a thick streak of bad boy in him. He wore Miller shirts and smoked roll-your-own cigarettes that gave his lips a bittersweet taste. Kerry approved. I don't remember how it started but soon we were pashing in his bedroom every time I went to visit. The next thing I was 'on with him'. We used to catch the train in to school together and as we sat—he reading the form guide and I reading my school books—our knees would bump. It was romantic in a pragmatic, public-transport kind of way. He made me feel safe. I could believe that my feelings for Kerry didn't exist.

It was all panning out just the way Kerry had hoped it would.

Before she left home my sister used to catch the train to go to secretarial college and every day I worried about her. She was a very pretty girl. And petite. A prime target for marauding sharpies. But as it turns out she wasn't the one who got 'picked'. I was. Me, in my prissy convent-girl uniform.

There were three types of trains—the new sleek silver trains, the slightly older utilitarian blue trains that had lots of standing room, and the very old red rattlers, relics from the 1920s. They had the friendly feel of Thomas the Tank Engine, and some of the romance of the Orient Express. They were beautiful, with wood panelling, curved brass luggage racks, pressed-metal ceilings and dark green leather seats. You could slide the slatted wooden shutters up and down in the window by grasping the leather strap in the brass catch.

It was a hot day and as I stood on the melting platform with my friends, waiting to catch the train home from school, I hoped I got a red rattler because the doors weren't centrally locked and you could stand in the open doorway, letting the hot wind blow up your skirt. Riding on a red rattler also provided a reasonably plausible excuse for losing your regulation straw hat: 'It blew off my head on the train, Sister.'

I was thinking about Sasha. We were seeing less of one another now. Our romantic encounters on the train were more infrequent, and I didn't know why. It made me uneasy. Was it something I had done?

Finally a rattler rattled in. One by one all of my friends got off at their stops and by the time we got to Croydon everyone else had disembarked. Or so I thought. The rattlers had a long bench seat that faced towards clumps of banquette seats with a long aisle that ran between them to the bench seat at the other end. I was seated right in the middle of the t-intersection, facing this aisle.

So far I had managed to ride the rails without ever having to confront violence directly. I was a convent girl during the week and a pretend sharpie on the weekends. But, on this particular day, I was most definitely a convent girl. I heard her before I saw her.

'What are you fucken starin' at?'

I knew this phrase. Everyone did. It was the dead-eyed challenge of the predatory sharpie. My heart did a 120-volt jump. I looked up to see a sharpie chick with bleached blonde hair and four-inch corkie platforms staring at me with hate-filled eyes. Her friends were seated behind. I had done nothing to provoke this hatred—except to exist. She leaned forward, right into my face. 'I said, what are you fucken starin' at?'

There is no right answer to that question. It is not a question. It is a psychopath's foreplay, prelude to a beating. I knew that it was simply my presence that pissed her off. My hat, my gloves, my stupid uniform. She turned to her friends and sneered.

As she pulled herself up to her full height on top of her corkies I braced myself. Just at that moment the querulous old train, God bless it, lurched forward and the sharpie lost her four-inch-platform footing and was sent reeling the full length of the carriage, her arms windmilling furiously. If you have seen the YouTube footage of supermodels falling off their platform shoes, you'll know what I'm talking about. Her friends ran to pick her up. And I did the worst thing possible. I burst out laughing. Hell hath no fury like a sharpie chick scorned.

The rattler pulled into the station and before she could stand up I bolted out the door and to the safety of the guard room, shaking. I knew how close I had come. And I knew, absolutely, that I would never have it in me to be a true sharpie chick.

In 1974 no one wore seatbelts even though we were supposed to. Chris had come to pick us up from tennis in the Kingswood. The family car. Boring. I was sitting behind Chris, and Kerry was sitting behind the vacant front passenger seat. We were wearing our tennis gear: bobble socks, short skirts, frilly undies. I was wearing a baby-blue cardigan. It had been raining for days and the street was wet and oily as a mackerel's back.

The other car materialised. One moment it wasn't there, the next it was making a right-hand turn into the service station, cutting across our lane, and we were sailing into it. Sailing is what it felt like. An effortless glide followed by the brutal jolt of collision. Like a daydream followed by a slap in the face.

When the car came to a halt I could not understand where I was. After a moment I realised I was jammed down behind the front seat, on the floor, facing the rear window. The impact had flung me forward into the car radio and then back. Chris had blocked most of my flight. But there was no one sitting in front of Kerry. I struggled out of the trough and looked across at her. She lay completely still. Her face was smashed and swollen.

Jadwiga, c. 1933

Mieczysław, c. 1920s

Dad at the tiller, c. 1932

A tree full of Szubanskis, c. 1936.
Dad is perched on the tree at far left

Dad and Danuta

Dad holding his father's hand. Warsaw, 1935

Mieczysław and Mini-Me, c. 1935

Danuta and Andrzej just before
the war. Danuta (above)

Burying a comrade, Warsaw during the uprising. Dad is at centre left, hands on hips

Luke and Meg McCarthy
with my mother (r) and her
sister Mary, 1926

Mum and Dad get hitched, 1949

Mum, c. 1949

On the back of the photo:
*To Margaret, excuse my tongue 1947*

Gran, Mum, Barb,
Dad and me shortly
before we left Britain

Outside our house in
Croydon, c. 1972. The
cat's name was Seamus

Barb, Chris and me at the motel, shortly after
we arrived in Australia

# A CASH FREEZE ON FREEWAYS AS LABOR STEPS IN

**The Sun**
NEWS-PICTORIAL
44 FLINDERS ST.    PHONE 63-0211    BY AIR 7c  6c
15,660    Melbourne, Tuesday, December 12, 1972    80 Pages

**654,598**
Average Daily Sale

Your color calendar — inside

I'll lick 'em all...

WEATHER—Bureau City forecast: Fine. Mainly sunny. Sea breezes. ● Expected top temp. a warm 24. Yesterday's top, a mild 21. ● Details, Page 74.

**A CASH freeze on inner suburban freeways has been announced by the Federal Government.**

Federal freeway money will be spent instead on streamlining public transport and building new cities.

The new policy was revealed in a telegram sent last night to a meeting of the United Melbourne Freeway Action Group.

The Department of Urban Affairs and the Transport Department will hold the freeway money until after an inquiry into roads.

The inquiry will examine the economic efficiency, social and environmental effects of freeways.

The Government is likely to call on the states to halt their spending on planned freeways.

Victoria spent $11 million of its $43.5 million federal roads grants on freeways in 1970-71. In 1971-72 the State got $50 million.

Yesterday's telegram was signed by the Labor spokesmen for the two departments, Mr Uren and Mr Jones.

## Efficient

They said Federal freeway money would be spent on building an efficient and rapid public transport system.

The money would also be used for building new cities rather than "ripping out the guts and charm and booting the poor out of the old ones."

The telegram said: "We feel that the money could be better spent by upgrading the rapid public transport system, slowing down the growth of the central business districts of the cities and creating other centres on the outskirts.

"This would ensure a balanced transport load."

In Melbourne about 1500 people attended the public meeting on freeways at the Town Hall last night.

The Metropolitan Transport Plan was released in December 1969, and proposed freeways of 307 miles for Melbourne.

The cost $2616 million.

The Victorian Government is now revising freeway plans and a cut-back in spending is expected.

Continued Page 2.

## Lillee's partner — Jeff WHO?

NSW right-arm fast bowler Jeff Thomson last night gained a Test berth after only five first-class matches.

Thomson, 22, will partner Dennis Lillee in the Second Test against Pakistan in Melbourne on December 29.

Two squads were chosen because the First Test starts in Adelaide on December 22.

Thomson, 6 ft. 1 in. and 13.10, could hardly believe it when he was told of his selection last night.

"I bowled badly in the last game against WA," he said.

● Report — Back Page.

**POKING** your tongue out — as everyone knows — is the greatest possible aid to concentration.

Just ask Magda Szubanski, of Croydon State School.

It helped make this backhand volley over the nets at Kooyong a winning shot.

Magda was playing in the under-13 singles match in the annual school tennis titles.

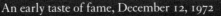

An early taste of fame, December 12, 1972

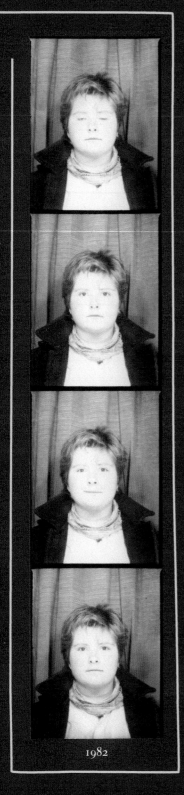

1982

Karl Marx's tomb, Highgate, 1982. Not quite ready to dump the ideologies

Christmas with the Szubanskis, 1982—not long after I announced I was dropping out of uni

'Kerry? Kerry?'

There was no response.

'I think Kerry is dead,' I screamed.

'Get out of the car.' It was Chris. Get out of the car. He grabbed my elbow and fixed me with the intensity of his stare. His eyes were black as iron bolts. 'Go to the service station and call Mum and Dad.'

'But what about Kerry?'

'Go to the service station. Call Mum and Dad.'

Dutifully I walked across the wet asphalt and it was only as I walked through the puddles that I realised I had lost one of my tennis shoes. My bobble sock was saturated. I felt no emotion at all. Not one. In fact, I now know, my first response to shock tends to be excessive courtesy. I knocked on the glass door of the service station. 'Excuse me, I'm sorry but we have had an accident. Can I please use your phone?'

The attendant looked at me incredulously. There were, after all, two car wrecks strewn across the apron of his service station. I rang Mum and Dad. They had guests, their Scottish friends Wilma and Bob, over for dinner.

'Hello.'

'Oh, hi, Mum, it's me,' I said.

'Where are you? Are you coming home?'

'No. I'm in the service station on Hewish Road. We've had an accident. Can you come?'

I have no recollection of what was said after that. But as I sat on the vinyl chair waiting I became aware of a warm, sticky sensation. Blood was seeping from a gash at the top of my leg. I still felt no pain. Only sickening dread. And I have no idea how long I sat there, waiting for my parents, not knowing if Kerry was alive. Eventually the ambulance arrived. Kerry had been flung forward and hit either the window or the dash. She had two broken arms and her jaw was swollen like the bum end of a butternut pumpkin. But she was alive.

I was taken home, patched up, given a cup of tea and put to bed.

Slowly, like a baby opening its fist, feeling returned. As I lay there in the dark I began to shake. I didn't know what to do. So I got up and walked down the hallway, slid open the frosted-glass sliding doors into the lounge room, and stood there, shaking.

'Oh my god, lassie!' exclaimed Wilma.

Mum rushed over. 'What's wrong, hen?'

They fussed over me and put me back to bed. And then I began to sob. Deep, shuddering sobs. Wilma was a nurse, and she took charge. With brisk, matronly efficiency and great gravity she took my hand and leaned over me. 'Och, ye poorr wee thung. Ehvry mussul uhn yurr boady wull be aykung.'

It was probably the aftershock, and the incongruous thickness of her accent, but when she spoke I burst out laughing. And laughing. Pretty soon it was clear I was hysterical.

Despite having a Scottish mother I had never been able to get a handle on the accent. In that instant I mastered it. Wilma's thick-tongued tones were engraved into my ear and brain and motor memory and from that day forward my Scottish accent was pitch perfect. Her comment became a family catchcry. 'Ehvry mussul uhn yurr boady wull be aykung.'

Things were never quite the same after the accident. It seemed to signal the end of something and the beginning of something new.

Kerry and I drifted apart. We began to let go of one another. And then Sasha dumped me. He never told me why. I don't really know which rejection hurt more. Sasha or Kerry. One was public and humiliating, the other private and shameful.

I do know that my life was changed. I began to let go of Croydon. And, like Eliza Doolittle, I could never go back to the me I had been before 1974.

# FOURTEEN

When you are fourteen the inner life of any adult is impenetrable, but that of a nun seems even more mysterious. What desires, what dreams, what imagined futures could a nun possibly have? Surely none that bore any resemblance to my fraught adolescent torments.

Sister Agnes was young and pretty and given to staring. She would set an assignment for us and then, once all our heads were bowed and her thoughts were again her own, she would stare. All through class her slightly sad, bright blue eyes would drift to some un-seeable place in the middle distance. Sometimes they would shimmer brightly as a tear rose to the surface. And, as she stared, I would stare at her. Wondering what it was that haunted her, that drew her gaze to the place where, sooner or later, all troubled minds go. The thousand-yard stare.

I was developing a hopeless crush on Sister Agnes even though I knew nothing about her. Her habit concealed her shape, her style, her personal tastes. It even made it difficult to determine her age. She was an enigma. But some fine filament of sadness connected us and I felt that she might be the lifeline I was searching for. I wanted those slightly sad, bright blue eyes to see me, I wanted to draw that gaze deep into my soul. I wanted her to save me.

Since my sharpie makeover the previous summer my academic career had gone right off the rails. Being in the cool gang at school was my entire raison d'être. Then one day at the end of class Sister Agnes motioned for me to stay behind. Such one-on-one attention thrilled me in a way that I chose not to examine too closely.

For a long while she fixed me with her melancholy gaze. 'Magda,' she said. 'What are you doing? Your grades are a mess. You are close to failing and you have become sullen and uncooperative. I am at a loss to understand. I can only think that you are being influenced by the wrong girls. I want to help you, Magda. Tell me, is there something wrong?'

This frank line of questioning was unexpected. It pierced straight through my defences, but it didn't even come close to getting at what really bothered me. Running with the 'wrong crowd' was the least of my worries. What got to me was that I could tell she really cared.

'I don't know, Sister.'

'You must have some idea.'

I wanted to have an idea. But how could I possibly explain the tangled web of desires and needs that had led me to this place? How could I tell her that this pathetic, misdirected, one-girl rebellion was the fight of my life? I didn't even understand then that nearly failing maths, pretending to be a sharpie, detonating the good little Polish girl was my only hope of finding myself. That if I didn't do this I would be lost forever, a phantasm like Echo who, with no words of her own, could only imitate and fade.

I couldn't explain so I did the only thing I knew how to do: I radiated dumb insolence. I rounded my shoulders. I drew my wordlessness around me like a cloak and turned myself into that monstrous cliché—the monosyllabic teenager.

'These girls, Magda, do you really think this is the sort of company you should be keeping?'

Silence.

'Magda?'

Shrug. 'Dunno.'

There is a strange alchemy that works on your soul when a nun, especially a hot young nun on whom you have an adolescent crush, exhorts you to rise to your better self.

'These are not bad girls, Magda,' Sister Agnes went on. 'They are just misguided. They need to be influenced in the right way. Sit down.'

All the badass in me, admittedly not very much, melted away. I sat.

'You have many fine qualities, Magda. Perhaps you could use them to influence these girls, to guide them onto the right path. I'm sure they are all nice girls if shown the way.'

A mission. She had given me a higher calling. Something worth fighting for. Every little Polack freedom-fighting corpuscle in me responded. I knew she was right. I knew, deep down, that I did not really fit with the bad girls, with their Farrah Fawcett bangs and 'bad-boy' boyfriends. Besides, ever since kissing Kerry I had begun to suspect that it was me who was really, truly bad. Much more bad than any of those caustic little bitches ever dreamed of being. Beyond confession or absolution, I was a sinner bound for eternal perdition. Perhaps being good would save me from the seventh circle of hell. Perhaps there was a glimmer of hope.

'I need you to do the right thing,' Sister Agnes continued. 'Can I rely on you, Magda?'

Sister Agnes with her blue eyes was both my damnation and my salvation. I stared back at her with a disastrous combination of admiration and infatuation.

'Yes.' I accepted her challenge. I would try to change these bad girls for their own good…and mine.

But how do you drag a pack of feral fourteen-year-olds onto the path of righteousness? I hadn't even been in the tough gang for long. I decided to start with the leader. Elise Carver was the epitome of tough-girl chic. Her eyebrows were plucked so thin they barely existed. Her eyes were dark, mascara-ed pits of rock'n'roll sedition. Her hair was a longer version of Bowie's Ziggy Stardust look. Her socks sagged insolently round her ankles in languid defiance of school rules. The singular thing about her was her utter lack of effort. Elise didn't give a fuck. I am a natural born flaming enthusiast, a closet Kumbaya Christian. Elise's absence of exertion sucked me in like a vacuum sucks up a naked flame.

My mission to save Elise ended with a whimper. One day we were all standing in a group outside the library. The others were bitching viciously about some girl and that was when it happened—I didn't join in. It was a form of passive, non-violent resistance, I suppose, and astonishingly effective. Suzie Cameron turned to me and issued a sneering appraisal. 'You never say anything mean about anyone.'

'Well, I just think maybe we shouldn't be so critical,' I stammered, wrenched between the desperate desire to fit in and Sister Agnes's call to my higher self.

From that moment I was unceremoniously dumped by the cool girls. Elise and I never spoke again and it became clear that Sister Agnes had sent me on a social suicide mission.

So began my inexorable slide down the many snakes and ladders of the convent-school caste system until I found myself at the bottom of the heap among the Untouchables. The new girls. The girls who smelled funny. The girls, worst of all, who were rumoured to be lesbians. So far I had managed to evade detection. But I knew that if anyone ever learned the truth about me I would slip through the cracks from purgatory into absolute hell.

This was *Lord of the Flies* and I had an inkling of what it was to be Piggy. I was—as one girl put it while she informed me that she and her gang didn't want me hanging around anymore—'like a kicked dog with its tail between its legs'.

I had gone from high school hero to zero.


You come to dread recess and lunchtime when you are an outcast. For me they became an agony of killing time. Of dithering. Of slow minutes spent trying to decide where to sit. I would stand there holding my lunch, frozen with indecision. Oozing blood into shark-filled waters. I thought they would go for me but they never did. Worse, they shunned me.

I have never felt so pathetically alone in all my life. There was only one place I could go. The library. Haven of the social reject. The last resort of the friendless. Books became my refuge but I was wary. Ever since reading Leon Uris I was frightened of what I might find in books. Besides, I couldn't concentrate. The only book I could manage was *Gone with the Wind*. I persuaded the nuns to let me have a day off school to go into town and watch the movie at the Forum. I quickly developed a fangirl crush on Vivien Leigh.

Away from school I fell back on my tried and trusted form of self-medication: TV. Old black-and-white movies were my favour-ites—*Casbalanca, Andy Hardy, Some Like it Hot, Philadelphia Story, Stage Door, All About Eve*. And Hitchcock—I watched *Dial M for Murder* until I knew the dialogue by heart. I had a debilitating infatuation with Grace Kelly.

To feed my growing addiction required planning and research. My father got up at five every morning so he had first dibs on the *Age*. Every Thursday I would get up before him and nab the *Green Guide*. I would take it to my room and scour the TV schedule. Most of the really good movies were on in the middle of the night. Once I had found what I was looking for I would set my alarm clock. It was the old-fashioned kind that went off with a deafening clang, like a robbery was underway, so I muffled it with bobble socks and sweatbands stuffed inside my tennis racquet cover.

Then, in the dead of night, I would creep through the small, sleeping house and into the lounge room, slide the glass doors shut, plug in the headphones and sit glued to Grace Kelly or Ingrid Bergman or Susan Hayward. I would watch the same films over and over again. I still do. I have seen *Some Like it Hot* maybe a hundred times.

I understand now this was classic self-soothing behaviour. And a little OCD. But it was also a safe outlet. I was far too scared to express my loves in real life. Old movies presented an arena for all of my pent-up feelings to find their expression. I sublimated my desire, I projected myself into the hero and through this transposed self I wooed and won some of the most beautiful dead actresses of all time.

I was in love with the lead actresses but I identified more with the character actors and actresses—Celeste Holm, Peter Lorre, Alastair Sim, Claude Rains, Margaret Rutherford, Mildred Natwick, Peter Ustinov, Maggie Smith…Their quirkiness. Their accents. Their timing. They became like an extended family of aunts and uncles. Many of them were inherited loves from my parents. But soon I began to develop my own tastes. *Cabaret, To Kill a Mockingbird, To Sir with Love, Butch Cassidy and the Sundance Kid.* I had a huge poster of Robert Redford on my wall. I wasn't sure if I wanted to kiss him or be him.

Needless to say my schoolwork suffered even more. I was exhausted not just from depression and anxiety, but also from the sleep deprivation. I slipped further and further down the social ladder until finally I hit rock bottom. Lost and rudderless, I went with the class grifters to the department store at Camberwell Junction and stole some cosmetics. And we got caught.

Luckily I had nothing on me—when the manager went to call my parents I stuffed all of my booty into the hem of the cubicle curtain.

My mother was furious. 'Oh for God's sake! What were you thinking?' They were worried now. They asked me what was wrong. My confidence was so low, my shame was so great, I couldn't bear to tell them.

So they brought in my sister. 'What is it, Mag, what's going on?' she asked with tender concern. And it all came pouring out. About school, and being friendless and dumped. Not the other thing. I knew I could never tell anyone about the other thing.

I begged my father to let me change schools, to start afresh. He made an appointment to see Sister Rosemary, the headmistress at Siena. She ran the school with a benign and wise efficiency and my father admired her greatly.

'Don't take her out,' she advised. 'This sort of thing happens. It will blow over. Just ride it out.'

My father was not a socially anxious person. He had no way of empathising. And perhaps, compared to what he had been through, this looked trivial. He didn't remonstrate with me or chastise me but he washed his hands of me. I was wiped. I was no longer a good Polish girl. I had done the one thing he could never forgive—I had failed. Two things: I was also becoming fat. Whenever I asked how he was he would say, 'I'm not as well as I look,' raising the spectre of his cancer. I was not allowed to change schools.

I was like a wild, caged thing. I needed to escape. So I made myself sick. I went to bed with my hair wet. I would soak my nightie in cold water and run out and stand in the freezing night air while my parents slept. I willed colds and flus and tonsillitis into being. I caught chills and fevers. I was hoping for pneumonia but it never came. I did damage my lungs, though. They became my weak spot. And years later I finally got the pneumonia I had prayed for. Too late.

*

That year, 1975, something in me broke.

I was panic stricken, cracking ice. Possessed by the demon shadows of feelings I didn't understand. An inexorable quiet frenzy built inside me. I was the girl in Stravinsky's *Rite of Spring*, dancing myself to death. A crash of cymbals, a sharp slice of strings. And then silence.

I smashed like a dropped vase.

And the numbness came. It felt as though I had fallen down a mineshaft and nobody noticed. I could hear voices but I didn't know how to tell them where I was or how to find me or what was wrong with me. It was as though the very 'me' of me had fallen down that mineshaft and all that remained was the hollow shell of a human being.

While Sister Agnes was right—I hated the way the mean girls bitched about everyone—I paid too high a price for my moral revolution. We are social animals, and nothing terrifies us like the threat of exclusion. Being cast out from the herd means death. A little piece of your heart never quite recovers. And I was now in no doubt about the nature of my secret sexual feelings.

# BECOMING A FAT LESBIAN

There is a word. An awful ugly word. A name. A label. I am at the bathroom sink. I have locked the door. I can hear my family outside. The TV somewhere in the distance. I stare at myself in the mirror for the longest time. I start silently calling myself this word in my head. I am too scared to say the word aloud in case saying it makes it true. If I take that word outside of my head, and put it out in the real world, I might never be able to make it go away.

I slide the mirror of the bathroom cabinet open. There on the shelf are the tablets. I have a plan. If I do it, then the whole revolting mess will just go away. If I do it, then they would know. I want them to know something is very wrong. But I could never tell them what it is. I want them to help me. But no one can help me. I bury that word deep down. Because it's an evil word.

*

I wasn't the only one who hated lesbians back then. Everyone did. There were two girls at Siena who were rumoured to be lesbians. The story was that the nuns had decided they were 'too close'. Their parents were called to the school. They were allowed to stay, on condition that they would no longer be friends. We all thought this was best for everyone. I don't know how we found out, but word went around the school like a dose of impetigo.

I also don't know if any of it is true, but everyone was disgusted. Including me. I prayed that the scandal would provide a decoy so no one would notice that my gaze sometimes lingered, that my cheeks flushed at inappropriate moments.

There are some remarkable souls in the world who manage to elude homophobia. Who feel no need to cure, eradicate or even explain. Jean Genet, for instance, who said, 'I'm a homosexual…How and why are idle questions. It's a little like wanting to know why my eyes are green.'

For some reason, be it genetic or chemical or the love they receive early in life, such people are immune to society's contempt. They have an inner resilience that makes them indifferent to disgust and allows them to ride out the storms of shame and hatred.

I wasn't one of them. My resilience curdled at the slightest unkind word. The dread of being cast into an even deeper well of loneliness was more than I could bear. Going to the bathroom cabinet and staring at my mother's sleeping tablets became a habit. I prayed, 'Please, please, I will do anything, anything, I will bear any hardship, carry any cross—but not this one. I will die if need be. Please don't make this my cross.'

My prayers went unanswered. I should have trusted my three-year-old self. God was not my friend.

Just as my father would rather have died than lose his leg, for me, disapproval and isolation, the consequences of people knowing I was a lesbian, were a fate worse than death. I cemented my soul to a false self. It wasn't that I lied—I *became* a lie.

It was impossible for me to tell anyone what the problem really was. And at that point no one in my family was listening. My mother was clinically depressed, my father was fleeing his own demons, my brother had sunk into a monosyllabic rage at my father. My beautiful sister had left home.

I became morose and dull. I wept constantly but they were strange affectless tears. Had I been taken to a psychiatrist this would have been diagnosed (and was, retrospectively) as depression. And if I'd known then that I would be stuck in the pit of my breakdown for another five long years I probably would have taken the pills.

Helen helped. Helen was the new girl. She had no one to sit next to, and I sensed an opportunity. Helen was brusque, driven and ridiculously intelligent. While I moved like a deep-sea diver, Helen's speech and movement were rapid. She was a natural speed-reader. She had high, broad Prussian cheekbones and light blonde hair, which always ran free from its braids. Her shirt tail always flapped loose behind her. She seemed to have more hours in the day than the rest of us. She took extra subjects in her spare time and aced them. I am not sure that we especially liked one another at first; our friendship was born of loneliness and necessity. But it gathered momentum and turned into one of those intense, pubescent, fervidly artistic female friendships. Helen was smart and wanted to be a writer. She wrote fabulous poems for the school yearbook.

Together we carved an eccentric niche for ourselves and slowly I began to rehabilitate. Then, as we all matured, the key indicators of social capital changed and Helen and I gained currency. The next thing we knew we were kind of cool.

She was the writer and I, she decided, was the actress. She wrote me copious letters, more for posterity's benefit than mine, always addressed to Dame Maggie Edith Evans.

We created 'art happenings' and the nuns allowed us to do 'radio' broadcasts over the school PA during recess. Like pre-Raphaelite nymphs we would link hands and dance around the mysterious 'Mound' in the middle of the schoolyard. It was in fact just a heap of dirt left behind from some minor excavations. But in our imaginations it was transformed into a druidic shrine of no small significance.

We started our own school rag, entitled *Untitled*, the back page of which was devoted to a spoof of a silly TV soap, *The Young Doctors*, which we called 'The Young Teachers'. It was a scurrilous commentary on the goings-on in the staff room.

Helen's a lesbian now but we were not in love. We were just in love with the theatrical expression of ourselves. We were that fierce thing: young women beginning to feel the power of life flowing into them. I asked Helen recently if she knew she was a lesbian when we were at school and she said, 'No. No idea.' I was gobsmacked. This was the one area in which my awareness was ahead of hers. I had assumed for decades that our 'secret', undeclared even to one another, was what bound us. But no.

In every other sense Helen was a long way ahead of me. She knew what she wanted and she had the tenacity and brilliance to get it. Her dynamism and passion gave me definition. I hitched my rickety wagon to her thoroughbred horsepower. I was the Watson to her Holmes.

Year nine was when the Great Hunger started. There had been rumblings in earlier years when my hormones kicked in. And now, as the truth of who I was became inescapable, my hunger became ravenous. My brother had a job at the Brockhoff factory and would bring home huge tins of chocolate biscuits. As part of my nocturnal TV ritual, I would grab fistfuls of biscuits, rearrange the remaining ones to disguise the missing, and pad out to the lounge room. Sometimes I would pour a small snifter of Bailey's from the sideboard, taking a moment to top up the bottle with milk.

I had begun to 'balloon', as people so charmingly put it. I was becoming a fat person. I watched with relief and despair as my flesh armour thickened. I crawled deep into the folds of myself and hid there.

I made valiant attempts to beat my hyperphagia into submission. Many years later my school friend Nikki Worth reminded me of an incident I had completely forgotten. That year, she told me, the other girls were teasing me about my weight. So I put myself on a spartan diet, lost a stack of weight, said, 'You see! I could be thin if I wanted to be. But I don't want to.' Then I promptly stacked it all back on again. Point made.

It is weird but I can scarcely remember this. Nikki said it was one of the most strikingly wilful things she had ever seen and so she never forgot it. 'I just thought, wow! What an incredibly strong character.'

I didn't believe I was strong. I knew I was weak. The hunger was a bottomless void. Naturally I blamed myself.

I was bursting the banks of my uniforms. Dresses were let out again and again and eventually even my blazer would not fit. Since I could not do anything about my weight and was too ashamed to tell my mother about my blazer I improvised wildly and found a loophole in the school rules that said you didn't have to wear your blazer if you were wearing a regulation raincoat. So I took to affecting an indifferent, eccentric manner. Rain, hail or shine, in four degrees and in forty, I wore my raincoat with dash and bravura. And no one ever questioned it.

I had never imagined this as my future. Who does? And, while it was me, it didn't feel like it was me. I felt as though I were possessed by some evil spirit. No one knew very much about weight loss back then. The consensus was: eat less. But I didn't seem to be able to do that. I was plagued with questions that I could not answer, except as condemnations. I called myself cruel names: weak, greedy, lazy.

That was how we thought about fat people.

Mum enrolled with me at Weight Watchers. I even read the biography of one of the founders, Jean Slutsky Nidetch. It didn't work. I was taken to doctors and dieticians and quacks. In a form of acupuncture, I had appetite-suppressing staples punched into the bony part of my ear that supposedly controlled the urge to eat. Another guy gave me his patented weight-loss 'rocket fuel'. Nothing could curb my appetite. I was driven to eat by a ravening hunger that would not leave me alone, that even woke me in the middle of the night.

How could medicine, both conventional and alternative, save my father from cancer but be helpless to save me? I was getting fatter and there was nothing anyone could do. I was the Incredible Bloating Woman. There was no telling where this would end. The belief that I was feeble-minded, that I would crumble at the first sign of pressure, had me by the throat. It became who I was.

Two years dragged on. I managed to scrape through classes but I could not concentrate to read or study properly. Every one of my report cards complains about my lack of application. I was in an academic tailspin.

How weird, then, that in year ten Helen, Anna Rogers and I were selected to be the school representatives on *It's Academic!*—Channel Seven's TV school quiz show. For some reason I could never fathom, Mrs Cother chose me to be captain of the team. We made it through to the series final—despite the fact that in one of the rounds I made the shocking error of misspelling 'tournament'. I left out the *n*. I had played in so many you'd think the word would have been seared into my consciousness. So whether or not this was a subconscious middle finger to tennis I will never know.

I had continued to play tennis on and off throughout. But I was battle-weary and tired of constantly losing. And I hated the increasingly competitive edge that had eroded the camaraderie of my gang of friends. So at the age of sixteen I became the tennis equivalent of a conscientious objector. One night at the dinner table I announced my intention to quit.

'Don't be ridiculous. Why would you do that?' My father peered over his shooter's magazine.

'I don't like the competitiveness.' I braced myself. I expected a fight. I wanted a fight. But my father barely raised an eyebrow.

'Well, if that's what you want.'

So it was a pyrrhic victory. He had given up on me anyway.

At the end of year ten we all faced a crossroads: humanities or sciences. This one decision, more than any other, would determine the rest of our lives. Did I want to be a doctor? Despite the fact that I was losing my faith in medicine I enrolled in straight sciences: physics, chemistry and maths.

As for my crush on Sister Agnes, that was beyond the reach of medicine of any kind. I think it was around that time that Sister Agnes left the convent. I believe she got married.

# GRÜBER

For some reason I never had after-school jobs or pocket money like other kids. When the new McDonald's opened down the road in Ringwood a frisson of excitement ran through the surrounding suburbs and all of my friends applied for jobs. Some of them got them, too. Mandy Plunkett, I seem to remember, did. But I didn't. I applied, but I had no practical skills whatsoever. All I was good at was watching TV and eating Brockhoff biscuits. Nothing terribly employable. I have to say my parents weren't encouraging. I don't know why.

When I was sixteen I made a break for freedom. I attempted to escape the thwarting, to self-activate. I went down to Arndale shopping centre on Mount Dandenong Road and asked every single shop if they had any work. Finally the café owner said yes and I was employed as a dishwasher. This was the first proper job I had ever had. I lasted two days and then he sacked me for dithering.

So I gave up and went back to watching television. My apathy and lethargy grew worse. Mum attributed it to the hypoglycaemia. She had decided that sugar was what ailed us. My sister had blacked out one day and so she went to a new naturopath whose name was Grüber. For years that name had skittered across the surface of our lives like a bright, attractive but elusive fishing fly. In old war films. On a dentist name plaque. And now here it was again…Grüber.

And every time, 'Jesus! Not "Groobah"! Grüber,' my father would gripe. 'It's a German name. There is an umlaut!' So when Dad corrected us yet again about this new Grüber I asked, 'Why do you always do that?'

'Because that is the proper way to say it.'

'Well, does it really matter?'

'Don't be so bloody ignorant.' He whisked away my plate and started doing the dishes. 'I knew a Grüber during the war.'

'What? A German?'

'No. Grüber was a Czech. But he was in the German army.'

'Who was he?'

'Nothing to tell.'

'Who was he? Tell me!'

Mum piped up from the dining room. 'Oh, for God's sake, Peter, just tell her who Grüber was!'

And so he told me the story.

After the Warsaw Uprising failed my father was cattle-trucked out of the city to Stalag 344, near Lamsdorf in Silesia. It held mostly Russian prisoners and was renowned as one of the worst. 'It was built on a swamp. They treated the Russians like slaves. The Brits were treated a little better. We were treated like the Russians.'

Late in 1945, as the Soviets advanced, the Germans retreated. And they dragged the POWs with them. My father had good feet: perfect arches, of which he was very proud. He could walk for miles. Which was just as well because he was now part of the infamous Lamsdorf

Death March. Hitler's motive was to walk the prisoners to death.

'Aie! It was that bloody cold! Unbelievably cold!' It was in fact the coldest winter of the war. 'We walked for three days with them. And the pigs! If somebody was sick…they just shoot you. And quite often the Allied planes would shoot at us too. They had no idea, they thought we were Germans.'

'So what did you do?'

'We escaped.'

'How?'

'We just walked away from the line.'

'What do you mean? What did the German guards do?'

'What could they do? They were losing the war. They couldn't keep an eye on all of us.' He picked a crumb from his plate and gave me a patronising smile. 'It wasn't very dramatic, Magda.'

'So where did you go?'

'We hid in a haystack in a barn. The Germans came in and started sticking their bayonets into the hay. But we were that deep in we almost suffocated. And then once they were gone about ten Poles popped out of the hay!'

The truth lies somewhere between my taste for the dramatic and my father's liking for ironic understatement. The mortality rates on the Lamsdorf Death March were comparable to those of the notorious Bataan Death March.

Along the way the escapees happened upon some bicycles. Four of them shared three bikes and they rode across Germany.

'We went to a farmhouse and there was an old Pole who had lived all his life in Germany, together with his German pal. They were in their eighties or nineties. And this farmer hid us. But the German guy had a grandson who ratted on us and the Germans came and got us.'

'How old was he?'

'He was just a kid. He was maybe seven. He didn't realise. His grandfather slapped him across the face. Anyway, the kid had told a passing column of German soldiers and their prisoners about the men hiding on his grandfather's farm. And the leader of that German patrol was Grüber.'

'What was he like?'

'About five foot nine. Darkish. Quite a good-looking man. Quite well presented, with an air of authority. I said, "You're bloody *Volksdeutsche*, aren't you?" and he said, "I am a Czech." He was leading a motley bunch of about a dozen German soldiers, and maybe sixteen prisoners—Poles, Czechs, Russians. There was even an Englishman from Liverpool. Grüber used to make the Russians pull the sleds with all the baggage on them. He told us to put our bags on the sleds but we said no.'

So my father and his friends began walking. And walking. And walking. From time to time Grüber would stop them and scout ahead. If there was a German column he would come back and march his little band in the opposite direction. Or he would go up to a farmhouse and arrange for the men to sleep in the house. In actual beds.

'Normally you were lucky to sleep in the barn between two pigs for warmth. Most of these Germans were very nice, you know. They would feed us—we used to have potatoes in jackets! And you could see they were genuine, not just because they knew they had lost the war.'

After a while my father and his Polish friends began to suspect something. They quietly took Grüber aside. 'Eh, mate. We know you are up to something. What is it?'

So Grüber told them that he had grown up in these mountains. He knew every pass, every trail. And he had a plan. 'We will walk until the end of the war.'

And so that's what they did. A ragtag multinational bunch of mutual enemies tramped across the Carpathian Mountains in the early months of 1945, dodging German patrols and biding their time until they could return home.

'What did you all talk about?'

'Football. And films. *Captain Blood* and things like that. They were old men like *Dad's Army*, doddery old fools. There was one old boy who was really old. He said, "What am I doing here? I'm a schoolteacher. What do I know about soldiering?" I said, "Never mind, Grandad, let's have your rucksack." We used to carry their backpacks and their rifles for them.'

'What? The Polish POWs carried the rifles of the Germans!'

'Yes.'

'Why?'

'We felt sorry for them. Poor old bastards.'

Eventually my father and his friends met some Polish girls who were working in a factory. The girls told them the conditions weren't too bad and the men fancied their chances were better with these girls than with Grüber. Grüber let them go. They were caught and sent to another POW camp, before ending up in Luckenwalde. In April 1945 they were liberated by the Soviets.

'What was it like to be finally free? It must have felt amazing!'

'I would not have wanted to be one of the people who lived in the nearby town after the Russians were liberated.' My father corrected my naivety.

'Why?'

He looked at me like I was a fool. 'The Soviets gave the Russians twenty-four hours to do as they pleased. Jesus!' He shook his head. 'I couldn't believe it. Decent people were doing things they could not even have *thought* of a few hours earlier. They went completely mad.'

'What did you do?'

'I agreed to stay overnight in a German home among single women and young girls.'

'Why?'

'Because the presence of a former prisoner of war was the only way to protect them.'

'From what?'

'That's enough, you don't need to know any more.'

I felt very proud of my father for that. Still do.

'And did you ever find out what happened to Grüber and the others?'

'They spent the last few weeks of the war in Grüber's home town. Skiing.'

'Ha ha! And Grüber?'

'I can't remember exactly. It was either the Germans or the Russians, the day the war ended.'

'What?'

'Shot him.'

# SALAD DAYS

In 1976 the nuns announced there was to be a school musical. It was to be an original piece of work called *Soul Happening*, written by the English teacher Patsy Poppenbeck and her rotund husband Dr Ralph Poppenbeck, who was cast in the plum role of the Devil. When the announcement was made our hearts sank. We were brutal teenage girls and Ralph Poppenbeck was not rock-god material.

We were not kind about poor Ralph. In fact after he and Patsy Poppenbeck first got married, whenever we walked past her classroom we would take a moment to stand outside and bark 'Ralph! Ralph! Ralphralphralph!' like small yapping dogs, and then run as we heard the rapid clack of her furious march to the door.

If this musical flopped there would never be another one. If it succeeded I was going to audition for the next one. Ralph Poppenbeck carried all of our pubescent theatrical hopes on his wide and sloping shoulders.

For two nights only, the assembly hall was transformed into a theatre. There was moody lighting and the rows of green vinyl fold-down seats had been pulled out from the walls. As I took my seat next to Sharon Pesavento I did not feel terribly hopeful. The lights were dimmed, a hush fell over the crowd, the band struck up and red satanic light filled the proscenium arch. And then Ralph Poppenbeck strode onto the stage in tight black and red satin…

Ralph Poppenbeck was smokin'! Seriously smokin'. He exuded devilish cool and a sly, sexy, scary charm. It was thrilling. As I watched that plump fellow strut and shimmy across the stage like a rock star I glimpsed the transformative power of art to take the drab grind of life and turn it into a thing of pizzazz! It was chemical. In an instant all of those movies and TV shows that had been my salvation seemed within reach. Just as when I was eight I thought I could touch the moon from the top of our hill, I now felt I could reach out and feel the flickering, insubstantial world that lay beyond the silver screen. A plan began to hatch in my brain. Maybe I could be a writer, or even an actor?

I told my father I wanted to drop out of school. There was a family conference.

'Don't be stupid,' my father advised. 'Don't quit. You have to have something to fall back on. Look at Jonathan Miller.'

Jonathan Miller—doctor, sculptor, director, television presenter, later a knight of the realm—was my father's polymath of preference. He was also a comedian, having started out with Peter Cook, Dudley Moore and Alan Bennett in *Beyond the Fringe*. My father dangled the prospect of Miller in front of me.

'You can do all of those things, Maggie.'

He was right. But he was wrong too. I had cheered up a little over the years but the depression lingered like a London fog. It was my playfulness that saved me and I clutched at it like a drowning woman. I became the class clown. I was a good mimic. It was not long before I was 'doing turns' before each class. In those few emancipated moments before the nun arrived and rapped her bride-of-Christ wedding ring on the desktop, the girls would clamour for me to do one of my impressions. In terms of schoolyard politics, class-clown status is a form of diplomatic immunity. At long last I was safe.

Siena was a middle-rung Catholic convent school, but the nuns expected nothing short of academic excellence. They were Dominicans, the Order of Preachers, renowned for their intellectual ferocity. This was a group of well-read women. Some of them, I suspect, were career nuns who had entered the convent to get an education. Others had been missionaries and suffered from lingering tropical ailments. A few had doctorates and were scholars. But more than anything they were a living example of a community of women who were capable, efficient and intelligent, and who lived and exercised power independent of men. They were feminist theory put into practice.

But they still had to do as they were told, of course. By Rome and by the priest who lived in the priory across the road. Still, some of the nuns intimated that there should be married clergy, even women clergy, and that, quite frankly, some lone priests were 'strange' from want of companionship.

Our patron saint, Saint Catherine of Siena, was one of twenty-five children. (No wonder she became a nun and theologian.) She was our role model. She had a masochistic twist in her nature and some odd ideas. Like all nuns she was married to Jesus but rather unusually she believed that, in place of a wedding ring, she wore on her finger the invisible foreskin of Our Saviour. She enjoyed the mortification of the flesh. She once drank pus from a cancerous sore. This was the example of ambitious selflessness to which we were supposed to aspire. In class and by example, the nuns tried to impress upon us the importance of social justice. In an effort to jump-start our sense of community we were bussed over to a local Catholic old people's home to help with the feeding. It backfired. The odour of mouldering humans and food made me dry retch. I felt like I was being shown the ghost of Christmas future and vowed to die young.

As we matured so did our appreciation of our teachers. There was Joan Fahey, the wall-eyed, battleaxe senior-year English teacher. I loved her. She was tweedy and sturdy and had a bullshit detector like no other I have ever encountered. Her turned eye would scan the room like a CCTV camera, forcing total compliance as it was impossible to tell exactly where she was looking. To my amazement she was fond of me. She wrote in my report card that I was a 'gifted student with quite a flair for writing'. But her praise did nothing for my shattered confidence. Only praise from my father felt real and true and that was, of course, withheld. Still, I wrote a piece for the school magazine about a man who watches his wife burning to death in their home. It was called 'Courage'—and its grim themes were eerily prescient.

There was Miss Valentine, the resolutely single European history teacher who lived with her cats. I hated European history. All that mediaeval cruelty got inside my head and messed with me. Madame Grinyer was the French teacher. She would have us over to her house and cook us delicious French meals while her husband introduced us to the brilliance of Woody Guthrie and Pete Seeger.

There was the slinky-hipped physics teacher who sashayed along behind the desk like she was in an ad for Kool cigarettes and who went away at the end of one term as Mrs Butler and came back the next as Ms Ajayoglu, having discreetly divorced her husband and reverted to her Afghani maiden name. After class had begun she called me down, as I secretly hoped she would. 'What's wrong, Magda?'

'Nothing, Ms Ajayoglu.'

'You know you can talk to me.'

'Yes, Ms Ajayoglu.'

My parents didn't beat me. I was fed and clothed. How to explain that the world seemed…bleak? Pointless. That the love I felt was of the variety that dared not speak its name.

And then Hurricane Warwick arrived.

Warwick Taylor was the new year-eleven English literature teacher and he was as flamboyant and brilliant and extravagant as only a parochial who has seen the world can be. His drooping moustaches and shoulder-length red hair gave him the look of a musketeer. His physique was like John Wayne's—large and imposing, perched precariously on too-small feet. He would begin each class by rolling up his sleeves to reveal his pale, freckled skin and long fingernails, perfect for strumming the guitar. And then, his arms flailing like an impassioned conductor, he would launch into a reading.

Warwick was in the grand pedagogic tradition of educators who change lives: *To Sir, with Love*; *Dead Poets Society*; *Good Will Hunting*. We were utterly captivated and would never be the same again. And we knew it.

Warwick Taylor awakened my soul to the wonders of art and literature. Poetry had always irritated me. It was not factual. It was messy. It was about emotions. And because my emotional landscape was such a dead zone I found it hard to relate to such delicate profusion. I was both attracted to and repelled by the realm of the senses. The notion of a self-conscious storyteller using aesthetic tricks was like lying. Prufrock's timid mediocrity frightened me, and Stephen Dedalus's precious epiphanies were of no use to a suburban girl, quietly asphyxiating in the vacuum of her own life. But Warwick's flaming enthusiasm burned phrases into my mind forever. 'Like shining from shook foil.' I began, at sixteen, to love the sound of phrases I couldn't yet understand. It is fair to say that without Warwick I would not be writing this book.

Just as Warwick saved English literature for me, Sister Mary Mechtilde killed chemistry. God bless her. She was old and wore a practical white apron over her habit. She was even more fastidious than my father, who also ran a lab. I think she had been a missionary somewhere and perhaps she had some form of OCD. She would scrub her cheeks until they were literally red raw. She was full of behavioural tics that we quickly learned to exploit.

The floor of the science lab was a chequerboard of black and white tiles. Sister Mechtilde could not commence the class until we were all arrayed perfectly within alternating squares, like a human chess set. This provided us with a very simple way to delay the class. Once she was satisfied that everything was in order she would turn to face the blackboard and we would quickly rearrange ourselves. She would turn around to find us in minute disarray and a flight of confusions and disturbances would flutter across her cheeks like frightened birds.

We thought we were geniuses for devising this plan. But soon the nuns got wind of it and one day Sister Rosemary flew in in a flap of white scapula and rapped her ring furiously on the counter. 'Girls!'

We stood to attention, giggling. We thought we were hilarious.

'You are very cruel. Sister Mary Mechtilde has some…problems.' The kindness on Sister Rosemary's face silenced us instantly. We felt like a bunch of little arseholes.

'Sister Mary Mechtilde will be going away for a little while. Miss Carter will be taking the class.'

I felt ashamed but a small flame of hope flickered. Maybe Miss Carter would make science interesting; maybe my old dream of becoming a doctor didn't have to die.

Things were looking up. Miss Carter was young and hip and pretty. The telltale stick of white chalk dangled from her fingers like a cigarette or a joint. Miss Carter gave me my first true lesson in chemistry—she was a catalyst.

I did not grow up in a party political household. My parents were swinging voters. They were sympathetic to the underdog and the worker, approved of many of Gough Whitlam's reforms and were pleased that Australia was leaving behind the stultifying Menzies era. They found the country's over-identification with Britain ludicrous, and knew all too well that the feelings were not reciprocated. But from time to time they became so exasperated with Labor that they had to vote Liberal. *Plus ça change.*

It was Miss Carter who galvanised me into political action, and via the most unlikely means: the periodic table of the elements. I hated the periodic table and everything it stood for. Dmitri Mendeleev's meticulous tabulation of everything in the whole wide world was the cross on which my hopes of being a doctor were being crucified. Then Miss Carter furtively mentioned the political and social significance of number 92 on the periodic table—uranium. She told us about dangerous by-products with half-lives of 250,000 years. Seen from this fresh perspective the periodic table, that killer of childhood dreams, acquired meaning and appeal. It was about energy and life and power.

Soon after, Anna Rogers and I went down to Camberwell Junction, where there was an army disposals store. I bought my first pair of khaki pants, a canvas mesh tote bag and a Hawaiian shirt. Then we caught a train into the city to join one of the big marches against uranium mining. It felt like my Woodstock, my 1968. But what I realise now is that it wasn't uranium or environmentalism or politics as such. It was the sense of agency. Of coming together to change things. My true passion, in retrospect, was the mob. I was bewitched in the same way as when I first heard an entire football stadium singing 'You'll Never Walk Alone'. The thousands of voices united, the wave of sound that rolled and splashed around the arena like the surf crashing into a narrow inlet. The possibility of soul-filled connection with masses of people…It was spiritual, mystical. I still long to be like one of the starlings on Ot Moor, joining in their daily murmuration: a discrete individual but also selfless, swirling and tumbling, twisting and turning in perfect synchronisation with hundreds of thousands of others.

Anyway, not even Miss Carter could save chemistry for me. It had to go. At the end of year eleven, I announced to my parents that I was dropping sciences. I would do a complete 180 and study humanities in my final year. All the totems of my childhood—the white lab coat, the stethoscope, the scalpel—went up in a puff of incendiary rebellion.

I don't know exactly what my father felt. As usual his feelings revealed themselves to me only by their absence, in the form of silence. He never dwelt on disappointment. Like the crumbs on the table, it would be swept up and disposed of before you even knew what was happening. I had nothing to back me up except my gut instinct. Art was my new destiny. So I slipped the chains and escaped. And who had I learnt this Houdini trick from? My father. 'Clive of Poland'. The little Englishman. His reinvented life was partly forced by circumstance, but mostly self-created. He didn't want me to be like him. But I was.

We had made it to year twelve, with all of the prestige associated. Our class now were leaders. We had power and privilege. We had a common room. We were allowed to smoke. In this gentler environment I formed new friendships. I had a core clique. We were Warwick's favourites: Helen, Genevieve, Anna, Nikki, Izabella, Madeleine and I.

Genevieve was the religious one. She came from a large Catholic family and was fiercely smart. Anna lived with her divorced mother. This was still slightly shocking but none of us cared. Both of her parents were terrific. Her father was urbane and groovy and introduced me to the brilliance of early Bruce Springsteen. Nikki was cheeky. In the library checkout book she added an extra Jane Austen novel to the canon: *Pride and Prejudice*, *Sense and Sensibility*, *Sex and Sexuality*. And her father was Jewish. Madeleine was the cultured one. She had lived in England for a year and her father was music critic for the *Age*.

At the time I was obsessed with Maggie Smith's performance of Miss Jean Brodie—her hilarious haughtiness, her poignant self-delusion, her idealistic pursuit of 'beauty, art and truth' in the education of her 'gels'. Her switch from angry to steely to impassioned to dignified to high-handed and finally hurt and humiliated was like watching a Romanian gymnast execute a perfect routine. And the language! 'She thinks to intimidate me by the use of quarter hours?' All executed in that diamond-hard Scottish accent. There was something about Maggie Smith, and not just the accent, that reminded me of my mother. Years later, when I met Dame Maggie, this perception was confirmed—the same unfeasibly soft heart protected with sharp but funny porcupine needles. Anyway, at convent school I would quote her at the slightest provocation. Chrysanthemums were forever after 'such serviceable flowers'. I had nailed her 'my gels are the crème de la crème' speech. We began to refer to ourselves as Warwick's 'gels'. Well, I did.

Warwick announced he would be directing a new school musical—*Salad Days*. *Salad Days* is standard high-school theatre fare. It is reasonably funny without demanding the skill required for Coward or even Gilbert and Sullivan. Perfect for ham-fisted amateurs. It is about a young couple who are given a magical piano that fills people with an irresistible urge to dance, which results in toe-tapping classics such as 'Oh Look at Me, I'm Dancing!' There are spaceships and an old tramp who turns out to be the uncle 'we don't mention'.

I decided to go for the role of Lady Raeburn, the middle-aged dowager. Auditions were held in the assembly hall and they were public. This meant that I got to see several girls try out before me. With every attempt my confidence grew. For once my early English accent would be an asset and not a handicap. I *knew* I could do this. And I was right: I got the part.

Boys were bussed in from brother Catholic schools to play the male parts. That was how I first met Andrew Goodone who, back then, was a plump, nerdy *Glee* type. I was astonished when I saw him many years later transformed into a raffish stand-up comic. And no matter how many times I saw him on stage, with a scotch and a fag in hand, saying 'fuck' all over the place and being dark and dangerous, I could not shake off the image of that sweet young boy, just as when two photographic negatives are accidentally developed together and the images hover ethereally in the same frame, each haunting the other.

Warwick was a perfectionist. A theatrical slave-driver. He tried to impress upon us the rigours and disciplines of the stage. He drilled into our bogan brains that the correct pronunciation is not 'pi-A-no' but 'pee-AH-no'. Not 'dance' as in 'ants' but 'dahnce' as in 'aunts'. He made us rehearse until late into the night. Our parents would simply have to understand; it was the transpersonal god of beauty, truth and art that demanded this sacrifice. Inch by inch, he dragged us up to his lofty standards.

Meanwhile, my official studies were flatlining. Dear Miss Valentine exhorted me to pull my finger out.

'Magda,' she would implore, 'I still think you may be able to pass. If you would only study.'

But I couldn't. No warning sound ever reached me. It was as if all normal feelings were contained in a bubble. I could see but never feel them.

Finally, after all of our hard work, the play opened. The instant I stepped onto that stage I could feel it. All of the disparate, confusing parts of myself formed into a meaningful whole. I had been plummeting headfirst towards oblivion. Now, with a snap, the chute opened above me. When I had my solo I felt like a conductor, leading the audience. I was surprised how gentle it was. The slightest gesture, the lightest touch on the surface would cause a ripple. I could feel the bonds of belonging begin to regenerate.

I wasn't the only one having a chemical reaction. When I stepped out onto the stage, according to my mother, my father slapped his forehead and then his knee. 'My God! My God!' He shook his head. 'She looks *exactly* like my mother!' His voice trailed off. His nose reddened and he began to fidget. What must that have felt like for him? To see this bizarre theatrical reincarnation of his beloved mother, from whom he had been exiled for thirty years? Another strange palimpsest of images and realities.

Mum said he looked like a little boy, grinning from ear to ear. Then he turned to her and said, 'She's got It.'

After the show my father was beaming brighter than the Otway lighthouse. 'Well done, Maggie! Well done, love!'

He hugged me tight and kissed me on both cheeks. I had waited a long time for this approbation. We all had. 'You were really excellent, hen,' Mum joined in. 'And funny!' This, coming from my mum, the funny one in the family, really meant something. But I knew. I could feel it. I was no longer an outsider flailing on the periphery of life. I was standing right at its red-hot centre. This was the birth of my creative self.

And finally I was indisputably better at something than my father. Comedy. My father couldn't tell a joke to save himself. He would get the sequence wrong, laugh before he started, mangle the delivery and fluff the punch line. I had found an escape route from all those years of humiliation on the tennis court. He knew it too, and was happy for me. But I knew instinctively I had to keep my dream away from him or he would kill it. Slowly, stealthily and absolutely. Without meaning to. Just as he had crushed my brother's dream of being a racing-car driver.

Besides, when it came to getting into drama school my parents were clueless. So I pinned all my hopes on Warwick. I knew he was the only person who could help me. We arranged that after the exams

I would go over to his house and he would mentor me. My new dream was about to take flight.

But first there was the small matter of European history to attend to. I had slipped so far behind that even dear old Miss Valentine had given up on me. My only hope now was swot vac—the three weeks of study time before the exams. I didn't like coffee but I got a large tin of instant and locked myself in my bedroom. I effectively did my entire year twelve in those three adrenaline-fuelled weeks. For years after, the first blossoms of spring would always be associated with sheer panic. I sat the exams and waited.

As the days grew longer and warmer, the prospect of university and a very different life drew closer. Much as I longed to escape the narrow confines of high school, the dizzying freedom ahead spooked me. Let off the leash, who would I be?

Perhaps it was this sense of impending liberty that prompted me to visit my sister. I couldn't bear to keep my secret any longer. I had become a stranger within my own family, a minority of one. I could not carry that word on my own any longer. Lesbian. I hated that word. It turned my heart to lead. It sounded like a slur even if you didn't know what it meant. Only one person in the world could hear that word and still love me. Maybe. I hoped.

So in the dog days of summer I went to visit Barb, who was by now married and living in Scoresby on a new housing estate with her husband and a small baby. Everything was new. The grass was short, the fences were bare and there was not a single tree over three feet tall. The shadeless suburb baked in the noonday sun. And as we sat on the berber couch drinking our cups of Moccona I prised open my heart.

I remember years ago watching an old black-and-white movie, *The Man in the Iron Mask*. An innocent man, the twin brother of the King of France, is imprisoned and forced to wear an iron mask for years. I knew how he felt.

The moment I opened my mouth to speak I started to cry.

'What's wrong, Mag?'

I felt like I had rocks in my throat. 'I have to tell you something but please, please don't tell Mum and Dad. Promise me.'

'OK. I promise.'

The word was still safely vaulted up inside me. But once it was out, I could never take it back. Between juddering sobs, I said it. 'I think…I think I might be a lesbian.'

I had never heard anyone utter that word except as an insult. I felt like I was the only one in the world. I don't know if Barb knew how much rested on her response. Tears came to her eyes.

'Oh, Mag. I thought maybe. Do you know why?'

'I have no idea. I just know I am.'

'Well, I still love you.'

It was as if I had been told I wasn't going to the guillotine. Barb hugged me and we sat crying together. And, for the first time since I could remember, I felt I was not alone.

For me and the gels, now that the torture of exams was over, before results were announced in the papers, it was time to plan our futures. My dream of being an actor had grown. I wove hopes and dreams and imagined lives around it. Warwick was the man who would open the door to this new life, and now the day of my meeting with him had finally—*finally*—arrived. We had arranged that I would come to his flat in South Yarra. As I walked down the hill from our house in Croydon I knew that I was striding towards my destiny. I caught the bus, two trains, another bus and then walked up Punt Hill. All up it took me about two hours but I didn't care. As I entered his apartment block I could see my new life shimmering before me, like a mirage.

I saw the note from the end of the hall. A small white rectangle on the front door. As I got closer I could make out Warwick's flamboyant handwriting. *Something has come up*, he flourished. *So terribly sorry…* and so on.

I took the note from the door, scrunched it up and put it in the bottom of my bag. Then I walked back down Punt Hill and caught a bus, two trains and another bus home. I never heard from Warwick again.

The exam results were announced. My marks were enough to get me into Arts at Melbourne University. There was one minor miracle—European history. I topped the class.

# THE CHERRY ON THE CHRISTMAS PUDDING

'It is a sin to waste the God-given gift of a good brain.' In our house that phrase was like Chinese water torture. My father believed in brains the way other people believe in gods or lottery tickets—if you get a good one you are set for life.

I was not convinced.

I chose to go to Melbourne University because I lacked the imagination to go anywhere else and because my friends Helen and Anna went and because at the heart of the campus is the Old Arts Building—an oasis of modest neo-neo-gothic grandeur that was in fact built after World War I. I have always been a sucker for anything remotely gothic. If I can't get the real thing then mock will do. It feels like the embodiment of my life—gloomy rudiments overarched with vaulting optimism. The extreme excitability of the mediaeval soul always seemed a good fit for my own emotional lability. But I never felt I had a right to be at university. Like Virginia Woolf I half-expected a bat-like beadle to flap around the corner and shoo me off the turf. This was no place for an ex-wannabe-sharpie from the outer suburbs.

Siena Convent had an excellent academic record but a feeble social one. When I arrived for Orientation Week I knew Anna and Helen and nobody else. The kids from the wealthy Catholic schools—Xavier, Genazzano, Mandeville—already knew one another from dances, parties, polo matches and skiing trips. Their world was alien to me. And the prospect of meeting other lesbians filled me with longing and dread. But where? How?

I didn't have a clue. The wide open spaces of my unconventional life made me agoraphobic. I clung to the shores of what I knew best. Food. For want of a better idea I spent most of my first term sitting in the Student Union on my own eating Smarties. I was functionally friendless and desperately lonely, which made me a beacon for every Christian group on campus. But for all their talk of forgiveness and unconditional love I knew this warm embrace did not extend to lesbians. No, the campus Christian Union was not the place to lay down my burden. Or meet other lesbians. I could feel myself slipping into the void. I began to think about suicide. I would stand on the train platform and stare at the tracks for longer than was healthy.

Academia, I was discovering, failed to excite me. But it did achieve one thing—it got me out of Croydon. If the travel to school had been hard this was worse. From Croydon to Parkville took me nearly two hours each way. Train timetables dominated my life, leaving little time for study. So it was arranged that I would live with family friends, the Bartniks, in Ivanhoe—not far from where Mum had been a live-in nanny. From there uni was just a quick bus ride up the freeway but most of the time I used to hitchhike.

Bob Bartnik was a Polish Quaker. He was tall and charismatic. He and his wife Margaret had three boys, which made me, perhaps, a little like the daughter he never had. I adored Bob. He was funny and freethinking. He was the same age as my father but I was never clear about exactly what he had done in the war. I don't know if he felt the need for redemption. I just knew he was different from my father. We had lots of chats. Bob thought I might like the whole Quaker thing. He would tell me about pacifism and the lovely belief that there is 'that of God' in all human beings. He used to take me to Quaker meetings and I was duly impressed—aside from the fact that the womenfolk did the washing-up. Presumably that has changed since 1979.

The meetings were held in a big old red-brick house in Malvern. The meeting room was arranged in concentric circles. When we entered we found a group of people sitting in silence. There was no altar, no priest, no music. No incense. No hierarchy. Just people. And your own soul. I loved the idea of this stillness but not even Bob and the kindly Society of Friends could help me.

Helen joined the Socialist Club and I joined the Feminist Club. The Feminist Club met in the Women's Room. Weird to think of feminism as a club, as if it were a hobby like bushwalking, stamp collecting and the Friends of Monty Python Society. Aside from my high school anti-uranium activities, I was not at all political, but a general sympathy for the underdog led me towards the Women's Room. Plus I hoped that where there were feminists there might also be lesbians.

The Women's Room was tucked away at the end of the corridor on the top floor of the Student Union building. With my heart pounding like a frightened chihuahua's I summoned my courage and pushed open the door. It looked homey, like a lounge room with a few old armchairs and couches scattered about. The walls were covered with screen-print posters and handwritten notices about dances and fundraisers and rallies. A group of women sat around chatting. They flicked their eyes in my direction and smiled but no one stopped talking or said hello. Sitting in the corner was a pretty woman with close-cropped, tight curly hair. She wore immaculate white overalls that were more fashion statement than boiler room. Pinned to the bib was a lesbian badge. A lesbian. A real live lesbian. I felt like an explorer glimpsing an endangered species. She was tiny: frangible and fine-boned as a black cat. But she exuded a kind of quiet power—the power of being herself.

I took some pamphlets, browsed through some of the books on the shelf and began acquainting myself with feminism.

I started attending meetings. At first I was too nervous to speak. It was the 1970s and in those days politics was an extreme sport. It was not for the faint-hearted. The 'personal was political'. Uncompromisingly so. And its language and attitudes were still vaguely Stalinist. No one would be caught dead eating at McDonald's, shaving their armpits or wearing lipstick. The atmosphere was earnest, angry and confrontational. People called one another out over the slightest transgressions. Like any other utopia-in-waiting there were strict rules. So I just watched, listened and learned.

Despite all this the Women's Room soon became a safe haven for me. I liked the political types I met there. They were misfits like me. It took me a while to understand their jargon, their talk of 'patriarchy' and the 'division of labour' and 'dialectics' and 'paradigms'. But eventually their politics started to give shape and form to the non-specific dread I habitually felt. It was the beginning of explaining myself to myself. Most importantly, I was not alone. I now had friends. For the first time in my life I felt vaguely normal. Gradually my life began to feel viable. And the weight, as they say, began to fall off me.

Before I knew it I had a gang—Cate, Elaine, Katrina, Judy, Julia. We would go to Women and Labour conferences and on Reclaim the Night marches and on interstate trips. We attended salons modelled

after the great Parisian soirees of legendary lesbians Gertrude Stein
and Natalie Barney. I became best friends with Elaine, who was one
of the most eccentric people I had ever met. While the rest of us wore
a uniform of Japara oilskins and Doc Marten boots she wore op shop
bright pink, floral, flared jumpsuits and big floppy hats. She came from
Violet Town, a tiny place a couple of hundred kilometres north-east
of Melbourne on the Hume Highway, and although her parents had
sent her to an exclusive boarding school in town she retained the air
of an outsider. Her parents were Scottish and she was gentle but with
a sharp, harsh humour like my mother's, which is no doubt why we
clicked. We had a compatible kind of crazy.

Sometime around then Helen and I came out to one another. It
was a relief. I didn't feel so alone. I had developed a minor crush on
Lorena, who was in my fine art class. She was of Italian stock and
I used to go over to her parents' place in Bulleen, where her father
would ply me with his eviscerating home-made grappa. Then one
day she told me that she and Helen were now dating. 'How do you
*feel* about that, Magda?' she asked, as we always did back then.

We were standing on the corner of Grattan and Cardigan streets.
It was a bright sunny winter's day, the kind of brilliant light you get
on the snowfields. Everything felt illuminated. And what I felt was
the blankness rising up to engulf me like a poisonous gas.

What did I feel? I had felt something, once, I supposed. If so it
was now gone. Anything I said now would be pure guesswork.

'I don't know.'

'What do you mean?'

'I don't know what I feel. I don't feel anything.'

'But you must feel something?'

'Not really, no. I mean, I could name an emotion for you but it
would be like a blindfolded person playing pin the tail on the donkey.
I might hit the target but it would be a fluke.'

Lorena laughed. And it became a running joke, 'Magda and her absence of feeling'.

Actually, my feelings were an unregulated mess. I ricocheted between feeling nothing and feeling everything. As I wrote to Helen a bit later, when she and Lorena had gone travelling, *You know how I get drunk at parties and kind of explode because I keep so many things— especially my sexuality—bottled up all the time? I have done just that. And lost a friend.* I still hadn't told any of my new uni friends that I was a lesbian. They were feminists but that didn't mean they wouldn't be creeped out.

By now, second-wave feminism was becoming my religion. The cornerstone of it all was consciousness raising. CR was designed to cast a light on the 'dark continent' of the female psyche, to raise us out of our denial about our oppression as women, and to open us up to our feelings. But this presented me with a problem. I didn't know what I felt. My feelings had been invalidated for so long that they were stillborn, lifeless things.

The first CR session I went to was in a large terrace house in Carlton. Maybe twenty or so women were arranged around the lounge room. A few of them conformed to the caricatured stereotype of feminists—short hair and overalls and nary a bra between them. Many just looked like 'ordinary' women in jeans or Laura Ashley frocks. There was a hint of patchouli oil in the air and a large selection of herbal teas.

One by one the other women spoke of their feelings—of how it felt at work or in class to be sexually harassed or belittled or passed over for promotion. Slowly, the Mexican wave of revelation swept around the room. Until it reached me.

I sat there, frozen. I was like the planet before creation—a tangle of nameless, shapeless ephemera. In the place where my feelings should have been there was a vast expanse of nothingness. The only emotion I could identify was a queasy fear in the pit of my stomach. A fear of being exposed.

What could I say about patriarchy? About men in general? About my father? About myself? It was like the old days in confession. The pressure was on to come up with something. I said a couple of feeble things and the talk moved on.

How could I explain what I hadn't even begun to understand myself? That I was locked in the Jedi mind trick of my father's denial? That I was the victim of a victim. All I knew was what I feared—that I was not like other human beings and I was devoid of normal emotion. And there was no way I was going to let these women, kind and patient as they were, see that.

My letters to Helen and Lorena were full of tortured agonies about my 'repressed sexuality', as we called it then.

Finally I told Elaine. She was superb. Kind, caring, supportive. I wrote: *Elaine and I were sprawled on the mattress in the Women's Room chatting about our families and how there were some things we just couldn't tell them. And I just poured my heart out and told her about myself, my repressed lesbianism—everything. She was amazing! I know it shouldn't 'be an issue' as you put it but somehow for me it seems to be. It just seems to permeate everything I do and contaminate the way I relate to other people. Elaine is rather worried about my excessive guilt complex actually.*

In the midst of this confusion I had my first sexual experience with a man. He was a sweet, shaggy-haired, Ned Kelly–bearded hippy Labor lefty. I rather enjoyed it, in a disconnected way, but I got up and went to a party rather than spend the night cuddled up. I did offer him the option of coming with me.

I tried again with the attractive boyfriend of a friend. (At her suggestion. Those were the times; she was in love with someone else.) But he was drunk and couldn't get it up. He had a rather small penis, which was a complete non-issue for me but seemed to bother him.

'Now you know,' he said, 'why I am a feminist sympathiser.'

Meanwhile, I moved out of the Bartniks' and into my first student house, a plain little single-storey thing, squished in among a row of terraces on Brunswick Street in North Fitzroy. It was owned and lived in by two Italian socialists, Sonny and Gianni Giannini. The Giannini brothers were not *so* socialist that it precluded them from being property-owning landlords. The migrant love of real estate apparently trumped ideology.

They were as unalike as two brothers could be. Gianni was a svelte, elegant Euro communist—I seem to remember the phrase anarcho-syndicalist hovering around him. He was an intellectual who argued from his head while Sonny was a stocky Stallone lookalike who did all his thinking with his great big heart. Sonny was a conductor working for the heavily unionised tramways. The Giannini brothers would argue outside my bedroom window for hours at a time about the best way to bring about working-class utopia. Sonny would become more and more impassioned while Gianni kept his cool. Against the rising tide of Sonny's heartfelt diatribe Gianni would try to get a word in: 'Let me give you the scenario. Let me give you the scenario! Would you let me give you the scenario?'

I never did get to overhear the scenario.

They were good guys. Sonny and I used to ride our pushbikes around Carlton, going to see movies at the Bughouse Cinema in Faraday Street, wending our way back through the quiet streets, circling the fountain at the Royal Exhibition Buildings. And in the warm soft night, as the moonlight glittered on the great domed roof of this symbol of empire, we would amiably conspire better worlds together—his socialist, mine feminist—like a couple of Bolsheviks who had snuck into the Tsar's Summer Palace.

But I was a useless cook and a hopeless housemate so eventually the kindly brothers had to ask me to leave.

For one short but memorable term I lived with Henry and Graham, who was the president of the Australian Union of Students. He was always travelling and hardly ever home, and when he was the house was full of student politicos crashing on couches and any available floor space. Henry was a student Labor apparatchik. He was gay and he was a plump, kind, pleasant fellow. Great company and good to talk to. He also played political hardball. The rumour was that he had a dirt file, a locked filing cabinet in his room allegedly filled with scandal and muck about every student politician of every political persuasion. He was politically savvy enough to know that these hatchling politicos were the potential future leaders of the nation. One drunken night Henry showed me this political Pandora's box, hinting obliquely at its terrible hidden power, but since he would not let me see its fabled contents I cannot confirm if it was full of political vice or just his uni essays.

By the end of first year I had spent so much time finding myself, or at least looking, that I had not opened a single book. My grades were disastrous. I was staring down the barrel of total failure. Not only would this leave a permanent blotch on my academic record, it would also mean the loss of my student allowance. With exams only a week away, drastic action was required. There was only one possible option—I would have to drop out. Clear the slate and start again.

Many student households dispersed over the summer, and so I found myself back at the Bartniks' for a spell. My parents came over for a visit. We sat in the cosy lounge room making polite chitchat. Dad sat a few feet opposite me on the brick ledge next to the woodfire heater. Mum was in an adjacent armchair, smoking. 'So how's uni going?' she asked.

'Well, I need to talk to you about that actually.'

Mum leaned forward like a fox on the scent. 'What is it?'

I looked around at the Bartniks. Margaret smiled cheerily. Bob beamed. They were oblivious of the betrayal about to unfold. Despite my conviction of the rightness of my course of action my hands began to sweat. 'Well, I've decided to drop out.'

'Oh, good God.' Mum lurched back in her seat.

'What do you mean?' asked Bob.

'I don't understand. Why would you even think about doing such a thing!' Dad protested.

'Because I know I am going to fail. It's better to drop out.'

'What do you mean you are going to fail? Have you not been studying?'

I squirmed. How to explain? I had at last connected with my tribe. Something in me knew that this was more important than getting an H2A for fine art. I knew in a way that my parents never could that my life depended on me *not* sitting my exams.

'It's not like when you were young, Dad. Uni is free. It's flexible. You can drop out and it's fine! It's much better to drop out than to fail. Everyone does it. And it's free!'

'Ach! You have no discipline. It is always the same story with you. You just need to apply yourself.'

'That's not true!'

He wanted to protect me. But I knew his efforts to do that would in fact destroy me. As for my mother—she never even had a chance at an education. No one dared dream such a thing for her. But she did dream it for me. She was, after all, the one who taught me to read.

My father sighed. 'I am not as well as I look.' He rubbed his leg, playing the cancer card again. Now, in a deft pincer movement, Bob mentioned how the young son of a man they knew quit uni and how, within a month, the father had dropped dead of a heart attack. I felt my head swim. Was I killing my own father? I was just a kid, only eighteen. It never crossed my mind that I could tell him the real reason for my failure—that I was trying to come to terms with the fact that I was gay. In my family, only my sister knew. And no one knew about my suicidal thoughts; that I looked longingly at train tracks and pill bottles. Not even Barb.

I put up the force field of stubborn indifference and denial. I shut them down and laid my trump card on the table. 'It's too late. I've already done it.'

My father looked like he had been electrocuted. 'What?'

'I've already dropped out.'

'Ach, Jesus!'

Mum dragged like a navvy on her cigarette. My father looked as if I had horsewhipped him. His elbows rested on his knees, his head hung low, shaking in disbelief. 'It's a sin,' he muttered, 'to waste the God-given gift of a good brain.'

Over the summer break I got a job at a small diner just up the road from the Bartniks' and around the corner from the Camberwell tramways depot. In those days the tramways served as a kind of catchment area for people who had fallen through the employment cracks. The ranks of the conductors were a circus of colourful lefties and non-conformists. On the trams you could get away with piercings and weird hair and all kinds of other personal eccentricities. There was one French guy on the Fitzroy line who became famous for his mime and magic routine.

Our little diner became the café of choice for this raggle-taggle bunch of intellectuals and artists. My favourite among them was Laszlo the Hungarian tram driver. He'd been an art historian and intellectual back in the old country. I had, after a fashion, studied art history in my first year, so we had lots of conversations about art and politics. But I was also fascinated by him because he was from a similar part of the world as my father. I plagued him with questions about life under the communists and his answers did not fit neatly with my naive left-wing assumptions.

The café was co-owned by a lovely Greek man who worked so hard he literally became delusional. I came into work one day to find Spiro muttering to himself and trying to shoo away a fluffy toy dog. There were a few other waitresses but the main one was Gerda. She was an artist. I liked her. She had a dark, dramatic bob and looked like Pola Negri. She used to flirt a lot with Laszlo and I suspected they were having an affair. I used to confide in her about my budding but, as yet, theoretical lesbianism. One day just before Christmas we went for iced coffee at a rival café.

'So, Magda, don't you think it is about time your lesbianism became practice rather than just theory?'

'Umm, yes, I suppose so.'

'So what are you going to do about it?'

'Oh, umm, I dunno.'

'I could help you with that.' She eyeballed me over the top of her creamy iced-coffee, playing with her straw.

'I don't know what you mean,' I stammered. I didn't want to presume.

'Well.' She licked the cream from her straw. 'I suppose I was wondering if you were going to be the cherry on my Christmas pudding.'

I wasn't. Which, looking back, was probably a mistake.

# POLITICALLY CORRECT POO

As I had promised my parents, I re-enrolled for the following year. Among other subjects, I took the drama elective. Despite my ardent politics a tiny ember of artistic hope still flickered. Until the fireball incident. Our teacher gave us an exercise: we were to imagine that we were fireballs. Some people were brilliant at it. I wasn't. I was painfully self-conscious, and halfway through my fireball sputtered out. I loved the theory—Artaud, Grotowski, Brecht. But I quickly realised that whatever talent I had wasn't suited to drama school. I stopped going to class.

I finally found a home with my friends Sue and Marc and Peter in Palmerston Place. A bright sunshine yellow and brown, two-storey terrace right opposite uni. Sue was a botany student. Marc was a dapper Frenchman who was studying computer science, I think. Pete was tall and handsome and a rising star of the left intelligentsia. They were a really great bunch and were good-natured about my lack of domestic skills. We used to go and see bands and movies and march in rallies together and smoke pot around the heavy wooden kitchen table. (Well, the others did. Pot does not agree with me. It makes me feel insaner.) I was the house clown. I would do impersonations and accents and try to make them laugh while they toked on the joint. They would roll back, sucking in hard, furiously waving their hands at me to stop, trying not to let any of the precious THC-laden smoke escape their lungs. We had some great laughs around that kitchen table. And they would always say, 'You should be on the stage!' But I was haunted by my failed fireball.

We would sometimes go to see comedy at the Last Laugh in Collingwood. The Laugh was already an institution and all the greats of alternative comedy, including overseas acts like French and Saunders and the guys from The Young Ones, played there. I longed to be up on the stage but I still hadn't a clue how to go about it.

I loved all things edgy and unconventional. It was the era of great northern English post-punk-cum-new-wave music. Bands like the Buzzcocks, Magazine, Joy Division, Gang of Four and Howard Devoto. Songs with dystopian, sexually transgressive titles like 'Orgasm Addict', '(Love Like) Anthrax', 'Homosapien' and my all-time favourite, 'Love Will Tear Us Apart (Again)'. 'Ever Fallen in Love (With Someone You Shouldn't've)' became my anthem. We would have parties and pogo round the lounge room until the walls shook and our retinas nearly detached.

Then one day Pete did something slightly shocking: he decided that he was going to teach himself to cook. It was a rare thing for men to have culinary expertise in the 1980s. Pete had prematurely greying lambswool curls and long fingers that were never intended for manual work. He was a natural intellectual and he later became an academic. He approached the task the same way he would an exam—he bought a cookbook, he followed the instructions and he made osso buco. And it was really good. He had taught himself something useful. I, on the other hand, had taught myself to play the spoons and 'Camptown Races' on my teeth. And swim. I did teach myself how to swim. But this was a hallelujah moment. I grasped the liberating notion that you could decide to do something, even something you had no aptitude for, and learn it. All it took was time and persistence.

But of course the osso buco was more than just a tasty dish; it was the beginning of Pete's emancipation from the oppression of leftist politics. It was a statement that he enjoyed bourgeois tastes. The osso buco was a goddamn declaration of independence! And I admired him for it. Politics back then made tyrannical demands of people. Many households were run along party lines. There was one Maoist household where a resident was accused of being a bourgeois individualist for wanting to take a shit with the toilet door shut. Even poo had to be politically correct.

We always think that history is made by kings and generals. But it is ideas that make the world. These are the currents that our lives bob along on like corks on the mighty oceans. If we do not control them we become victims of history. Somewhere along the line I began to realise that knowledge is power. That if I was going to have a hand in the running of my own life I was going to have to enter the realm of ideas. I was deeply into feminist art theory at the time. I wrote to Helen that it was *not in order to promote the 'cause' but rather because I like ideas.*

We had inherited a post-Holocaust world where humanity's vilest act was no longer inconceivable. It had happened, and we were different because of it. The previous generations had got it all so heinously wrong that we felt we had to scrap the whole thing and start again. We wanted to cure humanity of the human condition.

But heads without hearts are cruel things. Especially young heads. I was becoming hard. My father's refusal to see that socialism would cure all of the world's problems not only infuriated me—it convinced me he was stupid. We started to argue. He tried to warn me about the dangers of all thought systems.

'The war cured me of all the "isms",' he said. 'Nazism, communism, socialism, patriotism, nationalism, capitalism. I have seen them all. The problem is human nature. People. Shit always floats to the top.'

I couldn't hear him. I believed he lacked the intellectual sophistication to grasp the big picture. He did not come from one of the historic nations. Poland was an uncomfortable anomaly. It was oppressed not by capitalism but by communism. Solidarity, the non-communist trade union that began in the Lenin Shipyards in Gdańsk in August 1980 and eventually helped topple the Soviet Union, had partnered in its struggle for freedom not with a worldwide workers' revolution but with the reactionary, backward Catholic Church. What could my father possibly know about the fight for freedom as it was being fought now? On one of my visits home to Croydon he cautioned me, 'It was the radical intellectuals who gave credence to the Communist Party in Poland in the 1930s. They paved the way.'

But to me, at eighteen, Poland was a political inconvenience. South America was where it was at. I wanted to be an urban guerilla. I fantasised about going to Nicaragua to fight with the Sandinistas—the revolutionary poets. I read their poems, listened to their songs.

Then a letter arrived from Helen. She had been to East Berlin and seen the reality of life behind the Iron Curtain: harsh, repressed, menacing. This rattled me. Maybe my father was not so wrong. I ricocheted between arrogant certainty and feeling like a naive fool. I wrote back to her, *I dreamt I went to visit my relatives in Warsaw and everything was fine except there was a wall at about a ten-mile radius and you could never leave.*

Poland, with its inconvenient truths, began to drive a wedge between me and my newfound friends. My father wanted to protect me from that part of me that was most like him: my idealism. He could see how brightly it burned inside me, so he tried to extinguish it with ridicule. And when he flagged, Mum would pick up the baton. 'My God, you're *just* like your father,' she would taunt. '"Sister Hannah with her banner!"'

I still wanted to be that pretty young resistance fighter I had seen in my father's picture book all those years ago. All my parents had at their disposal to stop me was wit, mockery, manipulation.

'Don't be the first one up on the barricade,' my father warned me.

'Why? Why are you so afraid to take a stand?'

'Because I know what will happen.'

'What?'

'You will turn around to find there is no one there behind you. During the war the ones who joined the Nazis had the life of Riley. My parents did the right thing, they fought the Germans, and they lost everything. You don't understand what a ridiculous world it is.'

I wasn't listening. I was looking for an arena in which to deploy my revolutionary fervour.

Around the end of first year I had volunteered for the Women's Refuge Referral Service which was housed in the Women's Liberation Building in West Melbourne. Several times a week I would ride my bike over to the centre and spend a few hours working the phones: taking calls, placing desperate women and their children in refuges and emergency accommodation. I began to feel my life's work and my heart's desire were aligning. But what I really wanted was to work in a refuge.

The women who worked in the refuges had an aura about them. Whenever I saw them it was as though they walked in slow motion. They were uncompromising warriors on the front line, bravely confronting patriarchal violence in its most dangerous domain—the family home. They were changing the world. And it was dangerous work. Sometimes the violent husbands would attack the workers.

I can never be certain if it was compassion, idealism or recklessness that drew me to it. I was by now nineteen, the same age my father was when he joined his unit. Like him I was angry and full of despair. But a bright fire of idealism burned within me, so intense it felt originary. I felt it was mine and mine alone.

In the middle of second year uni I applied and was accepted. I think perhaps I was the youngest worker in the state at that time, and I certainly felt it. I was kind of like a team mascot. But at least now I was a refuge worker.

I was still studying part time and my old student diary from 1980 reads like a socialist-feminist debutante's dance card—it is a whirlwind of rallies for the homeless, squatters union gatherings, meetings with government ministers, May Day marches, street theatre rehearsals, screen-printing sessions and women's dances organised by an entity known as 'The Coven'. All interspersed with reminders to go to the laundromat.

The refuge was run by a collective—us. Lots of the workers were lesbians and they became mentors for me, in work and life. I especially loved Barb. She wore fedoras, smoked long, thin cigarillos and had a great sense of the ridiculous. Once, when a rather earnest worker was complaining of her 'industrial deafness', Barb teased her, 'Oh! You incurable romantic!' and winked at me from beneath the brow of her fedora. The other woman, who was very literal, didn't get it.

The locations and identities of the refuges were completely secret. The refuge I worked at was called Matilda and its location was never any more specific than the vague designation North West Region. The large, rambling old brick home had, from memory, four bedrooms, each of which contained several beds and bunks. There would be one family per room. The women and their families would stay until we could organise a Housing Commission flat for them. We had to find the women new identities—names, drivers licences, schools for the kids. They often had to leave behind everything they knew—home, family, friends.

Every few weeks a new family would arrive at the refuge. The women were bruised and broken, the kids fractious and scared. The worst was when the kids were hurt. That cut deep into your soul. The work was confronting and frightening. But also a real privilege. Seeing these women and children slowly mend made me feel worthwhile, although some of the socialist feminists at the refuge would have considered such talk dangerous. Sentimental, victim-saviour bullshit.

A lot of the work at the refuge was sheer drudgery: shopping for food, buying toilet paper, going down to the Department of Social Security. I struggled with the practical stuff. And I was too young to truly empathise with the women. But I really loved chatting with the residents, getting to know them and their kids. And finally I found a way to be useful. One of the workers had a friend who had a house in the country, at Blackwood, where we would take the kids on camp. I would do childcare during the day and at night by the open fire I would spin long nonsense yarns, doing all sorts of accents and funny voices. We would all laugh and fall about, and the kids would scream 'More! More!' And something in me clicked. Something about this felt very right to me.

The whole point of the refuges was to empower victims, to give them a voice, to hear them. But it was a delicate balance. Eventually I learned that it was often the ones who loved to talk who came to rely too heavily on the social life of the refuge and struggled later on. Out on their own, in a commission flat with just their kids to talk to, the loneliness got to them. Despite our best efforts, some failed to escape the complex emotional hold of their abusive partners. That was gutting. The strain on the workers was tremendous and it was a running joke that every couple of years a worker 'burned out'. Which is a euphemism for having a breakdown.

But it was this element of danger that held me transfixed. Danger, the presence of death, crackled around my father like an electrical field. We will all die, certainly. But he and his family had stared death down. He had goaded it, tempted it. His proximity to death made him the most alive person I knew. And so I always wanted to do the risky stuff.

One of the women in the refuge was named Mai. Small and steely, she mostly kept to herself. Her husband had been an intelligence officer for a brutal Southeast Asian dictatorship. He had beaten and threatened to kill her and the children many times. On one rare occasion, when he let them out of his sight, Mai grabbed the kids and ran.

Frequently women like Mai arrived with just the clothes on their backs, and we would have to make a trip back to the house to get important documents and clothes. I was given the job of looking after Mai with another refuge worker named Sue who was in her mid-twenties, which made her seem to me like a proper grown-up. She was a lovely, unflappable kind of a girl. We had to collect some survival essentials for Mai. We had asked for police support but none arrived. It was no surprise. The police attitude to domestic violence was often indifferent and we did a lot of our work unprotected.

We waited until the middle of the day when Mai was pretty sure her husband would be out of their flat. I pulled the van up carefully outside the block. It still had a dent in the sliding door where I had scraped it along the side of the refuge while trying to reverse shortly after getting my licence.

It was an eerie day. The clouds were high and thin and bounced a glary, blinding light around. At the back of the flats was a large, desolate paved yard that served several adjoining blocks and was open on two sides to the street. In the middle of the busted-up concrete, among the weeds and the plastic bags that drifted like mutant jellyfish, was a Hills Hoist. On its lifeless metal branches hung the washing left behind when Mai and the children had run for their lives a few days earlier.

'I'll go in with Mai,' Sue said. 'You get the clothes.'

'Are you sure you don't want me to come with you?'

I wanted to help but I also wanted to be tested, to prove my worth.

'No. I need you to keep an eye out in case he comes back.'

Sue and Mai tentatively approached the house. I reluctantly went to the Hills Hoist. Clothes pegs ricocheted through the air as I yanked the tiny onesies and child-size jeans off the line. The keys to the van were in my fist, ready to go, and my eyes darted around the scene. Nothing. Then a scream.

'Run! Run!'

Sue and Mai came flying out the back door of the unit. I dropped the basket of laundry and we bolted to the van, jerking at the buckled door. It was jammed.

'Fucking fuck!'

We gave up on it and all piled into the front and I slammed the van into first.

'What happened?'

'We got some of the stuff and as I went round the corner into the lounge room he was standing there behind the door, pressed against the wall holding a hunting knife under his chin like this…'

She indicated a good nine inches' worth.

'Jesus!'

As we rounded the corner Mai's husband emerged into the court-yard. He was smallish, slight. There was no sign of the knife. He didn't run. Even more creepy—he walked slowly around the yard and then disappeared down the street.

After a while we returned. Finally the police arrived. They went in and spoke to the husband, who had by this time come home. A very young copper came out and favoured us with a patronising smile. He rocked back and forth on his heels. 'I have spoken to Mai's husband and he has assured me that he will not bother Mai again.'

'You don't seriously—'

'No,' he cut me off. 'He has given me his word.'

The subject was closed.

Refuge work was all-consuming. I was totally immersed in the cause and the politics. I had my first proper lesbian sexual experience with one of the workers there—an older woman who was, of course, kind and gentle. I had a few flings actually, but the pieces of my lesbian jigsaw didn't magically fall into place, not then.

Because I wasn't in love with any of those women. I was falling in love with Jane.

Jane was in my philosophy tutorial. She was cool and arty and as beautiful as a Rosetti. Her most striking feature was her curly hair, which she wore short and swept up so that in profile she looked like Nefertiti. She dyed it purple. She was tall with pale eyes and fair skin, the kind of Irish looks for which I have a fatal weakness. Our version of dating consisted of taking speed and talking for twelve hours non-stop about existentialism and Merleau-Ponty. Which was no small feat given that I knew next to nothing about either.

Jane had grown up round the corner from Siena. She had a dysfunctional (Irish) Catholic family history similar to my own. Unlike everyone else, who lived in grotty share houses close to uni, Jane lived alone in an art deco studio flat across the river in South Yarra. She was sophisticated. She smoked Sobranie cigarettes and decorated her apartment with beautiful black-and-white photographic portraits. She worked part-time as a nurse in a psych hospital. She was a poet. She was like my Jungian shadow, my unlived self, and she reawakened in me my passion for art.

In truth, ideology had begun to chafe a little. My thoughts longed to roam more widely. I had a delightful friend named Yvonne who had left Northern Ireland because she couldn't stand the atrocities on both sides. When a friend declared that Yvonne lacked a 'political analysis' of the Irish situation it left me fuming. *I never want to disregard people like Yvonne, who is really marvellous,* I wrote to Helen, *simply on the basis of their lack of a political-feminist or whatever analysis! I feel as though I need to be stronger in my own right rather than under the auspices of sisterhood and the Women's Movement.*

I suspect Jane was drawn to my brand of grass-roots political activism as I was drawn to her intelligence and artistic self-realisation. Our first kiss happened on a trip to Sydney for a conference. We had driven up with the gang from the Feminist Club. It was my first time in Sydney and I was buzzing with excitement. On our last night we were camped out in the offices of a women's bookshop in Glebe, about six of us sleeping on the floor. As the others drifted off around us Jane and I whispered to each other, our heads leaning closer and closer. And when, finally, we kissed it was as though a dream I had long ago abandoned had come true.

As we drove back down to Melbourne with the others, Jane and I sat in the back seat of the station wagon and in the darkness I surreptitiously rested my hand between her legs. The mere thought that I was allowed to touch another human being in such an intimate way made my heart soar. I was twenty, I had a girlfriend and I worked in a women's refuge. And although I didn't know it then, it was perhaps the happiest I have ever been in my whole life.

Jane was my first love and it was a sweet, innocent love but bruised, too. We attracted and repelled one another like two damaged magnets. A riot of hitherto repressed feelings began to erupt, but love takes practice. My desire to love and be loved was well in advance of my capability. It was like running on broken legs.

Loving Jane was like loving a cat. She was absolutely her own person and I never felt completely sure that she loved me. This provoked my already rickety feelings into spasms of insecurity and jealousy—a new word in my emotional lexicon.

But jealousy was very uncool in the women's movement, and non-monogamy was virtually compulsory. Jane was always hanging around with our friend Jenny, and I began to suspect something was going on. Then one day Jenny invited me over for dinner. There was something she wanted to discuss. At the end of dinner we moved to the lounge room. I started to feel tense.

'So, Magda, there is something I wanted to tell you.'

'Yes?' I waited for the axe to fall.

'Well.' She stared into my eyes. 'I am in love with you.'

'With *me*.' I choked on my peppermint tea, certain I had heard wrong. 'You're in love with *me*?'

'Yes. With you.'

I had not seen this coming at all. It was the first time anyone had said those words to me—and they were wasted on me because I was so besotted with that elusive object of desire, Jane.

As always my studies ran a poor second to my emerging emotional life. By this time my father had given up all hope of me ever completing my degree. I had worn him down. But I had also worn myself down. After two years at the refuge I was sliding, as predicted, towards the inevitable burnout. The stress, the frustration and the vicarious trauma had taken a toll. This was not the depression of my youth. The pendulum had swung, and I was becoming manic—not clinically, but close.

'You never sleep!' Jane observed.

She was right. It was as though my internal clock was broken and kept skipping over the sleep setting. I couldn't read: books got too deep in. I couldn't handle having yet another voice inside my head. At night, too wired to lie still, I would crawl out of bed and sit wide awake in the armchair. Then I would go out and drive around for hours.

My parents had no idea what was going on. I hardly ever visited or spoke to them on the phone. I had started wearing overalls, stopped wearing bras and cut my hair short and spiky. I looked like a proto-typical baby dyke and had come very close, once, to telling Mum. In one of our rare phone calls I tentatively mentioned that several of the workers at the refuge were lesbians.

There was an icy silence. 'You're not one, are you?'

My mother is like one of those lollies that alternate from sour to sweet and you are never quite sure which you are going to get. The venom in that sentence could have killed an elephant. I stood in the hallway of my share house and picked at the yellow paint on the wall. I could tell her. I could just tell her. And it would be done. I would be free. And if they cast me out, so be it. I was tired of dragging the madness around.

But it wouldn't be fair. The timing wasn't right. She was having a sour day. It would be like getting a tattoo when you're drunk. I would forever be gay and she would forever be sour about it. But maybe there would never be a right time...

I took a deep breath. 'No. No, I'm not.'

I felt a wave of regret, and relief. And the chasm between us widened.

So only Jane had an inkling of my mental state. She was perhaps the first person who showed me what I looked like to others and began to explain me to myself. 'You cannot stand to be alone with yourself for even five minutes,' she teased me. She was wrong. I couldn't stand to be alone for a single second.

Now I was being seen. And it was terrifying. It was the real reason I couldn't study—I couldn't be alone in my head, with my own thoughts. It wasn't safe. But Jane's words were like a challenge. She enjoyed her own company. She could study and think. Was this what I would have to do to be with her? Sit still?

My room in the house in Palmerston Place was on the second floor and my desk was at the window overlooking the laneway. It was a tranquil spot. A one-way street with little traffic. And a silence that reverberated. I sat. I opened my textbook, *Introductory Philosophy*. And it started—the voices in my head. A pack of rabid dogs, barking mad, tearing my mind to shreds. Jane would find me out. She had already glimpsed the truth.

'Inside your head is like a radio with all these different stations.'

She had seen the sideshow, the circus of colour and movement. But what if she saw the mad motor that drove it?

I got up, left the room and never sat at that desk again. I ran. I dropped out of uni and asked my mother for a loan. And I bought a plane ticket.

# THRESHOLDS

There was a well-beaten path across the globe. You got a passport, an international drivers licence, an international student card, a youth hostel membership and a Eurail pass, and off you went, never knowing where you would end up. Some went via Asia, others via the kibbutzim of Israel. I decided on the conservative route. London.

I was twenty-one years old and had lived in Australia since I was five but I still didn't feel Australian. I wondered if Europe might provide the sense of home I craved.

My departure was a debacle. As usual I left everything until the last minute. On the day of my leaving, my parents and brother came over to Palmerston Place to help me pack up all my stuff. And Jane came to say goodbye.

Jane was not particularly impressed with the abrupt and dramatic nature of my departure; no doubt she was hurt. In my lovestruck fugue I secretly hoped that my absence would make her heart grow fonder. Of course no one in the family knew about Jane and me, so our last kiss was like our first one—furtive. I pulled her into the lounge room downstairs while Mum and Dad and Chris clomped about in my bedroom above.

That final kiss was perhaps the sweetest of them all. And it was not my imagination—a tear came to her eye. I took that tear to mean that she would wait for me. Even though I had no idea of when, or if, I might return.

It took thirty-six hours of flying to get to London. I arrived in June 1982. Within days a letter arrived from Helen, exhorting me to *go ahead, create your own new woman—but do it by yourself—anything formed under the shadow of an ideology, for me anyhow, is mean and limited*. It wasn't just my crazy head and broken heart I was running from—it was those ideologies.

I crashed with my friend Janne, who was living in a squat in Islington. Janne had worked at one of the sister refuges and we had become great friends. Whippet-thin with black curly hair and a high aquiline nose, Janne was a game girl, up for fun and adventure. The squat was just around the corner from Upper Street and the famous punk rock venue the Hope and Anchor pub, where the Sex Pistols had shot to notoriety screaming 'God Save the Queen' and 'Anarchy in the UK'.

The squat was not nearly as squalid as I had hoped it would be. In my romantic imagination I envisioned mattresses on floors and reggae riots and police raids and punk revolution. But the Islington squat was just like a normal share house, only with power and water hooked up in a makeshift, illegal and potentially fatal fashion. It was a four-storey place and my digs were in the basement. It was fine in summer but as the days grew colder I felt sure the damp walls were crawling with tuberculosis.

I spent a month or two going to pubs, listening to post-punk bands and visiting Karl Marx's grave at Highgate Cemetery. In August I caught a northbound train, full of all kinds of dreams of homecoming. I was going to stay with my mother's cousin Molly, one of the Edinburgh branch of the Lamont clan and a member of the cabal of funny cousins. On the way I stopped off to visit my auntie Kathleen and uncle Dominic and their respective families in Yorkshire. It was great to feel the shared humour and easy kinship of my beautiful cousins but Yorkshire was not my ancestral home. Scotland was the place of my dreaming.

I arrived in Tollcross and humped my backpack up seven heartbursting flights of stairs to the small flat where Molly lived with her husband George atop the Spudulike, a takeaway outlet that served baked potatoes. They were delicious and I lived off them for the entire time I was there. Molly was expecting me but when I entered the room she did not smile or even say hello. She swivelled her head round from the TV, gave me a vivisecting glance and in a withering, Jean Brodie-ish accent drawled, 'My God, what a weight you've got on you! Where did you get that? Your mother was always bone-thin!' With that she took a deep, hard suck on her Silk Cut, the purpose-built creases of her wizened face pulling tight around the fag end like a drawstring bag. And turned back to the TV.

I stood fatly in the middle of the room, the soles of my Doc Marten boots squeaking on the Axminster. I was fascinated to see that as she watched television she held her hand to her cheek, her little pinky resting lightly in her mouth—exactly the way my mother does. The way I do.

A few days later Janne arrived. Over tea (meaning dinner) she tried to make chitchat with Molly. 'Do you travel much?'

'No. I never leave Tollcross.' Followed by a deep, chest-rattling laugh.

But Molly's gruffness was only skin deep; her kindness went

down to the marrow. She practised that peculiar brand of harsh but prodigious hospitality for which the Scots are famous. It wasn't until near the end of our three-week stay that we twigged that the bed we platonically shared was in fact *her* bed, and that she and George were sleeping on a cramped divan in an alcove.

It was festival time, when the high seriousness of the city of Edinburgh gives way to the spirit of carnivale as every nook, cranny and telephone box is turned into a performance space. The streets are stuffed full of clowns, mimes, jugglers, comedians, musicians, as if they had burst out of a basement like escaped lunatics. Once again I felt the siren call of the performing arts.

Soon enough Janne and I had a regular haunt: the Royal Mile Café. Where, for a pittance, you could get a bolt-strong pot of tea and black pudding in a bun. There were two sisters who ran the place and the creatures they resembled most in the world were a couple of trolls from the Hall of the Mountain King. They were small and stout and hunched and had low brows and long grey hair that fell across their round shoulders and down their backs like a mohair blanket. They rarely spoke and never smiled. But a really good cup of tea is worth any amount of rudeness. And good black pudding? Well.

After the festival Janne and I decided to make our way over to Europe. We caught the ferry to Amsterdam, and hitchhiked via the terrifying autobahns to Berlin. We were so poor at one point that all we had to eat was a thin tube of Dutch mayonnaise. We slept in ditches and in the spare rooms of total strangers until we were picked up by Manny, a slightly impish, slightly tiresome German. He had a long, fuzzy grey beard and a nest of long, straggly grey hair. It was evident from his annoying antics—licking Janne's ice-cream, tickling her, showing off—that he fancied her. He drove us in his little old Citröen all the way to Berlin. As I sat in the back I felt as though I was watching Pepé Le Pew and the Cat.

West Berlin in 1982 was a cool place to be; perhaps *the* cool place. Nearly forty years after the war it was a city that was still simultaneously deconstructing and building itself. Everywhere there were war-torn buildings alongside new ones and it felt like the death of the old world and the birth of the new. It was the home of two of my favourite acts, Kraftwerk and Nina Hagen, the punk opera singer from East Berlin whom I loved for her deranged waywardness. Her unabashed mash-up of European high and punk low art spoke to my own tattered soul. Her album *Unbehagen* (Uneasiness) was the soundtrack of my trip. And the punk centre of it all was Kreuzberg, a neighbourhood full of punks and broken buildings and Turkish *Gastarbeiter,* 'guestworkers' whose status was provisional. The old buildings still had bullet holes from the war. The suburb was surrounded on three sides by the Berlin Wall, which cut across the city like a blunt scalpel.

One day Janne and I decided to visit East Berlin. It was easy enough to take a day trip and I was curious to see what a self-proclaimed communist country looked like. As we passed through Checkpoint Charlie the first thing I noticed about East Berlin was its terrible greyness. The streets, the buildings, the monuments—everything was stripped of colour. To my amazement the thing I missed the most was advertising. The lack of hoardings and billboards, of the flashing neon signs and bright lights that constitute the wall art of free-market capitalism, left East Berlin strangely soulless. It was a vast, grey desert. The desperation I felt to see a Coke sign was rather a jolt to my lefty worldview.

There was very little of interest to see or do: the 'highlight' was the *unbekannte Soldat*—the Tomb of the Unknown Soldier. We wandered around the guardhouse, had a look at the eternal flame, the only symbol of light and warmth in the whole city. Suddenly, echoing across the concrete from behind us, we heard a loud *thwack, thwack,*

*thwack* as a small group of soldiers goosestepped across the paving stones. A chill ran through me. I thought of what it must have been like for my Polish family to watch as thousands of silly-walking goons marched into Warsaw.

We retreated to the state-run cafeteria designated for tourists. It smelled like the kitchen of an underfunded nursing home. The food was disgusting, as grey and mean as the city itself, as though the flavour had been deliberately extracted. It literally lacked the spice of life.

I was quite unnerved by East Berlin and its deliberate eradication of all pleasure and beauty. It made me long for superfluity. And it made me apprehensive about what I might find in Poland, which had been living under martial law since December 1981.

Warsaw. Finally I was headed there, three days earlier than I had planned. Janne was going to Barcelona.

At the train station we hugged goodbye. I took her hand and poured all of my useless deutschmarks into her palm. 'Here. You take this.'

'Really? You won't need it?'

'No. I have a Polish promissory note in złoty. I'm fine.'

'Are you sure you don't want to come to Barcelona?'

'I'm sure.'

As I watched her leave, headed for sun and fun, I wondered if I had made the right decision. But it was now or never.

October 1982 was not a good time to be going to Poland. The country was in political ferment. This was the height of the Solidarity Movement—Poland's Arab Spring—led by Lech Wałęsa and a bunch of Polish intellectuals, and supported by the Polish Pope, John Paul II. Martial law had been in place, on and off, for more than a year. There had been massive strikes and in response the tanks had been rolled out and the borders closed. I had written to my aunt and uncle in Poland to tell them I intended to come, but now I had to make a move and pray that my timing was right.

Then it was announced that travel restrictions had been relaxed. This might be the only chance any one of our family would ever have to go back.

The authorities had stopped all flights in and out so the trains were packed, standing room only. I squeezed aboard. I had to prop my backpack upright in the corridor and half-stand, half-sit on top of it. Which I did, for the next eight hours. As the train clacked on into the dark eastern-bloc night I began to fall asleep standing up, waking periodically with my face in the chest of the bulky man opposite. He was very nice about it. The Poles are used to being cattle-trucked.

Soon I noticed a bearded, fine-boned young man watching me. He addressed me in Polish. I gathered he was asking where I came from. He was astonished to learn it was Australia. We quickly established that our lingua franca was French, and I silently thanked Madame Grinyer. He told me he was a student. He had been to visit family. The situation was *trés mal* in Poland. We chatted on and I told him about my famous cousin Magda, though I suspect he didn't believe this girl in her Doc Martens, happy pants and duffle coat was related to a movie star.

We crossed the border into East Germany. The train stopped and the door opened, letting in a gust of cold air. The chitchat ceased and a guard clambered aboard; the atmosphere in the carriage tensed. As he made his way along the carriage towards us my new Polish friend translated from German into French for me: 'Transit fee. Five deutschmark.' My heart lurched. I had given my last coins to Janne. I fumbled in my crappy little money belt but I could find only a few stray pfennigs. How could I be so stupid?

And so I had my first brush with Soviet-bloc bureaucracy. The guard didn't care that I was Australian or that I had travelled across the world to see my family. This was East Germany: everyone had a sad story. Everyone had had their family ripped apart. His indifference was infinitely dense. He truly did not care, I could feel it, if I lived or died. I realised then that I was crossing over into a place where none of the life lessons I had learned thus far mattered. The guard's word was final: I was to be put off at the next station.

My new Polish friend looked at me and then at the official. He sucked in his breath and turned to address the other Poles. I had no idea what he was saying. They all listened, nodding solemnly. They all looked at me. I could not read their expressions. Then an old man dug his fist into his pocket, leaned across and pressed something into my palm. One deutschmark. For him it must have been a substantial sum. I wasn't sure what to do. It felt wrong to take his money. But my new friend told me to accept his gift.

*'Dziękuję, dziękuję bardzo bardzo.'* I thanked the old man profusely in my terrible Polish. He didn't smile. He just nodded. One after another the Poles handed me their precious western currency. I wanted to die of shame. I handed the five deutschmark to the guard, who gave me a level stare and then placed it in his satchel.

As the hours wore on the crowd thinned. My new friend disembarked and I felt very alone. Finally I got an actual seat in a compartment. Towards the end of the journey a new conductor got on board. He wore a thick woollen coat and stamped his feet from the chill. Something about him immediately seemed more human. Eventually there was just the conductor, another passenger and me. As we sat rocking in the carriage the conductor fumbled in his pouch and pulled out a cloth-wrapped bundle and a blunt penknife. The cloth contained some Polish sausage, a small loaf of grey bread and some even greyer cheese, which he shared with us. Using fragments of my first-year Russian and sign language, I name-dropped my cousin, and her fame and beauty got me an extra slice of grey cheese.

As the dark night gave way to misty dawn, images of rural Poland began to emerge like a developing photo. I was eager to see the land of my forebears. The landscape was flat and unremarkable. Peasants still drove horse-drawn carts.

At last we pulled in to Warsaw station. It was a grim, overcast day. On the platform a man walked past wearing a Bolshevik cap, a loose peasant blouson wrapped round with a belt, and trousers tucked into calf-length boots. He looked like Omar Sharif in *Doctor Zhivago*. But otherwise people were dressed in cheap, outdated versions of western clothing. Which I found a little disappointing. I wanted it to be more Polish.

One of the conditions of entry into Poland was that you had to leave a certain amount of western currency in the form of a promissory note purchased before entering the country. I had this note safely in my money belt. Now I needed to find the exchange office. I saw a man in a railways uniform and approached him.

'*Proszę, czy ty mówisz po Angielsku?*'

'*Nie.*'

He brushed past me. The reply was so blunt I was taken aback. This social intercourse was like the gnashing of gears.

I went to the ticket counter. Behind the metal bars was a very old guy with white hair and a kind face. This looked hopeful.

'*Proszę, czy ty mówisz po Angielsku?*'

'*Nie. Po Polsku, po Rosyjsku…*'

My tiny bit of Russian did not encompass things like currency exchange and promissory notes. There was only one thing for it. Mime. The universal language. I showed him my note and rubbed my fingers together.

'Ach!' he spattered out an incomprehensible burst of Polish consonants. Clearly, I had not understood.

He looked around, checking to see if he was being observed, and

then disappeared. A moment later he appeared at my side. He took
my hand and led me to another office. He pointed at his watch and
shook his head. This, presumably, was the office for the collection of
promissory notes. And it was closed. He looked at me pityingly and
went back behind his metal bars.

What to do? No one cared that I had come all this way. And why
should they care? The Poles were in the middle of a rebellion. People
were being shot, arrested, detained, interrogated. My timing was
completely off. But I could not give up. I had to persist.

A large woman in a grubby uniform was sweeping the floors.

'*Proszę, proszę Pani, czy ty mówisz po Angielsku?*' I asked.

She stopped for a moment.

'*Nie.*'

My brain was melting from exhaustion and panic. I sank down
onto a bench. I had come ten thousand miles, and now I was going
to be defeated by communist bureaucracy, indifference and my own
dismal language skills. Hot tears stung my eyes. Clueless. Why was
I always so clueless?

'*Proszę Pani…*'

I looked up to see the white-haired old ticket-seller guy. He waved
a small Polish coin and took me by the hand and led me to the phone
booth. '*Dziękuję. Dziękuję bardzo.*' I thanked him abundantly and
dialled my aunt and uncle.

The phone rang. And rang. And rang. I was muttering to myself
like a loon. 'Oh my God, don't tell me they're not home and I've just
spent my only groszy! Please God no! Please God let them answer.'

If there is any country whose people know that God does not
answer prayers it is Poland. How many millions of voices had cried
out to him in their moment of greatest need, only to be met by silence?

Then the ringing stopped and there was a voice on the other end.
Is there no end to God's perversity? Of all the prayers he could have,

should have, answered he chose this one?

'*Proszę.*'

'*Andrzej, umm jestem Magda.*'

Andrzej didn't understand. For a Twilight Zone moment he thought I was his own daughter Magda and rattled off something in Polish. I cut him off. '*Nie, nie Zawadzka, jestem Magda SZUBAŃSKI.*' Desperate that my groszy would run out I veered wildly into German. '*Ich bin hier jetzt…*'

In German '*jetzt*' means 'now' but in Polish it sounds like '*jesc*' which means 'eat'.

'*Co?*'

'It is Magda Szubański, I am here now!'

'Yes, yes,' he said in hesitant English, 'Magda Szubański will come in three days. Goodbye.'

'*No! No! ICH BIN Magda Szubański. Ich bin hier JETZT!*'

Bang! The penny dropped. His penny. Not the one in the phone.

'Ah! Magda! You are here now?'

'Yes.'

'Where are you, *kochana?*'

# WARSAW

Half an hour later Uncle Andrzej came clattering around the corner in his Russian-built Lada. The first thing I thought was 'He is so small.' Small and thin and spindly, maybe five foot six. So this was the man my father had hero-worshipped all those years. Four years older than Dad, he had been the first one in our family to become involved in the resistance.

He kissed me warmly and hugged me tight. And then he kissed me again.

'Come, we must be quick or there will be trouble.' He gestured at the guards. Andrzej may have been small but he was strong. He grabbed my backpack and tossed it into the boot of the car.

Andrzej came from a 'very good family'. In prewar Warsaw he was among the city's best dressed. His family lived in the same apartment block as my father's, and he and my aunt Danuta had been sweethearts since they were teenagers. He still had style. He was debonair in an uncontrived way. He wore his grey hair with its widow's peak swept dramatically back from his forehead like a handsome vampire. He was ironic, charming and naughty. He had a tiny hint of the old roué about him, and a wry sense of humour. One day over breakfast he told me that every day he and Danuta would read the obituaries to see who had 'given up smoking'.

As we rattled through the streets I wanted to cry—from relief, from joy. And from shock—my father's Paris of the East was a battered wreck. Warsaw in 1982 had about as much appeal as a multistorey carpark. It still felt somehow makeshift with just a few small pockets of old-world charm. It was exactly what its name sounded like—the nation's war wound. In the centre of everything, dominating the skyline, was the Palace of Culture and Science, a giant socialist-realist skyscraper. As we jounced past Uncle Andrzej waved his hand in contempt. 'Look! The Soviet Union's *gift* to Poland.'

My aunt and uncle's apartment was on what used to be called Miła Street. Pleasant Street. It was anything but. This was the very street after which Leon Uris named *Miła 18*. It was in the heart of the Warsaw Ghetto and it was on this street that the Jewish uprising of 1943 was masterminded.

Now it had a different name and was full of high-rise apartment blocks which were—as Andrzej pointed out—identical to the ones built in Bulgaria and Romania and every other Soviet satellite. The rickety lift clanked up seventeen floors. When I walked in the door Aunt Danuta grabbed me hard and kissed me on the cheek, again and again and again. No words. Just kisses and crying.

Danuta was in her sixties and she was a beautiful woman. She had blonde hair and green eyes, the kind of looks the Nazis exalted as Aryan but which are in fact typically Slavic. She had a fresh outdoorsiness about her that was somehow reassuring. She looked exactly like my father. Apparently so did I, because every few minutes she would lean across and grab my arm, tears in her eyes. 'I look at you and I see your father!' And the kissing and the crying would start all over again. At this stage she had seen her beloved little brother only once in nearly forty years, when he had visited briefly with my mother in 1977.

Other than that sentence, my aunt spoke virtually no English. She spoke Russian—all Poles were forced to learn it. Before the war she had been fluent in German—it was her most beloved subject. But when the Nazis occupied her city she refused to utter a single word of German until they left.

They asked me about my journey and I mimed my ordeal with the border guard. My uncle slapped his thigh in appreciation. 'Yes! You are an *actress*!' He beamed. I wondered if he saw in me the same talent he had recognised in his own daughter.

Aunt Danuta and Uncle Andrzej lived in a tiny two-bedroom flat that was spacious by communist standards. Andrzej had a very senior position in the merchant navy and for several years in the 1960s he had been posted to Shanghai during the Cultural Revolution. Their tiny flat was still crowded with exquisite chinoiserie. Two rosewood cabinets contained elaborately patterned duck-egg-green urns and plates. On the walls hung traditional weapons and papery fans and two-stringed erhu fiddles.

Across the hallway lived a couple and their daughter Małgosia, a tall, thoughtful girl who spoke good English. She was my age but (quite shockingly to me) she still lived with her parents. Absolutely no one I knew lived with their parents. I immediately thought, 'What do all the dykes do?' Moving out of home was the first step in finding your sexuality. When I wrote and told my friends at home, they were scandalised. In turn Małgosia was fascinated to know that I had left home at seventeen. 'Here everyone must live with their parents until they marry.'

'Is that for religious reasons?'

'No. Economic. And then you wait for an apartment. Sometimes maybe ten, twelve years.'

That first night in Poland I slept fitfully, overwhelmed by my own emotions, and the sound, through the thin regulation communist walls, of a man sobbing.

Early the next morning my cousin Magda, the famous actress, came over. She was as glamorous as I had hoped and was, I think, quite shocked by my appearance. I not only looked like a student and a bit of a punk, I looked like a lesbian. She was too polite to say anything but many years later, on a subsequent visit, she did remark that I had 'prettied up'.

I was very excited to be meeting my Polish namesake, my childhood idol. She was kind and attentive, fussing over her parents. She was, by all accounts, the perfect Polish daughter. But underneath the coquettish mannerisms was a wily survivor, a tenacious Mother Courage who had thrived in a repressive system despite never having joined the Communist Party. Never be fooled by a pretty Polish face.

Magda possessed a worldly sophistication that I longed to emulate. Her husband Gustaw Holoubek was considered to be one of the greatest Polish Shakespearean actors and is revered to this day. They were the Laurence Olivier and Vivien Leigh of Poland. Gustaw was also a senator in the Polish parliament and had been awarded a Knight's Cross. A man of principle and courage, he resigned in protest when martial law was declared. He was much older than Magda, about the same age as my father, and he was not 'classically handsome', as they say. But it was easy to see why Magda had fallen in love with him. The weight of his soul exerted the gravitational pull of a small planet, even in an indecipherable language. Her own soul's yearning to grow had clearly led her to him. When he died in 2008 Magda was inconsolable.

After we had eaten breakfast, Magda took me by the hand and

said, 'I am going to show you something.' I thought she might take me to a café or a museum. Instead we went for a short walk to a large, squat, heavy building. 'This is Pawiak, where the Gestapo would take Polish people before sending them to the death camps,' she explained. She went up to the guard. He recognised her and his manner changed instantly. She asked him something. Then we went inside and sat in a stark, chilly room.

The walls in Pawiak are thick. They muffle sound. They keep secrets. As we sat on a hard bench a voice came over the loudspeaker. Magda explained, 'He is reading out the notes the prisoners would write, maybe on a cigarette paper. Or a ticket. Whatever they could find. And then they would push them into little holes in the wall, or cracks. They were written for their loved ones, to tell them where they were, to tell them what had become of them. And to say goodbye.'

We sat there, the two of us, Magda holding my hand while I bawled my eyes out. Magda and Magda. The same name but completely different lives. She didn't cry. This was nothing new to her. 'I am sorry for this,' she said, 'but you must understand. This is our history, your father's history. This is what happened.' *Rozumiesz.*

But so much more history had taken place in the intervening years, forcing our lives along different paths, different destinies. There had been four decades of communist oppression. Recently Magda said to me, 'It wasn't awful all the time. We always found a way to have fun, to enjoy ourselves.' But there were times when it was awful. Both my aunt and uncle had been interrogated by officers of the dreaded UB, the *Urząd Bezpieczeństwa* or Department of Security—Poland's equivalent of the KGB. Former members of the Underground Army were seen as a threat to the communist government. Many of my father's wartime comrades were tortured, imprisoned, executed or sent to gulags.

Anti-communist activity in Poland was still no parlour game. One night a bunch of distant relatives came for dinner. In fervent tones they spoke about their desire to be free. One of them took from her pocket a tiny pin badge—it was the size of the white bit on my pinky fingernail. And inscribed in minuscule writing was the trademark red and white slogan *Solidarność*. The others shooshed her and made her put it away. I couldn't help but contrast it with the massive poster of the same image I had sprawled across my bedroom wall back in Carlton.

I wrote to Jane, *My cousin Magda and her husband (along with many other actors) no longer do TV work because of all the propaganda and so work in the theatre instead. If they were to stop work it would be seen as a strike and they would be arrested!*

My friends and I had never been orthodox—we had always been a little gang of ideological fringe dwellers. But Warsaw was pushing me off the edge. Every night I wrote copious letters to my parents, to friends and, of course, to Jane. I would try to explain the noxious blend of euphoria and tragedy but Jane was the only one who sensed there was something amiss with my mental state. She wrote to me that my letters *sounded sort of hysterical (of pre-overseas variety), as if it is all a bit too much. Is it? So what is happening in that travel-worn skull of yours?*

The truth was Poland had completely freaked me out. Socialism was My Thing. Not communism. I had no illusions about that, I knew what Stalin had done. But somewhere, deep in my idealistic heart, I harboured the faint hope that it might be possible to create a world in which Marx's maxim held true: 'From each according to his ability, to each according to his need.'

I needed desperately to believe in progress, in a world where the forces of fairness and equality would triumph and where misfits like me would be accepted. It was something I felt I could die for. In spirit, the Poles were a lot like the Sandinistas, except that they were fighting the very ideas that I believed in. After decades of communism they wanted nothing to do with Marx or socialism and would settle for nothing short of free-market capitalism. Worse than that, it was in the name of those ideals—the things I believed would save humanity from itself—that my Polish family had been persecuted.

Up until then, socialism had helped to explain me and the world I lived in. It gave me a friendship circle and a sense of purpose. But it was much more than that—it gave my untethered soul an anchor, and gave me hope. And now I was seeing, firsthand, the rotting black heart of it.

My father had been right all along. Goodness didn't stand a chance against the darker forces of human nature. I was being sucked into the black hole of Europe, a place from which no light emerges.

In Poland I started crying and I couldn't stop. I started crying that day at Pawiak and I cried myself to sleep every night I was there.

I wrote frantically to Jane, *Poland is the most alienating/depressing time of my life. If you listen carefully you will hear the people wailing and gnashing their teeth for a city that was slaughtered in the war. I don't know whether the Polish people love or hate war. They seem to keep a little bit of revenge tucked inside their cheeks like a chaw of tobacco and sometimes you will see them spit it out.*

Now I would say it was survivor guilt. By a fluke my father had got out of Poland and so his children had been spared all of this. I wanted to make it up to my Polish family for all they had suffered. But how? There was no plan. And no relief.

Not even in shopping. I could not buy my way out of this. I realised with hideous clarity how much I was a product of consumer culture. *Ah yes!* I wrote to Jane, *I would sell my soul to Amerika for tampons and chocolate bars and Coca-Cola and Levis jeans*. It is fair to say that shopping in Poland in 1982 was a bleak prospect. There was nothing to buy in the shops. I am not being hyperbolic; there was literally nothing to buy. One bra if you were lucky. Rows of shelves with no inventory.

But that didn't stop my family from lavishing me with treats. Each afternoon at three we would return home for *obiad*, which is the main meal. It usually involves some heavy, dark bread, a little cheese, maybe some fish soup. Potatoes. And always dill. It was always delicious. Eggs were rationed—two per person per month. As were pantyhose—one new pair every six months. In fact everything was rationed. There were queues for toilet paper. At the door of every public toilet sat a gnarly old woman, rationing it out, every bit as fearsome as a multi-headed hydra. You had to pay for your toilet paper and three sheets was the non-negotiable amount you were officially allotted. God help you if you had diarrhoea.

As we drove around Warsaw seeing the sights, Uncle Andrzej had the disconcerting habit of slamming on the brakes, jumping out of the car and racing across the street to stand in a queue. It didn't matter what it was for. What mattered was that it was short. Everywhere you queued for everything, all the time, not knowing what you might find at the end. One day Małgosia suggested we get hot dogs so we queued. And queued. And queued. Finally we got our hot dogs to find there were in fact no 'dogs' of any temperature involved. It was a bun stuffed with cheap and readily available mushrooms. Still, it was delicious.

The Iron Curtain would rise eventually, but what it had destroyed could not be repaired. The bonds of family had been severed, and would never be the same again. My fibres ached for something. I was conscious of a vacant space, a gap that could never be filled.

'What was our grandmother like?' I asked Magda.

She looked at me with frank pity. 'I am so sad you didn't know her,' she purred in her melted-honey accent. 'She was *such* a wonderful woman. My grandmother…' She stopped and corrected herself. She had never had to share Jadwiga with anyone else. '*Our* grandmother

was such a warm, loving, good person. If you had known her you
would have been so loved.'

But what is the love of someone you have never met, never
embraced? I had come all this way and I was grasping at thin air.
Everyone kept telling me how much I looked like her. But that just
made me feel even weirder, like I was some kind of science-fiction
experiment.

Danuta and Andrzej tried to make up for it. They fussed over
me, hugged me, handled me like a precious breakable object. They
brought in whatever family they could to meet me. Our closest family
member was cousin Rajmund, whom my father thought of as a brother.
I loved Rajmund instantly. He looked like a character from a Jean-Luc
Godard film in his smart trousers, short-sleeved shirt and suede boots.
He was funny, ironic and gallant. He was a journalist and historian
and also worked part time as a tour guide. And he spoke a workable
amount of English. As we toured the few remaining monuments of
the city he would give his spiel in his rich baritone.

One day Danuta and I were alone in the apartment. Andrzej had
gone to queue for food somewhere. She took my hand. 'Sit please.'
She disappeared for a moment. I could hear her ferreting around in
the bottom of a cupboard. Moments later she returned, her arms full
of photo albums. She sat beside me, opened the first album, pointed
at me and then at an image.

'Babcha.' Grandmother.

A woman stared back at me. A woman with kind, intelligent
eyes. A woman with a face just like mine. I tried not to cry but it was
impossible. Danuta patted my hand and muttered soothingly in Polish,
turning the pages of the album. Image after image of grandparents,
aunties, cousins, great-grandparents. The branches of my family tree
were no longer empty, they were full of names and faces. My aunt
gave me a small bundle of duplicates. We wrapped them in plastic

and I tucked them safely into my money belt.

A little while later Andrzej returned with a few morsels of food. The television was on. It was showing footage of young Arab men throwing rocks at tanks. Israel had invaded Lebanon. I had no idea what the anchorman was saying but suddenly Andrzej sprang to his feet in frustration and embarrassment, gesticulating at the TV. 'You see? You see this idiotic anti-Jewish propaganda we have to put up with!'

My family were Catholic but Andrzej's defence of Israel was staunch. I didn't have the heart to tell him that it was not only the Soviets who condemned Israel's actions, that many in the west did, too. So did I, especially after the massacres at Sabra and Shatila which had occurred only a month earlier, in September 1982.

'What does your father say about this?'

I remembered how my father told me when he was a kid they used to call him 'Jew lover' because he had so many Jewish friends and could speak Yiddish. His love of challah and halva and klezmer music. So often he told me how as little kids he and his best friend Wacek had planned to run away together to Palestine to fight the Arabs.

Everywhere in Warsaw the ghost of the Jews was present, a darker, infinitely more ghastly shadow of the Poles' own tragedy. The Poles had suffered—but they were still here. Before the war Poland had the largest Jewish population in Europe, roughly three million. Now they were almost all gone. Annihilated in the Holocaust.

I looked at my uncle's face—impassioned, indignant. This was a man for whom the Holocaust was not an abstraction. What would my father say about Israel? I didn't know. And here, standing on Polish soil, on the site of what had once been the Jewish ghetto, I was no longer sure what I felt. A truth that had seemed so simple in Australia, even in Amsterdam, quickly unravelled when pressed hard up against Polish reality. I felt moral certainty slither through my fingers.

I never did answer my uncle's question.

*

My visa was valid for two weeks. Soon it was time to leave Poland. Danuta and Andrzej took me to the train station and we hugged and wept. None of us knew if we would see one another again.

I couldn't wait to get back to West Berlin. I didn't just long for the west, I craved it like a junkie. I ached for beauty.

But I did not feel free. As the train clacked across the flat plain I felt a new sensation—the tearing of my heart. And perhaps I understood my father a little better.

The border still had to be crossed. This time I would be crossing from the wrong side—the eastern side. The scary side. My family had issued dire warnings. This was a place in which mistakes were not forgiven. Charm would be useless here. The train snailed up to the platform. I was in a compartment on my own. I could feel my heartbeat scudding through my veins.

The door opened and a beefy East German female shouldered through. She looked like an Olympic shot-putter doing her day job. I smiled. She ignored me. She was profoundly humourless. '*Reisepass.*'

'Oh, of course.'

I removed my passport from the money belt around my waist. '*Ich bin Australien.*'

I didn't want her to think I was Polish.

She didn't care. She flicked through the pages and gestured at my backpack.

'*Öffen.*'

She made me unzip all of the compartments of my bags. I was sure she was going to do a strip search. She pointed at my cherished parcel of letters from home.

'Give.'

I took them out. With thick, probing fingers she opened and examined every single one, checking there was nothing between the sheets of airmail paper. After a moment she reached across and pulled at my money belt.

'Give.'

With fumbling fingers I removed it and handed it over. She unzipped it. She dug her hand in and pulled out the packet of family photos. She unwrapped the plastic and rifled through the precious relics. And there, between a couple of fading photos, was a stray złoty note. It was illegal to remove currency from Poland. She pulled it out slowly, like a cat with a mouse. And then she eyeballed me.

'I…I…' I stammered.

I could feel my guts liquefy. I waited to be dragged off the train and hurled into prison. Her eyes were hard, unyielding.

Then she wagged her finger in my face. 'Tsk, tsk, tsk.' She replaced the note and zipped up my money belt.

The minute I hit West Berlin I headed straight for Kreuzberg. The decadent, deviant heart of the west. Someone had told me that there was a fantastic women's building in Kreuzberg where you would be assured of a place to crash. This one was arty and edgy, spanning about four storeys. I arrived in the dark of night and awoke the next morning to find myself surrounded by four floors of gigantic vagina imagery, which was a little too much even for me.

*This summer is* Frauensommer, I wrote to Jane, *and when I arrived at the women's building they asked if I was an artist and I said, no, I worked in a frauenhaus in Australia and they smiled and nodded because art and looking smart seem to be all the go here.*

That day there was a public performance of a haircut. One feminist shaved another's hair into a swooping, asymmetrical classic eighties do. 'Are these my people?' I thought. 'These crazy German feminists? Do I have more in common with them, now, than with my own family?'

*Magda has lost her feminism somewhere along the way,* I wrote, *and doesn't know where to find it.*

And why did Germany bother me less than Warsaw? Was this some kind of Stockholm Syndrome?

I wrote, *Oh how I love the sound of spoken German. Late in the night, the rasping voices of German women down in the courtyard.* And I thought of my aunt, who could never bring herself to speak German again.

Warsaw was a victim. Disfigured and damaged, it made uncomfortable demands on my compassion and my nerves. I was angry at Warsaw because I feared it would swallow me up with its misery. I was young. I wanted to live and have fun.

From Germany I made my way south to Italy. In the Boboli Gardens in Florence I bumped into some acquaintances from Melbourne, Richard and Sue. We formed a lifelong friendship in Florence, but not even great company and the many charms of Italy could stop a cloud of depression from descending. All the beauty and freedom just drove home my feelings of guilt. We went shopping one day in the markets in Florence. I bought a pair of red kidskin gloves. Impossibly soft. Implausibly cheap. I stared at those gloves, not knowing what to make of them. Not knowing if I had the right to enjoy them. They made me feel like Marie Antoinette.

I headed to the American Express office, hoping for a letter from Jane. Nothing. I had gambled that my self-imposed exile would jumpstart her heart, and I lost. Distance had severed the bonds between me and my Polish family, and I had let distance destroy whatever I had with Jane. I was beginning to learn that sometimes when things are broken they cannot be fixed. I wanted to see her, to talk to her.

I headed home on a cheap ticket via Malaysia. So there I was in Kuala Lumpur. It was durian season and the stench, like raw sewage, hung in the cloying air.

I decided to take a stroll near the hotel. As I made my way through the reeking markets I tried to reconcile all I had been through and what it meant to me. I was looking for some tiny sign of hope and humanity. I rounded the corner and there was a child, smiling broadly and playing with a toy. Heartened, I moved closer. It was not a toy. It was a dead rat which the little boy was cheerily swinging by its tail.

Something snapped. Gasping for breath, I ran back to the air-conditioned hotel and collapsed onto the bed, reciting over and over in my mind the horrors and sorrows of the world. I did not leave the room for forty-eight hours. I was ashamed of my weakness and aghast at everything.

On the plane I was seated next to a plump, genial Aussie woman. She asked me where I had been and it all just poured out of me. I told her about the women's refuge and Jane and Poland and my family. Everything. It gushed out of me. I was sure my intensity had scared her off but she smiled warmly and asked me what I wanted to do when I got back. There was something so encouraging about her open, friendly face that I felt I could tell her the truth, no matter how silly it might seem. 'I want to be an actress.'

It must have seemed ludicrous to her. I was a fat, dykey twenty-one-year-old with a bad haircut and happy pants.

She patted my hand. 'Oh!' she beamed. 'Good for you! Something tells me you'd be very good at it. I wish you luck.'

I needed a plan. I decided there were four things I would do: I would finish my degree in philosophy, learn to play the clarinet, get into acting. And I would win Jane back.

# THE KINDNESS OF STRANGERS

I arrived back just before Christmas and it was rather an anticlimax. Mum and Dad picked me up from the airport; my father, always physically affectionate, hugged me tight. He was pleased I had seen his family, he wanted to hear all their news. But that was all. There was no huge catharsis, no big emotional display. My great adventure was swallowed up by suburban life.

And I did not win Jane back.

When I returned from Europe there were a few desultory phone calls, some promised assignations that never materialised. I pined. I waited. My heart broke, slowly and painfully.

It was time for a new look. I ditched the overalls and dyed my hair black like Siouxsie Sioux (of the Banshees). I lined my eyes with heavy kohl kajal. I raided my father's wardrobe for car coats, tuxedos, dress shoes and brogues and his old leather briefcase. From St Vincent de

Paul I bought a heavy houndstooth coat. I went back to uni determined to show that I was a new woman.

True to my plan, I had enrolled in a subject called philosophy of religion. My distractibility was approaching clinical proportions and it was still a struggle to concentrate but I forced myself to read. One of the prescribed texts was *The Varieties of Religious Experience* by William James, the psychologist brother of the novelist Henry James. *Varieties* had an enormous impact on me. It was as if James had summed up the fundamental divide in my nature between buoyant optimism and a melancholy that dragged me under: 'To this latter way,' he wrote, 'the morbid-minded way, as we might call it, healthy-mindedness pure and simple seems unspeakably blind and shallow. To the healthy-minded way, on the other hand, the way of the sick soul seems unmanly and diseased.'

This was the fault line, the precise point where my mind bifurcated. I longed to have a mystical experience that would fuse these parts together. I yearned for an unequivocal, undivided mind and a soul of 'sky-blue tint'. A shadow lay across my soul. I could glimpse it, feel its weight. But what it was or why it was there I could not fathom.

I found James's pragmatism reassuring and steadying, in contrast to Nietzsche, that pyschopomp of misguided youth, to whom the ego was just a jumble of unrelated thoughts that only assume a semblance of order after the fact. As I sat in a corner of Café Paradiso by Lygon Street and examined my own fragmented mind, I felt this to be true. But if I was looking for ways to mend my broken heart Nietzsche couldn't help. Like most of the philosophy chart-toppers, his own personal life was an unmitigated catastrophe. He had few friends and even fewer lovers. If there is one thing Nietzsche *didn't* know about, it's love.

None of this was helped by the fact that I was also reading post-Freudian feminist theorists as well as Doris Lessing's *The Golden*

*Notebook*, the story of a woman's gradual loss of political faith and subsequent fragmentation. Actually, 'reading' is completely the wrong verb. I was devouring it. If I could have powderised and mainlined the thing I would have. I was falling off the mountain and that book was my only rope.

This did not go unnoticed. 'I saw you in the caf before,' said my friend Ros one day. She was a lovely older woman, a mature-age student who radiated a quiet, focused calm. She glanced at my copy of *The Golden Notebook*. 'Your eyes were burning holes into the page.'

Ros looked at me, her own soft eyes inquiring. A look that, I felt, saw everything and demanded nothing: was simply an invitation. But I had no answer. Even though I felt relieved to be seen by someone like Ros I simply couldn't name what I was looking for in those pages.

I was once again homeless. Two years earlier I had written to Helen: *I dreamt that I was moving house. I'm not quite sure which suburb but it is very old. There was a girls' school just across the road. I had the strange feeling of having been there before. Anyway, this house was perfect. The people were lovely and it had a strange yet familiar atmosphere about it. I knew that if I moved into this house everything would be just fine.*

My friend Katrina from the Feminist Club lived with her mother and siblings in a huge, rambling house in Walsh Street in South Yarra, next door to a girls' school. It was covered in stucco and ivy and reminded me of our house in Liverpool. Katrina was being sent to Paris for a year to be 'finished', and she suggested I move into her vacant room. The house was presided over by Katrina's mother, Helen-Mary, whom I had first met at the end of first year when I drank nearly an entire bottle of Johnnie Walker at her enormous kitchen bench and proceeded to entertain the family with accents and impersonations. On the whole I am a fun drunk.

Helen-Mary and I liked one another immediately. She was deliciously eccentric in the way that people from old money can afford to be. Her grandparents had acquired a double-barrelled surname—Scott-Scott—when one Scott married another. Her further-backs came from Adelaide (code for free-settler as opposed to convict) and once owned something like a third of Victoria. Helen-Mary had inherited the family home but not the money to run it.

She was asset rich but cash poor. Her life was a constant struggle with the second law of thermodynamics—entropy. She was always trying to get money to stop the house from falling in on her.

That house. It was like a house in a fairytale. It seemed to possess magical powers. There was an aura of enchantment about it. A sprawl-ing, stuccoed old-money pit, it had once been a grand home and before that an old stables. Now it languished like Blanche DuBois, a shabby shadow of its former gentility. The house exerted a strange, antebel-lum kind of charm on people. Even folks who only came there once would fall under its spell. It brought out the kindness of strangers.

There were eight bedrooms, several bathrooms and an elegant ballroom with floor-to-ceiling glass doors and sprung floorboards whose tactful mission had once been to cushion the footfalls of the society waltzers and jitterbuggers who twirled and shimmied across them. Now the ballroom was a rarely used TV room, and the house was full of family members supplemented by a bunch of hand-picked boarders. Helen-Mary and her kids, Katrina, Anna, Peter and Caroline, soon became like a second family to me.

I felt a very strong bond with H-M, who was also part-Scottish and part-Polish; her mother's name was Dorota. H-M was a beauty, and everyone said she resembled the French movie star Leslie Caron. Crossed with Björk. She was a divorcée. She had shortish dark hair and broad high cheekbones and my father always commented that she looked like a 'right Tartar'. She was…she felt incredibly European. She had a bidet. She spoke French fluently. She was the kind of woman who had lovers, not boyfriends. She had many affairs and was once engaged to a lord, until she broke it off. She was the first among my acquaintances who unabashedly went to a shrink.

Helen-Mary was a seeker. She searched and searched for something. Most likely a past that could not be undone, a past before her father died tragically and very young when she was an infant. Some wounds do not ever fully heal.

And yet there was a life force to her, a powerful optimism, a pluckiness. She was magnanimous and magnetic. She refused to submit to the stuffy strictures of the Melbourne establishment. She chose to befriend and champion the oddbods and misfits.

Her house was like a salon and she was always having some American New-Age guru or faith healer come to stay. There was a hot tub, a trampoline and an awful lot of nudity. I remember coming down to breakfast one morning to find a nude old dude, perched on one end of the massive island bench, holding forth on eastern philosophy. Which was all well and good except that his bare arse was plonked right on the food-preparation area. Much to the mortification of her children, H-M taught a very frank class in sex ed at their school. She was all for frankness in such matters.

My parents and H-M got along well. They thought she was very classy and when she and my father met it was deep talking to deep. They both stepped effortlessly into European roles. He kissed her hand and clicked his heels. She smiled graciously. H-M was the kind of woman who knew how to court a gentleman and tip a bellboy. In some ways it was as though my parents were handing me over to her to be 'finished'. Instinctively they knew she could give me things they never could.

Helen-Mary was a different generation from my parents. Perhaps her own struggle was what gave her a natural affinity with outsiders. With her warm and loving ways she became a refuge of acceptance. Her daughter was a lesbian and so it was no big deal to her that I was too. She was the most non-judgmental adult I had ever met. We all felt it, and many people I still know were part of that world. I first met the author Christos Tsiolkas in the lounge room there. It was a place of sanctuary. I told H-M about a troubled friend who had suffered a breakdown. We found her in her nightie, her hair unwashed, pacing the tiny hallway of her house, muttering to herself. And so she came to live with us. Seeing her recover was like watching a near-dead plant respond to water. When I had first moved into the house I prayed it would work its magic on me.

Helen-Mary, who was a brilliant masseuse with the gift of the healing hands, had a business called Body Care. For a while I worked there as a receptionist. We would start each day by deleting the pornographic messages that had been left on the answering machine overnight. There is nothing quite so funny as listening to amateur porn delivered in a nasal Aussie twang in the cold light of day.

One day she had a client named Cynthia who was a producer at the tiny Why Not Theatre in Carlton, one of several seminal theatres—La Mama, the Pram Factory. They were small but hugely influential, part of a self-conscious push to burst out from under the smothering influence of Britain and tell home-grown Aussie stories. Cynthia was producing a show inspired by Tod Browning's 1932 film *Freaks* and she wanted a circus fat lady. H-M immediately thought of me—which I guess is a compliment—even though I wasn't especially fat at that time. I was more of a circus plump lady. I didn't really appreciate comedy back then. I wanted to do drama but I didn't have the self-confidence. However, at H-M's suggestion I rang Cynthia and she invited me to meet the other cast members.

The theatre was a tiny space tucked away in a rabbit warren of buildings behind Lygon Street, where the Cinema Nova is now. The offices were upstairs in what had once been a funeral parlour. The other members of the troupe were Geoff, a tall, thin boy of about nineteen, and a pretty girl called, I think, Fiona, who was even younger. I felt immediately at home; it all went well and I got the role. Now all I had to do was write a piece for myself. I bought a small, lined notebook. I took up my pen and opened the book to a blank page.

My pen hovered and twitched over the page. I wrote a word and crossed it out. I wrote another. This too I redacted. I didn't know until that moment that a blank page possesses shamanic powers, unseen eyes that can strip bare all the secrets of your mangy soul. I didn't know that a blank page was a void that sucked up every feeling of worth and spat back every demon and dragon. It triggered the anxiety that was always circling.

Once again I was not sleeping. I was losing weight but not through any conscious effort. I felt raw, skinless, like an exposed nerve.

When I decided I had to tell someone I found Helen-Mary in the kitchen. She knew immediately something was wrong.

'Magda, are you all right?' She took my hand.

I burst into tears and told her how crazed I felt.

'Magda,' she announced, 'I am going to hypnotise you!'

H-M's bedroom was best described as a boudoir—an oasis of soft-furnishings, a plush bed, a dressing table with a triple-panelled mirror draped with necklaces and mala prayer beads. And an antique chaise longue. H-M instructed me to lie on the chaise. She had a beautifully modulated voice, rich and deep. As it flowed around me like treacle I felt myself melt into a state of relaxation. The jackhammer of anxiety fell silent. It was a strange new world.

Suddenly it seemed there was a way out, a tiny chink in the log-jam of my thought processes. I wasn't sure if this was the mystical experience William James had described, but it did give me a glimpse of something, a way of thinking. It was not the unyielding mind of my father. It was not the junkyard mess of my own head. It was the sense of being initiated into a non-judgmental consciousness, a respite from the human condition. For a moment I felt myself lifted out of the conflict zone.

The relief was temporary. The bone-shattering anxiety came back. I continued to function, to walk and talk, while inside I was pursued across a wasteland by ravening wolves. But I'd been given hope.

Then H-M's seventeen-year-old son, Pete, gave me a fantastic piece of advice. 'Don't judge what you're writing,' he said. 'Just write and keep writing. At first it will be crap but then it will get better.' So I began to write, clumsily at first, like a baby colt learning to walk. I wrote what I knew—undergraduate philosophy. By this time I had dragged myself through Sartre's *Being and Nothingness* and the works of Rudolph Otto, Bertrand Russell, David Hume, Joseph Campbell and others. And so my monologue, as it took shape, came to be about a woman who is unrequitedly in love with philosophy.

I felt the warm glow of satisfaction at a job well done. Instantly replaced with the excitement and anxiety of having to perform it.

On opening night the tiny theatre was filled with family and friends. My costume consisted of a polka-dot leotard and a yellow tutu. My jet-black hair was teased into a birds nest and my features were hidden beneath a thick layer of white-face make-up. I looked like I was opening for The Cure.

I can't remember the exact content of my monologue but it was essentially a love song to Jean-Paul Sartre and all the other philosophers who, my character felt, had let her down in her search for love and meaning. It was a parody of tortured undergraduate juvenilia. It was also true. And, despite its obscure subject matter, it went over surprisingly well.

I eventually stopped pining and my relationship with Jane settled into a lifelong friendship. We formed a band with her brother Simon and

My first performance, Why Not Theatre, 1983

Hippie and hipster. With Tom Gleisner
in a *D-Gen* sketch, 1985

Pixie-Anne Wheatley: in depth with Jeff Fenech, *Fast Forward*, 1989

Chenille and Janelle: with Marg Downey, *Fast Forward*, 1990

In costume as Margaret O'Halloran, Dogwoman, in 1999. The dog is my beagle, Jane Austen

As Esme Hoggett in *Babe*, 1995

With Steve and Terri Irwin, 2002

With Lisa McCune and Christen O'Leary, *The 25th Annual Putnam County Spelling Bee*, 2007

With Marg Downey and Martina Navratilova, January 2015. Di Fromholtz eat your heart out…

*This Is Your Life,* 1996

The Logies, c. 1999—and a genuine 1960s formal shirt

Rajmund (above); Magda Zawadzka (below).Warsaw, 2012

Before *The Project*, February 2012
with (l-r) my friend Fabienne, Mum, Barb

His Holiness

Coming out on *The Project* with
(l-r) Dave Hughes, Charlie Pickering, Carrie Bickmore

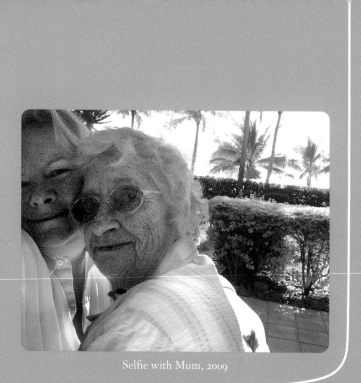
Selfie with Mum, 2009

The writer at work, 2014

some of his friends. It was called Uncle Torquemada. At the time we were all crazy about the eccentric spinster poet Stevie Smith who wrote *Novel on Yellow Paper* and, still one of my favourite poems, 'Not Waving but Drowning'. The band name came from one of her comic illustrations: a young girl is walking her little dog Beppo along with the Grand Inquisitor of the Spanish Inquisition, Tomas de Torquemada. Worried for the fate of her little dog's soul, the girl turns to Torquemada and says, 'Uncle Torquemada, does Beppo know about Jesus?' We thought this was hilarious.

Jane and I blagged our way into playing at a women's dance, even though only two members were actually musicians, and we agreed that the poster would include a warning that one of the band was a male. I was on lead vocals and Casio with Jane on percussion—clapsticks, basically—and back-up vocals. Jane and my old school chum Helen would write poems and I would come up with the music. I wasn't trained but I had a good ear and could compose a passable ditty. At the time women's music was folksy, worthy and spirit-crushingly earnest. We were a mad, ironic, dissident cabaret act, with a blend of poetry and dance beats. We did things like a cover of 'The Look of Love', with Jane as Jean-Paul Sartre—the famous googly eye was a ping-pong ball stuck on the end of some pipe cleaner—while I was Simone de Beauvoir sporting a towering trademark turban that would rival Marge Simpson. We only did two gigs.

One day, between tutorials at uni, I was sitting in the small cafeteria when a friend informed me that they were holding auditions for the university law faculty revue. In fifteen minutes.

I had heard of the legendary law revues although I had never seen one. Famous alumni included the likes of Barry Humphries. I wasn't studying law but that didn't matter, anyone on campus could participate.

'You should try out,' my friend said.

'I can't! I've got a tute.'

'Skip your tute.'

'It's in fifteen minutes! I haven't prepared or anything.'

Despite my fears I could feel the familiar buzz that the thought of performing gave me. I looked at the clock. I now had thirteen minutes.

'I suppose I could do my monologue.'

As a campus fringe-dweller I was not sure what to expect. I only knew that a professional comedian had been hired to direct the revue and conduct auditions. It turned out to be a skinny, funny-looking little guy called Alan Pentland, who would later play a big role in my life as Ferret, the sharpie-dancing boyfriend of my *Fast Forward* character Michelle Grogan. Alan had been in earlier architecture revues and had gained a reputation for quirky work. One of his acts was a striptease. He performed it with total commitment and it was hilarious to see this weedy little guy parody the moves of Gypsy Rose Lee. It culminated with him yanking off his jock strap to unfurl a six-foot-long foam rubber penis.

Anyway, I did my monologue but I could tell Alan was not impressed. He asked me to do something else: a parody of a ditzy girl sunbathing and being sexy. As a feminist I felt affronted: objectified and set up. But I did it, and I got into the revue. Alan told me later that it was not until I pushed myself out of my comfort zone that he was convinced. Doing the revue was terrific fun. My contribution was characteristically dark, weird and obscure, reflecting my obsession with Kurt Weill and Lotte Lenya. Helen wrote a poem called 'Song for Black-eyed Girls', and I put it to a kind of Weill-ian tune I had made up. It was a demented torch song. Alan loved it and I felt he understood my brooding Polish soul. He rehearsed me until my voice was hoarse and helped to bring out the hints of sexual menace in the piece. No one knew what it meant, including me, but judging by the applause it was a hit. The other piece I did was my alarmingly accurate impersonation of Benny Hill. And perhaps that strange juxtaposition sums me up.

Later I was approached to do the university national touring revue, *Too Cool for Sandals*. It was a year-long gig, and I was reluctant. But once again I got some great advice at the right time. From a woman who couldn't make a fist.

Finola was a writer who had no thumb. Her sister had chased her round the garden and chopped it off with an axe when they were both too small to understand. She was a friend of some avant-garde friends of mine. I liked her a lot and from time to time we would chat. I told her about the revue, which seemed far too mainstream and conventional for my alternative tastes. I thought maybe I should join the circus. Finola's response surprised me.

'Magda, I have known many people who, when the big time came knocking, shut the door in its face. They later regretted it and ended up bitter. My advice is—grab it!' And she grasped at thin air with her thumbless fist.

I didn't know what I wanted, but I knew I did not want to end up bitter. I had the grades to do honours in fine art but I deferred indefinitely and said yes to the revue. Besides, it was only a few month's work.

The revue was a blast. We performed at bars and unis all across the country. We did a long stint in Perth at the famous Pink Galah where, late at night, when everyone else had left the building, we would all play hide and seek in the dark. I've never laughed so hard in my life. The healing powers of comedy and good company worked their magic on me and the remnants of my depression lifted.

The tour culminated with a stint at the Last Laugh, the venue I had dreamed of playing and where, for a brief and incompetent moment, I had actually waitressed. The Laugh was owned by John Pinder, a bald, colourful, plain-talking man mountain. He was an old school impresario. If you imagine Cartman from South Park grown up and with oversized red spectacles you will have some idea of what Pinder was like. He was tough but fair. He could be brutal but his largesse and genuine love of comedy were winning. For a brief moment there was talk of him managing me. He believed in my talent but doubted my hunger and drive.

The eighties were an especially exciting time for comedy in Melbourne. For some reason the city gave birth to a whole bunch of funny people who got their starts in venues like the Last Laugh, the Flying Trapeze, Le Joke and the Banana Lounge. Sometimes the ground rises up beneath your feet and you are lucky to be in the right place at the right time. I was exactly where I needed to be.

# D-GENERATION AND DE PROFUNDIS

I can't remember how the call was first made. I had no agent so it must have come direct from Kris Noble's office. Kris had been a cameraman in the ABC studios at Gordon Street in Elsternwick and had risen up through the ranks to become a director. Frank Ward was a Yorkshireman who had started out as 'the only straight man in the chorus' of various light-entertainment musical productions. In his own words—'Hullo breakfast!'

Kris and Frank were now executive producers at the national broadcaster and had been to see *Too Cool for Sandals*. They wanted me and Michael Veitch to join the cast of an existing show which had just completed a successful TV pilot. The show was called *D-Generation*. This was opportunity knocking. And my response was to hesitate.

My equivocation had nothing to do with the quality of the show. The cast—Rob Sitch, Santo Cilauro, Nick Bufalo, Tom Gleisner, John

Harrison and my old tennis buddy Marg Downey—had already done a pilot and I thought it was fabulous. My doubts were about television itself. I had come a long way since the days when I sat glued to the screen watching Marcia Brady, when television was a friend and a mentor. To my mind television was now the propaganda wing of the oppressor, the belly of the heteronormative beast. By now I knew the gay cautionary tales, the terrible fates that awaited those who flew too high. My mind kept circling back to the victims. Alan Turing, the genius cryptanalyst who broke the Enigma code, helped to win World War II, and all the thanks he got was to be charged with gross indecency and chemically castrated. And, of course, Oscar Wilde. Poor bloody Oscar, the darling of London society, being spat on and jeered on the train platform on his way to Reading Gaol. I had read *De Profundis.* I did not trust the straight world or the glittering prizes it offered. Those men were geniuses and they had been crushed. What hope did I have? I said no.

Rob Sitch lived across from us in Walsh Street. The producers sent him to work on me. 'Look Magda,' he said, 'it's only ten shows, just a few months' work. The money's not great—it's the ABC—but it'll keep the wolf from the door.' The money was a good deal more than I had ever earnt but still I said no.

The mere thought of TV sent me into a panic. Some ragged part of my DNA whispered dire warnings in my soul's ear. *Keep your head down. Stay low. Stay small and you will be safe.* But there was another voice, just as strong. Wasn't this what I had wanted all along? To stand at the red-hot centre of the world? To feel the roar of its heart?

It was Helen-Mary, impatient with my dithering, who lifted the sword and severed the Gordian knot. 'Magda,' she said bluntly, 'the public has a very short memory.' Instantly I felt free. This was not something irrevocable, not some wrong decision I would be reckoning with for the rest of my days. I rang Rob and told him I was in.

*D-Gen* was filmed in the famous Studio 31 in Gordon Street. This was where shows I was addicted to as a kid, like *Countdown* and *Bellbird,* were filmed. It was great to see Marg again. Although we had led utterly different lives we quickly fell back into our pattern of gentle hilarity.

Despite that, the moment I stepped into that studio I felt like an alien. The show's title was a complete misnomer. The cast were the most clean-cut bunch I had ever met. After the polymorphously perverse types I had hung out with at uni, it was like moving in with the Waltons. They are lovely people but they are all still married to their childhood sweethearts. I was a Polish, Scottish, Irish, fat, short lesbian.

I clung to what I knew best—accents, mimicry. If it was not safe to be myself I could hide in pretending to be someone else. Then one day in a writer's meeting Andrew Knight, the head writer, made an announcement: 'We are not going to use any English accents. This show is going to have a distinctly Australian voice.' My heart sank. Sure, this meant a welcome reprieve from all the Monty Python imitations. But regional British accents were my stock in trade. I did not feel at all confident with Aussie voices and nuances. I was going to have to pedal bloody hard to keep up. My sense of humour had to find its way past a long succession of barriers: accent, sensibility, lack of shared knowledge. And, lastly, the sexuality barrier.

I don't know if the other cast members knew I was gay. They never said. And I could not bring myself to tell them. I can't explain why I felt so embarrassed. Plenty of my friends knew. I had lived an openly lesbian life at uni and the refuge. But exposure to the straight world revived and magnified my old anxiety. *There was something wrong with me, something defective. My mind was weak, that stupid jabbering idiot, that fucking fool of a thing. My mind was going to be the end of me.*

And then something weird started happening to my newfound lesbianism. Like some adaptive species of threatened coral, my sexuality retreated. My attraction to men increased. I began to homogenise. I became straighter. I grew my hair, I shaved my armpits and started wearing dresses. On a few disastrous drunken occasions I acted on my fleeting attractions to men. How could that happen? Was fear changing my sexual preference? Or was I just exploring a different part of myself? I was now twenty-four years old. How could I have found myself only to be losing myself again? Was there a real, irreducible me? Or was I just some kind of protean flux?

In 1986 the choices were gay, straight and bisexual. None of those fully expressed how I felt. The concept of sexual fluidity did not yet exist. Perhaps, if I was a different person with a different history, or if all this had happened twenty years later, I could have styled myself as a bold, if slightly confused, sexual adventuress. Instead, I used the harsh language of self-judgment I grew up with. Perpetrator, victim, collaborator.

I decided I must be some kind of sexual traitor, who had colluded in order to enjoy the benefits of a straight life. Never mind that I never once in my life felt I enjoyed any kind of 'heterosexual privilege'. I didn't understand that I was acting out a psychodrama. My role was written. I was predetermined and I didn't even know it.

This pasteurisation of my personality did not help with my comedy writing. Comedy is all about finding your voice. It's a difficult task, and it can take years. Your voice is best when it is formed where it is found. But what if you are trying to be what you are not? What if you don't know who you are?

Basically, my writing was crap. I simply didn't know how to convey my weird, queer world. Andrew Knight had not let a single one of my sketches through. The boys, in the meantime, were churning out material. So I went to Marg Downey. Despite the fact that Marg looks like the perfect straight lady she has a fabulously wicked streak. I had detected it all those years ago when we played tennis together. And now I was relying on it.

She came to visit at Walsh Street and we sat around for several hours drinking coffee, doing voices, trying to make one another laugh. It was a slow grind at first. Nothing came. It's always like that. But then I started imitating one of my lecturers at uni. Marg giggled. I kept on. Now I needed subject matter. In my Cinema Studies unit I had seen the work of a couple of experimental filmmakers who made short, obscure films that were, to me, hilariously boring and pretentious. The trickle became a stream. I started riffing, waffling on pompously. Then Marg started to roar with laughter, and I felt funny again. God bless her! It was like the old days with my mother.

We developed it into a mockumentary-style sketch about a young girl's journey through adolescence as revealed by a series of portraits of her shoes. Andrew loved it. Our next sketch was of an actress talking on a chat show about her first book—the big reveal being that it was the first book she had ever *read,* not written. I started to feel I was learning the craft of sketch writing.

Then came 'Lynne Postlethwaite'. Andrew Knight and another writer called John Alsop had stayed at a hotel in London with the world's least obliging concierge and they had written a brilliant sketch, based on her. It was an absolute gift. A middle-aged monster with an endless supply of justifications for her outrageous selfishness.

Not long before, I had been transfixed by the appearance of an elderly woman on the tram. Her hair and make-up looked as if they had been done once in the 1940s and thereafter just retouched, turning her face into a kind of living shrine to itself. I decided that was the look for Lynne. I had a character voice I'd been mucking around with and when I applied this to the script the result was magic. (Of course, it doesn't always happen like that.) I have no idea where I got that voice from—Lynne's long, drawn-out *Naooow*, the vampiric suck on her cigarette. But people constantly tell me that they know someone just like her—a frightening statistic for any demographer.

I began to appreciate the beauty of a catchphrase—Lynne's was, 'Tired, tired, tired, I said love, I said pet, I said please.' As the show gained an audience people in the street would quote the line at me. The success of the character was bolstering. It was the first time I felt solidly Aussie, my first experience I had of making an impact on the vernacular.

My initial inability to express who I truly was turned out to be the grain of sand in my oyster. I had to push myself to find the universal truths, the bedrock emotions that lie beneath all difference. I believe it forced me to create 'iconic' Aussie characters.

And perhaps the very things I feared held me back—my lonely childhood and queer sexuality—were in fact the perfect preparation for a comic actor. Years of midday movies in the suburbs had inadvertently schooled me in a style: Camp Sensibility.

But style is not enough. I needed to find my comedy tribe, and I was about to make two of the most important friendships of my professional life. Through Marg, I met Jane Turner and then Gina Riley.

Marg and Jane had been at Sacré Coeur together. Jane joined *D-Gen* in its second year, having made quite a name for herself on the comedy circuit. When Jane first came into the writers' room she reminded me of a startled bird. Fine-boned with quick darting movements, she was a completely different beast from me. But she was indisputably funny and a gifted writer, which made me feel a tad threatened. A fifth-generation Aussie, she had an uncanny ear for the vernacular. It was her birthright and I envied her that. Jane and I can be a little oil and water. We both love one another's work but we don't always mesh well. Jane has a completely different rhythm from me, as if one of us is doing a foxtrot while the other is trying to samba. Luckily we are deeply fond of one another and are capable of making each other cry with laughter.

Gina was a different story. I hated her on sight. She was working in an adjacent office on an ill-fated show with the unfortunate name *While You're Down There.* The dislike was mutual. I thought she was a crass show-off and she thought I was a stuck-up snob. We were both right but we finally overcame our pride and prejudice a year later when I moved in with our mutual friend, Tony. Gina and I completely fell in love over the phone when she would ring to speak to him and get stuck talking to me. Her spine-tinglingly accurate impersonations of Shirley Bassey and Agent 99 from *Get Smart* were the clincher. I have always been a sucker for a spot of good mimicry.

Gina and I didn't work together at first but we spent a lot of time hanging out at the kitchen table of the house she shared with Wendy Harmer in Fitzroy. We were becoming great friends but I still hadn't told her I was a lesbian. Then one day she said, 'So what's going on?' Sly smile. 'Anyone you like?'

'No. No, not really.' There was. I was having an affair with a straight girl we both knew.

'Then why are you blushing?'

'I'm not...I...'

Gina laughed. 'I know, you know.'

'Know what? I don't know what you're talking about.'

'Mag, I know you're gay. It's OK.'

'I'm...I...' I was now blushing beyond red and into the purples—tyrian and burgundy and puce.

'You are, aren't you? Ha! I knew it!' Gina must have seen the look on my face. Her tone softened instantly. 'Oh, you poor thing! It's OK, Mag.'

I knew it was OK with Gina; I knew she didn't care. Gina was a free-thinking atheist. She had lots of gay friends. But Gina wasn't the rest of the world. I still had not told anyone outside my uni circle. I still had not told anyone in the family except Barb.

It is hard to remember now how scary it was. Those were still dark days for gay people. Homosexuality had only been decriminalised in Victoria in 1980. Gay bashing was not uncommon. Friends of mine had been spat on, beaten up and hospitalised. I had been jeered at in the street, called a fat ugly dyke who needed to be 'straightened out'. In my uni days, bolstered by my feminism, with a support group around me, I had taken all of this in my stride. But now I felt isolated from the herd and my courage seeped away.

*D-Generation* got a second series with the ABC. With the money I made I moved into a ground-floor apartment in Park Street, South Yarra, around the corner from Helen-Mary's house. The street I lived in was lined with majestic terrace houses and looked like something out of *Mary Poppins*. My apartment was in a once-grand old house that had been subdivided. The rent was surprisingly cheap. My bedroom fronted onto the street and on warm nights I liked to sleep with the window open.

It was about 6 a.m. on the morning of 5 March 1987.

There was a huge, compact BOOM! Like the sound of a jet plane smashing the sound barrier, only right outside my window. I sat up, my body awake but not my mind. Something had happened. Something bad. What? A car crash? Too loud. Much, much too loud.

Another sound. Human, I thought. Then it stopped. Started again and stopped. A scream? A howl? A moan? It was the sound of a woman screaming. This was not like the screams and rants of the brawling junkies and drunks who pissed outside my window when I lived in St Kilda. It was a scream and a deep groan of pain combined. The sound the body makes when it knows it is dying.

'Fire!' A man's voice. 'Fire! Somebody call the fire department!'

Dazed, I stumbled out of bed and over to the window. It was half open. I yanked it up fully and stuck my head out. I reeled backwards.

'Oh my God! Jesus Christ, Jesus fucking Christ!'

What had been an elegant art deco apartment was now engulfed in a bright yellow wall of flame twenty feet high, licking up to the balconies above like a barrel wave in reverse, blackening the white plaster.

More voices. Male voices. 'It's all right love. We've got ya! We've got ya!' Some men were hauling the screaming woman from the ground below the balcony. She was naked.

'Oh my fucking God!' I could not believe this was happening.

The yelling man ran past.

'What is it? What happened?' I shouted.

'A bomb. They got her out.' He made a sweeping gesture across the bottom of his legs. 'But her feet are completely gone.'

He kept running. I don't know where.

What did he mean her feet were gone?

I ran to the phone, fully awake now and wired, my hand shaking like I had Parkinson's. I could not make my fingers dial the numbers, my hand spasmed and veered off uncontrollably. How weird. I noticed how weird that was. Pathetic. Weak. *Pull yourself together, you idiot.*

Eventually I hit 000. I quickly told the operator the details and got off the phone. Ever since my mother burned her hand I have been terrified of fire. As I ran out into the street towards the flames I was expecting commotion. The first thing that struck me was the silence. An eerie, terribly silent silence. The silence that comes from the absence not of sound, but of people. The only noise now was the roar of flames. Where was everyone?

I saw four bystanders across the road from the burning flat, maybe ten metres away from the flames. Even from there we could feel the heat singeing our cheeks.

The fire brigade had not arrived. There was no one else there, just us. And then, as we watched, a man emerged through the curtain of flame onto the balcony. Tottering, like a drunk actor making his entrance. He was completely on fire. His flaming hands were raised to his burning head like a soldier giving himself up to the enemy.

He started to talk. Evenly, calmly. He wanted to know something, 'Did they get her out?'

We started screaming at him. 'Throw yourself over the balcony! Just throw yourself over!'

'It's no use. Just as long as she's out.' His calmness made me feel crazy.

'Yes! They got her out. Just jump, just jump!' I screamed.

'That's good,' he said.

We stood there, the five of us and the man on fire. Neighbours, but total strangers. For a good minute or two he wobbled there, talking to us. He seemed to be beyond the reach of pain.

The man next to me couldn't stand it anymore. 'Where the *fuck* is the fire brigade!' We looked around, then someone said, 'Oh my God.'

On the balcony, still looking at us, the burning man wobbled sideways. He tried to right himself. Then he slumped like a condemned building and slowly toppled down behind the balcony.

The fire closed over him.

Eventually fire trucks and ambulances arrived. Police cordoned off the street. Traffic was diverted and trams were banked up down Toorak Road. Now the street was full—people and cars and thick fire hoses and news crews. A woman who lived in the back of our block and who'd seen nothing was giving a teary interview to a television crew.

I didn't know what else to do so I went to work as usual and filmed comedy sketches.

That night I went to Helen-Mary's, drank a bottle of whisky and howled. But I felt strangely hollow, as though I was not entitled to these feelings.

I called my father. I found his voice reassuring. 'Oh Jesus, that's rough. What can I say, hen? You just have to move on. During the war I saw Jews throw their children into the flames and jump in after them. You just have to put it behind you and move on.'

# FAST FORWARD

Late in 1988 Marg Downey, Jane Turner and I received a phone call from Steve Vizard. He was starting a new show called *Fast Forward* for the Seven Network. Opportunity was knocking again. Several of our colleagues from the Last Laugh had recently had unprecedented success with a show on Channel Ten—*The Comedy Company*. It was a massive popular hit and we had all watched with admiration and perhaps a little envy as the cast members became household names. What if *Fast Forward* could capitalise on that success?

Was that what I wanted? To be invited into the living rooms of the nation? How could I do that when nobody knew who I really was, when the idea of homosexuality made many people feel sick? Yet again I descended into the familiar spiral of fear and excitement, repulsion and attraction.

Marg and I spent the entire day on the phone, workshopping the decision. Marg said yes first. I followed shortly after. The money was stupidly good. And I trusted Rod Quantock, the head writer. He was an elder statesman of comedy for us. Besides, this whole thing could not last long. The comedy bubble was sure to burst.

The first episode of *Fast Forward* aired on 12 April 1989—my twenty-eighth birthday. Nothing spectacular happened. My life did not change. The ratings were initially low, so the axe hung over us. But over time they grew, until it became the top-rating show on TV, eclipsing even *The Comedy Company*. In the second year Gina Riley joined the team.

We were a pretty egalitarian bunch but in the early days the men tended to dominate. Some seasons passed where I languished for months without any meaty roles. The girls and I formed a natural—if somewhat powerless—power bloc. We found one another hilarious. We had a potent chemistry but as yet we lacked the confidence to work it.

The best way to get airtime was to write your own sketches. My fear of the blank page had diminished only slightly and now I decided it was time to slay that demon. Aside from us performer–writers there was also a team of dedicated writers—initially almost entirely male. The writers' room was on the ground floor of a building we called the Castle, a jerry-built two-storey structure on the corner of the Channel Seven studio lot. This small, airless office was a haven for the comedy boy boffins. Cast members rarely approached.

I could see no material difference between myself and the writers. What made you a writer was having the balls to call yourself one. That, and a computer of one's own. The girls and I would go down to the Galleon Café in St Kilda to write. We spent hours noodling around, making one another laugh—and penning sketches by hand. Consequently no one took us seriously. So I bought my first laptop computer. And then I pushed open the door to the writers' room and went in.

The boys were surprised to see a cast member, let alone a female one, in their domain; I seem to remember them blinking at the rare glimpse of light from the outside world. But they were very welcoming, and I soon realised that I could write just as well as they could. Or at least I wasn't any worse.

I learned three invaluable lessons in that room: 1) get the tools of the trade; 2) don't compare yourself with Shakespeare; 3) appreciate the beauty of impermanence. Cranking out twenty-six episodes a year of sketch comedy is the TV equivalent of making a Buddhist sand mandala—you cannot get attached to your beautiful successes or tragic failures because next week it will all be gone and you have to do it all over again. I found that incredibly liberating.

My main writing partner was Doug MacLeod. Doug had been a writer on *The Comedy Company.* With each new season of *Fast Forward* the challenge was to come up with new characters. Doug came up with a character idea based on my ability to do a Scottish accent—a thrifty Scotswoman who gives dubious 'canny recession tips'. I decided to name her after a dim-witted minor character in *The Prime of Miss Jean Brodie*—Wee Mary McGregor. Doug and I co-wrote the character and we made her cheeky, lascivious and tipsy. She was loosely based on the one time I had seen my mother tipsy, at Hogmanay, inciting a bunch of women to try and divest the lone piper of his kilt. Doug and I also took over the writing of Lynne Postlethwaite, the suburban gargoyle originally written by Andrew Knight and John Alsop.

Pixie-Anne Wheatley was the serendipitous product of my incompetence. We were doing a news spoof and they needed a female sports reporter. Marg could effortlessly reproduce the bizarre 'news-speak' intonation used by newsreaders but I simply could not master the art. So I made a virtue of necessity and Pixie-Anne, the ditzy sports reporter, was born. We made her the beneficiary of some high-level nepotism: her fictional father Sir Lance Wheatley owned the network.

The characters might have started in the writers' room but a lot of the magic occurred in the make-up room. The make-up artist, Barb Cousins, was an unheralded genius. I would spend hours with her, trying on wigs and funny noses and neck braces to bring to life the undercooked sketches we had often written in great haste. I would stare in amazement as my malleable features were transformed by the application of rubber noses and clever shading. I became Joan Kirner, Katharine Hepburn, Hoss from *Bonanza*. Yet again my identity seemed to be a shifting rather than a fixed thing.

It was on a plane trip to Sydney that I realised I was becoming famous. I was in character as Pixie-Anne, going to interview the boxer Jeff Fenech. As I walked through the airport I could feel the shift. Surreptitious gazes followed me; several people asked for autographs. It was slightly thrilling, I cannot lie.

But in the following months, as it gathered pace, I started to feel like I was strapped to a rocket. Magazine covers, interviews, endorsements. Suddenly I really was a household name, dogged by the horrible hollow feeling that the wrong 'me' had shot to fame. At night I dreamed that I was hanging on to the outside rail of a runaway train. I woke every morning feeling exhausted.

And somewhere along the way I developed a fear of flying. I had always loved flying. Ever since I was given my Pan Am captain's hat I had adored everything about it: the glamour of the air hostesses, the smart sophistication of the pilots, the natty miniature meals. The brilliant blue sky, the crystalline light, the dazzling sun and the pearly white clouds. It was the closest thing to heaven on earth. A sanctuary filled with possibilities, free of drudgery and strife. Even as a five-year-old I could feel my anxiety dissolving into the thin air.

But around the time of the bombing the fear began to creep in and seemed to spread in direct relation to my fame. As this little light of mine rose into the starry firmament, the fear became crippling. Eventually I was so riddled with terror I couldn't fly at all. It was the sensation of falling that I dreaded. The lurching butterflies in the gut. The sickening plummet. The phrase 'dropped like a stone' haunted me. I became a white-knuckle flier, relying on Scotch, noise-cancelling headphones and the occasional well-timed benzodiazepine.

It was the mask of my character that gave me courage. Safely hiding within a fictitious persona I could be brave. I could do things I wouldn't dream of without a wig and a costume. On a trip to the Gold Coast, it was decided that Pixie-Anne would go parasailing. Emboldened by the blithe ditziness of my character I went for broke. The comic's primal instinct kicked in: I would do anything to get the laugh—even dangle from a flimsy piece of silk held aloft by a breath of air. As I hung there I giggled and squealed in Pixie-Anne's piping catchcry laugh. It was a musical four-note laugh, like the song of a happy bird. It always felt to me like a bubble of joy rising from my belly, up through my chest and bursting out into the world. And for that short time my fear of heights and the whole world evaporated. I marvelled to discover that something so ephemeral could be a source of such strength. That silly, trilling laugh made me strong and brave; it made me happy.

The question was how to translate those feelings to my real life.

# SHADOW IN THE AMBER

In 1992 I decided to take my parents on a pilgrimage to the old countries, one of the best things I have ever done. Back in their childhood homes they were transformed, my father particularly. His pace quickened. He darted about full of energy and enthusiasm, showing us the haunts and hangouts of his youth. I could see clearly the young man he had once been.

Warsaw had changed too—I couldn't believe how much in the ten years since I had been there. All the way from the airport there were gaudy billboards along the side of the road, each one a giant rebuke to the communists who had been booted out in 1989. It was summer, the sun was shining and colour had returned. Everyone and everything was brighter and happier. Some traces of the old regime lingered, especially in the service industry, but otherwise the mood was one of brassy optimism.

We had a big family dinner at the Bristol, one of the few old hotels left in Warsaw, a short walk from the Old Town. The hotel staff made a big fuss of the family, probably because my cousin Magda and Gustaw were there. The meals arrived under silver cloches. A waiter stood silent and formal behind each guest. And then, with great drama and high seriousness, they simultaneously removed the lids, clicked their heels and left. It was fabulous.

That was the night my father's cousin Rajmund taught me how to drink vodka properly. 'It is a sin to mix vodka with anything,' he told me. 'Except caviar!' First you nibble the caviar on a little biscuit. Then you down the vodka in one gulp.

So I was keen to practise my new vodka-drinking skills, and planned to look up Agnieszka, the friend of a friend who had been at acting school with my cousin Magda. We arranged to meet in a cemetery on the first of August, the day when Warszawians gather to commemorate the uprising. It was a choking hot day and the air was filled with the smoke of tens of thousands of candles.

Agnieszka was a stunner, with auburn hair, green eyes and a white halter-neck dress that showed off her dark suntan to perfection. She stood in front of the cemetery and appeared to be posing—smiling, pouting, tossing her hair—for an unseen camera. I strained to see who was filming her. There, standing on a plinth in a pair of rather ripe runners, was a dishevelled-looking man with a palmcorder.

She grabbed me close. 'Marek, take a picture. Magda is *famous* in Australia.' She introduced the man in runners. 'Magda, this is Marek.' She shrugged. 'He is my ex-husband. Strange situation. But it happens.'

Agnieszka turned out to be the kind of magnificent creature that can only exist in real life. A powerful, sexy, fabulous Mother Courage who survived communism with nothing but her wits and élan and hotness. Like a brainy panther.

We arranged to meet up again and I rejoined my family. As we shuffled through the cemetery, something caught my eye. A long line of wonky headstones, uniform and yet misaligned.

'What does it say? Who are they?' I asked Uncle Andrzej.

'Girl scouts,' he replied. 'Among the first to be killed by the Nazis. Enemies of the Reich. This is how they frighten people. Killing girl scouts.'

My cousin Magda and her family had gone on holiday and we were staying in their apartment. A few days later Agnieszka and Marek swung by to pick me up and take me to a party at a bilberry farm in the Polish countryside. Agnieszka leaned back from the front seat and gave me a heavy wink: 'There will be lesbians there.'

The lure of the lesbians was strong, but nowhere near as strong as the alcohol. In fact, the bootleg vodka was so powerful I shot straight past tipsy, through flirty and into comatose. I have never been so drunk in all my life. I was seeing triple, quadruple even. I peered at Agnieszka out of one sozzled eye in a pathetic attempt to reduce my vision to double. She pursed her lips in a sensual pout of exaggerated Slavic pity. 'Oh. Poor Magdusiu. I think maybe Marek will take you home now.' The Poles don't judge drunkenness. They just drag it into a safe warm place.

I returned from the bilberry farm and staggered up the six flights of stairs. Just as I was trying to fit the key into the last of seven sturdy locks, my father opened the door. It was late but we had quite a long conversation before I teetered off to bed, confident that I had done a good job of concealing how smashed I was. My father had no patience for drunks.

The next morning, miraculously, I didn't feel too bad. In fact it would have been easy to pretend that the entire debauch had never happened.

'So it was a good night?' My father peered over his paper.

'Yes,' I said demurely, 'it was lovely.'

I began to describe the previous evening's events. My father gave me a wry smile and waved at me to stop.

'I don't need to hear it all again. You already told me.'

'Oh. Did I?'

He folded up his paper. 'Yes. In Polish.'

'Really?'

'Oh yes. Fluent Polish. You were very chatty.'

I don't speak Polish. Except, apparently when I am drunk. Fluently.

While Polish conversation swirled around us day and night my father would translate. Everyone was impressed by how good and how current his Polish was, especially as he had a foreign wife. Just as I had, my mother had tried valiantly to learn Polish years before. But of course she met with the same stubborn resistance from my father. As a consequence, she had spent years on the sidelines at Polish functions, warmly welcomed but never fully included. She could always feel the invisible barrier that kept her out. None of this was done out of malice. It was just…inevitable.

Uncle Andrzej said, 'Polish sounds like whispering, *sh-ch sh-ch sh-ch*.'

'Yes.' I nodded. An impenetrable wall of whispers.

One night, as we sat in the pinewood confines of my cousin's log cabin, surrounded by candlelight and the cheery warmth of the fire, the sense of claustrophobia combined with the feeling of being socially excluded overwhelmed my mother. The need to be heard, to speak her own language, became irresistible. Exhausted by the maelstrom of *szcz*s and *rzy*s and *wszystko*s, she began quietly lobbing random English words into the conversation, like non-sequitur grenades. And giggling.

'Knuckle.'

No one noticed except me.

'Hammer.'

As I cottoned on to what she was doing the giggles got me.

'Mum! Stop it!' I whispered furiously.

'Fence.' She paused. 'Peanut.'

It was naughty. It was like an impromptu performance-art piece about the social isolation experienced by a stranger in a strange land. We became a wobbling jelly of giggling helplessness. It was sublime. It was awful. It bound us together, and I felt I owed her that much.

Slowly the Poles realised. The conversation came to a halt. And the look of hurt on my father's face. Christ. For years he had been the stranger. And now, after only a few weeks, we did this.

We decided to do a road trip. We drove south across Poland's flat Masovian plain. We were going to Cracow first, via the famous salt mines of Wieliczka. And as always we sang. Rajmund's baritone was even richer and deeper than Dad's. It was hilarious—hearing him singing 'Chattanooga Choo Choo' with that thick, velvety Polish accent and his even thicker Brezhnev eyebrows.

The salt mines were built in the thirteenth century and go a thousand feet down into the dark bowels of the earth. To relieve their misery the miners carved holy statues into the walls, tiny dioramas depicting Our Lady giving succour to the miners. At the heart of the mine is an enormous cathedral carved entirely out of the salt.

Cracow was the ancient capital of Poland and, unlike Warsaw, was almost completely untouched by the war. The huge town square looks more Turkish than European, the markets in the Cloth Hall resembling a bazaar. That night as we sat in a café by the square, roaming gypsy bands serenaded us. We wandered about for an hour and followed the sound of bebop into one of the city's many underground jazz cellars.

It was a sunny day, the day we went to Auschwitz. A summer day full of bright blossoms and soft, warm air. A sombre, nervous mood overtook us as we left Cracow. It was my idea; the others didn't feel the need to go. But I wanted to see it.

Auschwitz concentration camp actually comprises several parts. Auschwitz I is the main camp and at first, when we pulled up out the front, I thought it looked like a little Noddy town—a small-scale village of red-brick buildings that seemed almost friendly. Until I saw that infamous sign. *Arbeit Macht Frei*. A chill ran through me.

We paid the entry fee and went in. I seem to remember Rajmund spoke to the guide. She took us through. The small lawns were lush and green, the pathways neatly manicured. And then we entered the buildings.

Many people have written about Auschwitz. There is no way to do justice to the horror. The great piles of human hair. The mounds of suitcases. The tiny shoes. The ovens.

We walked through slowly. Mum and I began to cry. 'Dear God,' I said. 'How can people do that to one another?' My father shook his head matter-of-factly. 'Well. This is the truth, Magda. This is what happened.'

Then we headed for Birkenau. Auschwitz II-Birkenau, the women's prison, is the grim one with the train line leading to the gate and the all-seeing guard tower. Birkenau was the extermination camp.

We parked the car. My father, Rajmund and I got out. But my mother refused. 'No. I have seen enough. I cannot see any more.'

'Mum, are you sure?'

'Yes, I'm sure!' And as my father opened the door my mother backed away from us, cowering into the corner like a scared animal, tears streaming down her face. With shaking hands she lit a cigarette. She frightened me; I didn't know what to do. So we left her there.

We wandered around by ourselves. Many parts of the site were destroyed. Blunt broken ruins, bits of concrete upended like outcroppings shifted by vast geological trauma. We walked through the barracks. Tiny, filthy, cramped concrete bunks. I kept looking at Dad, but there was no display of emotion. And I began to understand how he had survived the war. My father was brave. I never saw him show fear or horror. But it came at a cost. I remembered his reaction to the bombing in Park Street. It was as though the only feelings he could tolerate were the abstract ones. Injustice, a sense of right and wrong, unfairness. Sadness, grief—fear particularly—could not be allowed.

The Poles have become the custodians of hell on earth. It is hard. Being the world's shrine and cemetery, its monument to shame. My mother's response was the only one that was normal. But what, really, is the normal response to Auschwitz? Is feeling everything any more valid than shutting down, feeling nothing?

On the drive back to Warsaw I could sense my father's disdain. It was the slightest thing, the tiniest raising of his eyebrow. He was reproaching her—for what? her weakness?—and he was recasting her response as self-indulgent. A useless thing that was no help to anyone.

As a man his job was not to feel. It was to act, to do something. Maybe Izabella's father was right—feelings are what get people killed.

But dear God, if you cannot weep at Auschwitz?

I was thirty-one years old. I was a brave Pole. I felt the expectation to man up, and my emotions fell into step with my father's. They floated off like vapour. I felt, at that moment, nothing except irritation with my mother's weakness.

And for a moment I knew what it felt like to be my father.

We drove back up to Warsaw in silence.

When it was time to leave Poland we bought presents for the family back home. Along with vodka, Poland is famous for its amber. There are two stories of how amber is made. According to Ovid, amber is made from sunshine and sorrow. When Phaëton, the headstrong son of Phoebus the sun god, crashed and burned his father's fiery chariot and was flung headlong into the sea, his grieving sisters the Heliades were turned into poplar trees. And the tears they shed in sadness fell upon the banks of the Eridanus River where the sun's rays transformed them into amber. The amber fell into the river and was carried away on the tides to be worn by the brides of Latium.

The other version says that it was formed around forty-five million years ago when the great primaeval pine forests covered the area around the Baltic Sea. When a tree was wounded in some way, by disease or insects, it secreted viscous resin to cover and heal the wound. Some of the resin might drip into fissures in the earth or be buried by an earthquake or toppled by a glacier and pressed into the rocky sediment. Often flies and bugs would be trapped in the sticky substance and they too would be dragged into the underworld. There, over vast geological time, immense pressure and heat transformed the resin, causing it to fossilise and become amber. The heavy waters of the Baltic Sea closed over, and there the amber remained buried until tides and cataclysms loosened it. Amber floats in salt water, and so these chunks rose and continue to rise, back up to the surface, where they are caught by the waves and tossed onto the beach. Thus amber begins its second life—as a gemstone.

One of the first gifts my cousin Magda gave me was an amber necklace. It looked like a solid chunk of honey. Inside the amber was a shadow—a skinny, million-year-old insect that had drowned and was now trapped for all eternity in a golden coffin.

# HOLLYWOOD

When we came back to Melbourne I was frustrated and fractious. The producers of *Fast Forward* wanted to do another season but I was ready for something else. I had spent the last ten years churning out sketch comedy in airless, lightless studios and I needed to do something different. I left *Fast Forward* with no idea of what awaited me.

Then a big fat script landed in my letterbox. It had a one-word working title—*Quasimodo*. There was quite a buzz around the acting community about this script. It was co-written by George Miller of *Mad Max* and *The Witches of Eastwick* fame and Chris Noonan, who had directed the acclaimed TV miniseries *Vietnam*. I was a big *Mad Max* fan so I was very excited. From the moment I read the first line—'This is a tale about an unprejudiced heart and how it changed our valley forever'—I was hooked. It had elements of allegory, like Orwell's *Animal Farm*. It was charming and eccentric and had a brooding existential angst that I loved. At the same time it was a bucolic delight. The film was, of course, *Babe*.

I hadn't, at this stage, been offered a part. George and Chris knew I was good with accents: they wanted me to participate in a read-through to get a feel for how the script was working. Read-through actors are like the guinea-pig test pilots who never get to go to the moon.

I arrived with the other read-through actors at the Sydney studios of Kennedy Miller productions, situated in an old cinema in Potts Point. George and Chris escorted us round, as excited as a couple of kids with a new chemistry set. Before me were the beginnings of CGI, a jungle of mainframes and virtual 'skeletons' and 'plates'. I couldn't understand any of it. But George is a man with one foot in the future. A nutty professor with sprigs of wiry grey hair bursting out of his skull like tendrils of excess thought, he exudes a childlike curiosity and generosity.

He had first had the idea for *Babe* ten years prior, when he heard a reading of Dick King-Smith's book *The Sheep Pig* on a long flight. His prodigious imagination then set to work, envisioning a film for which the technology did not yet exist, and which he would have to develop himself.

Chris Noonan was very different. Quiet, gentle, purposeful. He had made various TV series but the thing that had moved me most was *Stepping Out*, his documentary about a bunch of teens with Down Syndrome putting on a show at the Sydney Opera House. It was magical and dignified. A film to make your spirit soar.

At the read-through we were asked to try different roles. They started by asking me to do a Scottish accent for the dog Fly—eventually played by the brilliant Miriam Margolyes. The moment I read Esme Hoggett I wanted to play her. But I was far too young and baby-faced—they wanted someone around sixty. Jamie Cromwell, who had already been cast as Arthur Hoggett, was in his mid-fifties. But my face has a strange malleability to it. Sketch comedy proved an excellent training ground for playing all ages and shapes of woman. Somehow I have always felt middle-aged, older than my years. This was one of those moments—rare—when you feel the planets align. I absolutely *knew* I could do this role because I knew Esme Hoggett: she was my mother and my grandmother all rolled into one. I got the part.

My screen husband Jamie Cromwell had a fascinating Hollywood pedigree. His father was John Cromwell, a legendary Hollywood actor-turned-director of the 1930s who worked with the likes of Bette Davis and Humphrey Bogart and was blacklisted during the McCarthy era. Jamie was a lovely man—kind, thoughtful. I liked him instantly. And he had that beatific smile. But you could still see hints of a rebellious young man whose star had not yet ascended and there was a feeling of something unfulfilled about him. He was quietly combustible, like dry kindling before the match is struck.

The film crew had taken over the rustic village of Robertson in New South Wales. It sits in a big wet patch perched on the edge of a dry continent above the Illawarra escarpment: coming from the sea road you wind your way up through coastal rainforest. Ancient ferns and eucalypts and brush cherries exhale their cool minty breath. The fecund smell of loamy soil fills your lungs. Everything is bursting with life. It felt like a good omen. I had just broken up with someone I'd been dating—a nurse, smart and witty with a look of Charlotte Rampling about her. We had a lot of laughs together. It had not been a terribly long relationship but Mum and Dad had met her (although they didn't know she was my girlfriend) and they liked her a lot. So I was carrying a bruised, if not broken, heart. I sensed that this film was the perfect place to recuperate.

The interiors were filmed in a reconditioned potato shed. The exteriors were down in the valley.

'Just wait until you see the house!' the production runner announced, beaming with pride as he showed me around the set. As we came over the rise I saw, nestled in the valley below, that iconic, higgledy-piggledy fairytale house. Its charm and beauty literally made me gasp. The production designer, Roger Ford, guided me around the crooked cottage and the barn while out on the gentle slopes the greensmen were hand-painting the sun-yellowed grass.

And I was introduced to Babe, the star of the film. The animal department was an enormous farm shed. It was like Noah's ark, filled with nearly eight hundred animals. There were geese and Indian runner ducks and jersey cows and draught horses and mice—and, of course, pigs. Chubby little pink pigs whose snouts had to be coated in sunscreen so they would not burn. Dozens of adorably cute Babes trotted around, snorting and wriggling their curly tails. In the final film there are forty-eight different Babes.

Funnily enough, a lot of the handlers were gay men and lesbians, perhaps because the head trainer had advertised in a Sydney gay magazine. (I hooked up with one of the handlers, which soothed my hurt heart a little.) Each trainer had to teach one animal just one trick—how to climb stairs or carry an alarm clock, for example. Months were spent mastering it. When it came time to film, the handlers would hide on the set behind a chair or a sideboard. Each had a pole about six feet long with a little food incentive attached at the end. These crisscrossed through the middle of the scene and were later digitally removed. Some of the trainers used whistles and strange little clacking things. There was none of the usual silence on set—it was a cacophony of neighs and oinks and bells and whistles. It was like trying to act in a zoo and I absolutely loved it. All the dialogue had to be re-recorded in post-production.

I spent about two months on the set. Each night after filming we would all go into an old farm shed and watch the rushes. The film was golden. Literally: through the lens of cinematographer Andrew Lesnie everything looked as if it had been dipped in honey and nostalgia. In my down time I would listen to the reassuring prattle of the chickens and the geese and the ducks, and the gentle lowing of the cattle. I felt like I was in a nativity play.

*Babe* also presented me with my first real acting challenge—the scene at the end of the film when a tearful Mrs Hoggett is finally won over. I was nervous but Chris made no fuss, he was gentle and, best of all, he had faith in me. In a strange way my recent break-up helped: there were tears just below the surface. Years later George Miller told me it was his favourite scene in the film.

After the film wrapped, Chris encouraged me to meet up with him in Hollywood. Johnny Friedkin, the unit publicist, came and picked me up at the airport. Johnny was old-school Hollywood. Over the years he'd worked on some of my favourite films—*Star Wars, Alien, Blade Runner* and all of Mel Brooks' movies. He was a little old New York Jew who once famously described Golden Globe voters as 'people who would cross the Alps for a hot dog'. We clicked.

Apart from the transit lounge at LAX when I was five I had never set foot in Los Angeles. But as we drove along the freeway past low-rise buildings and car yards and miles of bunting I had a sinking sense of déjà vu.

'Oh my God,' I told Johnny, 'this looks exactly like a giant Croydon.' I couldn't get over it. I had come all this way. I had finally reached the city of my fervid childhood dreams, only to discover I was back in the place I had run away from all those years ago—fucking Croydon.

The press conference went well, and so I decided to make a return trip with my agent at the time, Hilary Linstead, and my friend and fellow actor Jane Borghesi. Hilary had arranged a bunch of what are called 'go sees' with the major Hollywood agencies.

We went to CAA and UTA and William Morris and you name

it. I felt intimidated. The woman at CAA was polite but clear. 'You do realise that it's the pig's film?'

I met all sorts. There were men with hairpieces and women whose faces had the same extruded smoothness as outdoor furniture. Unlike Australians, the Americans made great efforts to pronounce my name properly. In fact they overcompensated, calling me Margdar. I felt like a Transylvanian extra in a vampire pic.

We went to the office of one weary studio executive. She had strings of letters behind her name, and she was over it. 'Why do you want to come here?'

'Well, I'm a biggish fish in a smallish pond back home and...'

'And what's so wrong with that? You want my advice? Stay home and be a big happy fish in Australia.'

Two very friendly guys at another agency had watched my tape. They said how funny I was but the conversation didn't go anywhere. They gave me tips about good places to eat and sights to see, gestures of hospitality offered smoothly, but there was something unnerving about it all. One of the guys laughed mirthlessly every time I said something funny, like a replicant who had learned the social cues but had no inner experience of actual humour. I couldn't tell if they wanted to represent me or not. The pleasantries abruptly stopped and they turned to Hilary.

'We would like to talk to you,' the mirthless guy said, 'if that's OK?'

'Of course.'

They turned back to me. 'Margdar, we're just going to talk boring business if you want to wait outside—'

'No,' Hil interrupted. 'Mags can stay.'

They swivelled their backs to me and, like two sharks moving in on their prey, formed their chairs into a phalanx pointed at Hilary. She sat back on the couch like the elder stateswoman she was, and it began. I still didn't quite understand what was going on.

They catalogued their successes, their clients, their goal to be the best agency in Hollywood. Finally it dawned on me that this was a sales pitch, the kind of flagrant self-promotion that simply wouldn't work in self-deprecating Australia. And then they moved in for the kill. 'So. If any of your clients are unhappy with their current US representation…'

Poaching. That was the point of this whole charade. Hilary had a very impressive list of Aussie directors and these guys wanted in. I was not their objective.

Hilary, a class act and a dab old hand, deflected them in a way that was so polite they weren't even sure if they'd been cold-shouldered. As we rode down in the elevator she turned to me. 'So?'

'Wow! That was something!'

'Yes. I wanted you to see that.'

This was the Hollywood I had heard of: the venal, shameless, ruthless, shark pool. It spooked me. I could already feel the tug on that part of my nature that is not guided by my better angels. I could feel that this town—more than any other—might make me mean and calculating. Once again I was ambivalent about success.

We needed to change our plan. We decided my strength was as a comedian. We needed to get to the funny people's agents. The kind of people who represented *Saturday Night Live* alumni. We arranged a meeting with one of the top casting directors. He was polite but perfunctory. We left him a copy of my show reel and went off to do more meetings and some shopping on Rodeo Drive. By the time we got back to the hotel that afternoon there was a message. It was from the casting director. We played it back. This is, word for word, what it said. I know because we replayed it about twenty times.

'Hey, Margdar, it's John. I watched your show reel…and it is… absolutely…hilarious.'

Encouraging. But the tone conveyed nothing. It was as if it was being read by an automaton. It reminded me of the time I went to a try-hard restaurant with friends and we were served ice-cream that had no flavour. It was the weirdest sensation: texture but no taste.

Was this a brush off? Or did he like my stuff? We analysed every word and every pause until it became increasingly absurd and soon we were gasping with laughter. It was a vivid illustration of two cultures separated by a common language.

It turned out the casting director's endorsement was real. He had arranged for me to go to one of the most sought-after management companies in Hollywood—Brillstein-Grey—which was how we ended up at the office of Bernie Brillstein.

Bernie Brillstein was the man who started *Saturday Night Live*, who nurtured the careers of John Belushi, Dan Aykroyd and Mike Myers and who ushered in the new era of rock'n'roll comedians. He helped make comedy dangerous, sexy and cool. The next day we arrived in the lobby of the building that housed his offices. I liked him immediately. He reminded me of some of the impresarios I had worked with in Melbourne.

I was assigned a manager who was already handling some of the most famous comedians in the world. People whose work I loved and felt a kind of kinship with. I was beside myself. There was discussion about building a show around me. But it would mean relocating to LA for six years.

'And of course,' he said, 'there is always *Saturday Night Live*.'

A couple of days later they took me to lunch at the Ivy. It was low key, discreet. There are cooler places to eat but being taken to the Ivy means you are being courted.

My new manager could spot the signs of power and wealth at fifty paces. An ordinary-looking man in a tight-fitting suit entered. Then another.

'Watch this,' the manager said.

Moments later a group of about eight women came in and sat down at a table in the middle of the room. They seemed similarly un-noteworthy, just a bunch of frosted blonde ladies who lunch.

'See that woman there?'

'Yes.'

'She is just about the richest woman in the world. She and her husband throw these unbelievable Christmas parties.'

He went on to explain the extent of her wealth. The parties sounded like something Gatsby would throw, only more tasteful: waiters glided past bearing buckets of Beluga caviar to a roll-call of Hollywood royalty; bevies of US presidents—past, present and future—presented themselves like eager starlets; a valet would take your car and when you collected it in the wee hours of the morning there, spread across the back seat, would be crisp copies of the morning's newspapers and an array of pastries for your breakfast. This woman and her husband were major philanthropists, legendary for their generosity, capable of changing national destinies and saving civilisations. I felt a strange pang of envy. What a safe harbour, I thought, sheltered from all the cruel winds of life. I longed to dock my little boat in such a place.

'And these guys,' he pointed at the men in suits, 'are her security. Her son was kidnapped.'

In an instant envy turned to pity. I looked at her. She had a kind face. No one is safe, I thought, no matter how rich or how famous. Warsaw is everywhere and we are fools to think otherwise.

'So, anyway, Margdar…'

I snapped out of my reverie. *So, anyway* followed by the use of one's name always signals the commencement of proceedings.

'We think you have the makings of a major network star.'

Silence. He was waiting for my response.

I laughed. Right in the gift horse's mouth. Like a clueless schoolgirl

I sat there giggling, an idiotic, frightened snigger. I couldn't stop myself. It went on, way past mildly awkward. He was very gracious about it. Gracious but baffled. God knows, I was baffled too. And embarrassed.

The twin pillars of my existence—work and sexuality—were once again at odds. I could not see how I could be true to both selves. But how can you be true to a moving target? I was an evolving flux. The only way to convey the impossibility of the whole thing was with this inane snickering.

Eventually I stopped and they moved on. The plan was to build a show around me and then move me across into movies. Several big-name stars had recently made the shift. But none of them was doing it with the baggage I carried. My head swam. I looked at the billionaire lady and her bodyguards. And I knew. This was my Everest. I was attempting to climb Everest without oxygen and with one arm tied behind my back. I wanted to run out of the room.

Although this took place only twenty years ago the world has shrunk exponentially since. Nowadays you can't watch a US TV show without hearing a faint Aussie twang from at least one of the actors. Back then there were Mel and Nicole and that was it.

I was going to get my chance to scale the loftiest peak in the acting world. I would touch the sky and the sun. I would soar, like Zarathustra. But I felt a tug and then a drag and it all came crashing down.

'What do I do about the gay thing?'

In passing my manager mentioned an up-and-coming young comedian who had her own show—Ellen de Generes. It was an open secret that she was gay. 'Nobody cares,' he said. But this didn't reassure me. And sure enough, in 1997, when she came out, she was cast into the showbiz wilderness for three years.

I felt like someone about to abseil off a cliff with a harness that doesn't fit. Almost involuntarily, I began to back away. I prevaricated so long that eventually Hollywood went and knocked on the door of someone who knew what they wanted. And my timid dream of being a big Hollywood star came to an abrupt end.

After I got back home to Melbourne the phone rang. Dad.

'Maggie, I thought I might drop over.'

'Sure. Is Mum coming?'

'No. Just me.'

This was highly unusual. Mum hates to miss out. I had rarely spent time alone with Dad since leaving home.

He drove to my house. I made a cup of tea and we sat up at the kitchen bench. I loved this time together, just the two of us. It reminded me of those early mornings before school when Dad and I would sit in companionable silence like a couple of old cats.

'So. Why did Mum send you?'

'She didn't.'

'Oh.' I was quite thrown by this. Dad had gone off script.

'I wanted to come.'

This had never happened before. Ever. I handed him his milky 'English tea'. The same as his mother drank.

'Have you got a bickie, love?'

'Sure.' I grabbed a packet of shortbreads from the cupboard.

He dunked his biscuit. He always dunked. We chatted for a bit. Then he said, 'What is it, Maggie? What is wrong?'

'What?' I was flustered by his candour and tenderness. 'Nothing. There's nothing wrong.'

'Yes, there is. Something is holding you back. What is it? What are you afraid of?'

I was shocked. He never spoke to me in such a personal, direct way. He had always been very respectful of my privacy. He and Mum both had. I didn't know that he was capable of such…psychological delicacy. Since I was a little kid I had rarely spent time alone with him. It was quite a shock to discover that he had been paying attention. And that he cared in a tender way. It struck me that he would have been a fabulous doctor.

As much as anything I was shocked by the accuracy of his diagnosis. But how to tell him what I really feared—that I would be outed and that my world would end? And something even deeper. That Hollywood had given me a glimpse of something hard in myself I didn't care to see.

'Nothing, Dad. I'm fine.' Urgent tears pressed up against my eyeballs. He must have been able to see them, surely. He was too discreet to say.

'Maggie, you have nothing to fear. You are capable of doing whatever you put your mind to.'

I wondered what he would have been like, what *we* would have been like—if I had seen this side of him sooner. I didn't even begin to know how to tell him what was wrong with me. For a moment the gulf between us had narrowed. But I shook my head and smiled; I said nothing. I still I didn't have the words to reach him. And soon, of course, we settled back into our habitual interaction. And it was as though this moment had never been.

You have to be strong to survive fame. Fame never saved anyone. More than anything Hollywood sat directly on the fault line of all my insecurities. I suspect it would not have been a good idea for someone like me, with so many cracks and fissures, to live in an earthquake zone. I need solid earth beneath my feet. Some small, quiet, healthy part of me knew that if I stayed in Hollywood things would not go well for me. The gulf between my real self and my false self would grow ever wider.

And this little Pinocchio wanted to be a real girl.

# AN OUTING

I have ridden many waves of fame and I know that no one is ever going to give you sympathy for being famous. The peaks are overwhelming. You feel invincible, full to the brim of the wonderfulness that is you. And at the exact same moment you feel as hollow as a Hallowe'en pumpkin. Then the inevitable troughs confirm every fear you ever had about yourself. You are a talentless fraud, a publicity puppet who will never work again.

I was never interested in celebrity. The red carpet has always been a necessary evil for me. I scrub up all right, but ultimately I hate wearing uncomfortable clothes. High heels make my bones ache all the way up to my skull; the Sisyphean task of putting on make-up only to have to take it all off again a few hours later seems the apogee of pointlessness.

It started innocently, as a favour. A prominent women's magazine asked if I would do an exclusive. I was extremely busy and really didn't want to do it. I hated interviews, for obvious reasons. But the editor pushed, and I was assured it would be fun and easy, and favourable. I agreed.

The day of the interview I had a hangover on top of the flu so my wits were not too sharp. But since I was doing this as a favour I felt safe; I wasn't going to be ambushed. I met the journalist at a restaurant. Even before we had exchanged greetings she slid an expensive bottle of wine across at me. 'Sorry, I've already started without you. This is delicious.' She smiled. We ordered and throughout the meal she kept refilling my glass. I decided to stop drinking. The interview wasn't going well. I began to feel uneasy and I clammed up.

Exasperated, she decided to take a new tack.

'OK. I'm going to say a word and I want you to say the first word that comes into your head.' She paused for effect. 'What is the first word,' she asked, 'that comes into your mind when I say the word "fear"?'

The word that sprang into my mind was *you*. But I decided to play possum. I hemmed and hawed like a hayseed until she changed tack.

'OK. How do you feel about your fame? People recognising you in the street…' She levelled a stare at me. 'The rumours…'

I had never known what I would say if I was asked point blank. I was confident I would make a mess of it. I *did* know that I would not lie; beyond that was anyone's guess. But now it came to me. I knew exactly the right answer.

'I don't care what people say. You can't control people. They can say whatever they like about me.' I shrugged. 'I don't care.'

She raised a sceptical eyebrow. 'Really? Because there are…' she paused. 'Rumours.'

'Oh. Really?'

'Yes.' She was waiting for me to ask what the rumours were. She couldn't contain herself any longer. 'One of the rumours is that you are…homosexual.'

She lingered over that last word, pronouncing it with the short 'o' as in homily. She was creepier than a Catholic sex educator.

To my astonishment, I was overcome by a strange sang froid that I didn't even know I possessed. I was, for the only time in my life, cool. 'Like I said, I don't care.'

She scoffed, tilted her head back and laughed. Then, like a tank taking aim, she lowered her gaze. 'You really don't care?'

I met her eyes. An even deeper calm came over me. 'No.' I smiled. 'I really don't care. And on that note—I have to go.'

I walked out. I'd surprised myself. I *meant* it. In my heart I did not care.

Later that night I cared, though. A lot. I had never understood until then why people in films banged their heads against walls in dramatic moments. But that night the emotional pain was so extreme I felt as though I was dying and giving birth to myself at the same time. I slid down the wall of my hallway gasping and weeping—and I banged my head against the wall. I pounded my skull with my clenched fist.

'You idiot! You complete fucking idiot!'

Barb was away. I rang Chris and explained what had happened.

'I am gonna have to tell Mum and Dad. And I was wondering if you could be there with me?'

In those days Chris sported a fuzzy ZZ Top beard that extended down his belly to his Harley Davidson belt buckle, and a long thin plait of hair that dangled down his back. He was not a bikie; my brother is his own man. He just loved, and still does love, anything that involves pistons and oil.

He didn't hesitate. 'I'm there for you. If they want to wear you like a bright shiny coat then they've got to be there for you in the bad times as well. If they attack you, I'll defend you.'

So this was it. Like it or not, I was coming out. I had learned from the experience of another friend. He had come out to his parents after a casual homophobic remark made by his father over dinner; after which it all went rapidly downhill. The father felt cornered into being a bigot and so became defensive, which in turn made the son even more adversarial. I wanted my parents to have the opportunity to be their best selves. I didn't want to back-foot them. We were not the kind of family that talks about sex. I had had years to come to terms with my sexuality—and God knows, *I* was still struggling. It was only fair to give them the same chance.

My parents had made the usual unthinking anti-gay remarks over the years. Every time Mardi Gras was on TV Dad would say, 'I don't care what they do as long as they don't try and shove it down my throat!' He had no idea of the impact of such harmless little comments, how they accumulated, like the dots in a pointillist painting, forming an unmistakable impression. What I didn't know was how deep they went. I was about to find out, and I was afraid because it is a nasty thing to be on the receiving end of someone's disgust. Unless you are thoroughly self-reliant it is difficult to be unaffected. The more you care about them, the worse it is. And disgust is an emotion that even well-meaning people sometimes have no control over.

Mine was probably the last generation in Australia for whom the idea of widespread public support for homosexuals was unimaginable. It is not so long ago that gays were subjected to aversion therapy— which is to say electric shocks to the genitals. Which is to say torture. The best we could hope for was not getting beaten up, being grudgingly tolerated and allowed to form gay ghettos in neighbourhoods where the rent was low and the crime rate high. We were inured to the meagre array of career prospects. Theatre, hairdressing and interior design for the guys. Stage management, security companies and social work for the women. Intangible prejudice pervaded everything. Talents withered. People led double lives and lived in terror of blackmailers.

The victimisation was one thing. The propaganda was almost

worse. We were blamed for the transience of our relationships, the illnesses we contracted, for pestilence, misfortune and bad weather. And, perhaps most damaging of all, we were told that we were predatory. That our sexual desires were not only unnatural but that we were child abusers. Even before AIDS we were seen as a contagious illness. In a supreme irony, proselytising Christian missionaries accused *us* of recruiting.

Lesbian characters in films or books were creepy, psychotic, jealous, scheming, neurotic, humourless, bitter, barren. Lesbian characters died—poor old Banford in D. H. Lawrence's *The Fox* gets killed by a falling tree; in *The Children's Hour* Shirley MacLaine hangs herself in shame; June Buckridge gets her 'just desserts' in *The Killing of Sister George*.

The dream of a long gay life filled with love was entirely absent from the culture we consumed. And worst of all, many of us internalised this bullshit. We took the loathing into ourselves. Some of us, God help us, believed it to be true. Like a greedy parasite this self-hatred attached itself to every other doubt and fear we had about ourselves, amplifying it, expanding it, giving it power. Until we were colonised by our own contempt for ourselves.

A lucky few escaped this scourge. Some, for whatever reason, never succumbed: for them being gay was not an issue. I wasn't one of the lucky few.

Coming out. It sounds like making your debut. But for gay people there was no party, no celebration, no welcoming into the bosom of our family and our community. We came out and then waited for the brickbats. We came out not knowing if, at the end of it, we would still *have* a family, a community. Some people were convinced that it would kill their parents. Some of my friends have been with their partners for twenty years and more, and their parents *still* don't know they are lovers.

That constriction, that inability to be open with the people we love more than anything in the world, corrodes the soul. My generation of gay people are sometimes like the walking wounded. As teenagers, closeted and terrified, most of us never learned to weather the ups and downs of dating. I for one am a classic case of arrested sexual development.

And the crucial difference between Lesbian Gay Transgender Bi-Sexual Intersex and Questioning people and other minorities is this: in every other minority group the family shares the minority status. In fact it is often something that unites them. But gay people are a minority *within* the family. A minority of one. It means, among many things, that gay children cannot draw on the collective family wisdom about how to deal with their minority status. No one else in the family has experienced what the gay child is going through. Worse still: all through our growing up, from the instant we realise we are gay, we live with the gnawing fear that our parents' love could turn to hatred in an instant.

So there we were. My parents were about to learn that I was not who they thought I was.

It was a Sunday night. Mum and Dad sat in their his and hers Jason recliners watching television. I was on the couch, Chris was on a stool behind the breakfast bar. Minutes ticked by. I felt acutely aware of the fact that this was one of those moments in my life that would change me forever. It felt like some sort of idiotic dare I had made with myself. One word would set in motion an unstoppable chain of events. I remembered the nervous tic I had as a kid, feeling compelled to make a noise for fear that if I didn't I would never be sure that I could. I thought: *I could stop this. I could stop the whole stupid thing. I don't have to do this.* I didn't have butterflies in my stomach—I had Bogong moths.

'Well, this is an unusual time for a visit.' Mum's piping voice chirped over the racket of the TV, which was adjusted to the right volume for Dad's hearing aid. Which is to say about a hundred decibels. 'Are you here for a reason?'

Behind the breakfast bar Chris eyeballed me over the rim of his mug of tea.

If I do it I will still have my brother and sister, I thought. At least I will have them.

I had a choice. I didn't have to risk knowing that their love for me was conditional. That they could only love me if I was straight.

And then I jumped. I didn't know if I was falling or flying.

'Can we turn off the TV? I'd like to chat to you about something.'

Mum perked up. 'Och, yes! We *love* to chat! Peter, turn the telly off.' She turned to me. She actually rubbed her hands together with glee. 'So! What do you want to talk about?'

And as if by magic the right words came to me.

'Well, about the fact that I'm thirty-two and there's never really been any mention of a boyfriend.'

Nothing terrible happened. I waited. Mum was blinking and thinking. Dad rocked in his chair.

'Oh, aye. Eh heh.' Mum leaned in. 'What exactly are we talking about?'

'Well...I guess we're talking about my sexuality.'

Dad rocked back in his recliner. 'Uh huh.'

Mum leaned closer. 'Oh, aye.' She leaned even closer. 'Which is?'

I wasn't quite prepared to say gay and there was no way I was going to say lesbian; there was plenty of time for the L word. Maybe in twenty years or so.

'Well, let's just say I'm not straight.'

Mum's head spun round to Chris. 'Do you know about this?'

'Course I bloody do! I've known for bloody years!' He winked at me.

Mum and Dad rocked on their recliners a while longer. It was terribly silent.

'Well, as far as I'm concerned,' Dad said at last, 'that doesn't change anything. You're my daughter and I love you.'

'Aye. Aye. We love you, hen.'

Dad put his hands up in a position of surrender. 'I thought so. I suspected.'

'Well, I didn't.'

'Really?' I'd had an inkling my mother knew.

'No! Well, maybe a wee bit. I just thought you were, you know, a career girl.' Her brow furrowed. 'Can I ask, why do you think you are…you know…what should I call you? Is "gay" the right word?'

'Gay is fine. No one knows why some people are gay, Mum.' I quickly added: 'But it's nothing you did or didn't do.'

They both gave sighs of relief.

'You know,' I continued, 'they think it may be genetic or…'

Dad leapt in. 'No one on my side of the family…'

'Oh right! So it's my fault is it?'

I slipped into referee mode. 'It's not about fault.'

Mum was still fretting about some detail. 'I just have to ask, have you been…*influenced*? I mean…are you sure?'

'Oh for Christ's sake,' Chris piped up from behind the breakfast bar. 'She's *thirty-two*! Yes! She's bloody sure!'

Mum flung herself back in her chair and threw her arms about theatrically. 'Oh OK. I just, you know, I'm the mother. It's my job to ask these questions.' She gave me a look of intense, kindly curiosity. 'Well, there are an awful lot of you about these days, aren't there? There seem to be more and more. Why do you think that is?' She stopped herself abruptly, appalled that she might be making a gaffe. 'Oh!' She leaned over and patted my knee tenderly. 'I'm so sorry, I hope that's not rude to you, I didn't mean to be rude.'

'Don't worry, Mum. It's totally fine.'

Then Dad said, 'Well, I wouldn't be being honest if I didn't say I am disappointed.'

That smarted. I had always thought Mum would struggle, she had led a much more sheltered life than Dad. He was worldly, had travelled; he'd had gay friends during the war.

He fumbled for an explanation. 'It's just—I wanted to give you away at your wedding. I wanted grandkids.'

'Well, you know, Dad, I still might have kids. Gay friends of mine have kids.'

We both knew the marriage thing was an impossible dream. And we both knew it wasn't about the grandkids.

But whatever his misgivings were he didn't dwell on them and he never let them come between us. As I was about to leave they both put their arms around me. 'We love you,' they said.

And we all bawled. The overwhelming emotion I felt, aside from love and gratitude, was shame. I had underestimated them. And as we stood there in the TV room, clumped together crying and hugging, I thought, 'How little we are. We are such little people.'

A couple of days later Mum rang me, all teary and querulous. The shock had worn off and the jitters had got to her.

'It's just that I worry, you know. I'm your mother. I have to worry.'

'I know, Mum. But the world is changing.'

'I'm not so sure, hen,' she said wearily, 'I wish it was but I'm not so sure. So. Do you have a girlfriend?'

'Not at the moment, no.'

'Well, what you need is someone classy like yourself.' She waited a beat. 'And for God's sake don't go in that bloody Mardi Gras!'

It's not just in comedy that timing is everything. I had come out at the right time, when we were all ready.

And then I waited for the magazine to hit the newsstands and my life to end. It didn't. The article was published. It didn't out me. I suspected it was only a matter of time. But in the meantime I had been given a great gift—my parents' unconditional love. My only regret was that I had ever had to doubt it.

# BIG GIRL'S BLOUSE

If not for my bruised heart I might never have created my most popular character ever—the lovelorn Sharon Strzelecki from *Kath and Kim*. After I broke up with the nurse I wanted to get fit and meet more lesbians. My (straight) friend Kaz Cooke was a member of a women's baseball team and kept telling me how much fun it was, so I joined up.

I had no idea. The camaraderie, the beers after the game, the nights around the TV watching games beamed in from the States, the analysing of stats and angles. But what I loved best was the selflessness of it. It wasn't the star players who impressed me. It was the volunteers. The indefatigable captains and little-league coaches who, without fail, would ring around every Friday to make sure there was a team for the next day. Who brought the equipment and collected fees and made up the shortfall out of their own pockets. I had experienced something akin to this in the theatre. But this was different. This wasn't work. It was sport. And it was everything that tennis isn't.

Sharon is the part of me that never got to play team sport.

She had her humble beginnings in *Big Girl's Blouse.* Late in 1994 Steve Vizard and Andrew Knight, the executive producers of *Fast Forward,* announced that they were going to do a series of one-hour specials. Gina, Jane and I were tired of scrambling for roles. We were keen to flex our creative muscles. We wanted one of those specials. We sat in our 'office'—my bright orange VW beetle—smoking and conspiring and working up the balls. Then we went up to Steve's office on the third floor of the Seven Network building and made our demand. If they wanted us for any of the other specials they would have to give us one of our own. Slightly reluctantly, Steve and Andrew agreed…*if* we could produce some scripts.

We went back to Gina's place and bounced off the walls, screaming and shrieking with excitement and terror. We suspected that they didn't think we could deliver. *We* didn't think we could deliver. And that brought out the girlie swot in us. So every day from nine to five we would sit around one another's kitchen tables because we had no other office, drinking strong coffee and writing. We had lots of laughs—we always do—but it was also hard work, slaving away down the comedy mines. But it was exciting because we were also our own masters.

To begin with the writing was terrible. We couldn't find our way in. The history of comedy had all been from the male perspective. Who were our role models? Apart from Phyllis Diller, Lucille Ball and Hattie Jacques I couldn't think of any. The boys could rely on tried-and-true comedy tropes. They could build on pre-existing structures—the work of Monty Python, Lenny Bruce, Richard Pryor. The list goes on and on. All great art movements are a reaction to what has gone before. That is what gives them energy and impetus.

We faced a void. We had to answer primary questions. What constitutes a genuine female voice? What did we want to say? There were lots of routines around at the time about specifically female issues—menstruation, tampons, pregnancy, boy trouble. We found all of that boring. We wanted to create a show that was as genderless as possible, that parodied and played with notions of femininity. But mostly, in truth, we just did what made us laugh.

There were also some widely held prejudices we had to overcome. When a friend of mine asked a male colleague if he found women funny, he sucked his teeth for a while and finally had to admit, 'Not really, no.' He was not Robinson Crusoe. I don't think this sentiment would fly now, in the wake of *Bridesmaids* and Tina Fey and Amy Poehler and *Absolutely Fabulous* and need I go on? But there is a simple explanation for why men haven't found women funny. It's because men only ever experience women in relation to men: they never get to see what women are like with one another. Shows like ours started to let men in on the joke.

Several weeks later we turned up at Steve's office again. He was heading overseas and had forgotten about our meeting; we only just managed to catch him. We thwacked a massive wad of scripts on his desk, and he flinched. He had no choice now but to give us a show.

*Big Girl's Blouse* was the making of us. It was the moment when we nailed our comedy voice. We created dozens of new characters. And we really started to play with language and accents. We had a mutual friend who was famous for her malapropisms. We incorporated those into the mix. The 1960s Australia we had grown up in was a 'piss-elegant' place, full of people 'putting on the dog'. So any kind of pretension became a big target. This led to 'noice, different, unewsuel' and 'look at moiye'. We parodied 1960s grooviness and housewifely virtue with the Patty Stacker sketch. Jane and I debuted Thalia and Evelyn, two fashion tragics. We trotted out our party pieces in a parody of *Home and Away* with Jane doing her Joan Fontaine, Gina doing Bette Davis and me doing Katharine Hepburn. It was like comedy gymbaroo for grown-ups.

I finally got to vent my tennis frustration. There was a documentary series that was a big deal at the time. It was called *Labor in Power* and it was about the leadership tussle between Paul Keating and Bob Hawke. I thought it would be hilarious to film a sketch in the same portentous style but make the subject matter a leadership spill in midweek ladies tennis. The sketch became something of a cult hit.

There was the Playschool sketch in which Gina played a balls-to-the-wall producer of pre-school children's TV who threatens to impale Mr Squiggle and says 'fuck' all the time.

Another favourite was the Michael Douglas sketch in which we lampooned the inexplicable spate of films (like *Fatal Attraction*, for example) starring him as a target for celluloid stalkers.

The freedom to do what we pleased was exhilarating. It also allowed us to emerge from behind the mask of our characters. In between sketches we would retreat to our 'bedroom'. There we would make comments and do jokes as 'versions' of ourselves. I found myself increasingly drawn to the realness of being me.

But of course the best idea of all was Gina's. She had been watching a program about bridezillas and thought it would be fun to do a parody. I wasn't too enthusiastic at first but when she and Jane showed me what they had written I thought it was great. They wanted me to play a role and so I drew on what I knew—sport.

And that is how Sharon came to life, as a sport-obsessed optimist.

In her early incarnation Sharon had a child. That quickly disappeared when we realised there was more to be gained from her single status. But Sharon's true belief is in sport, not romance. 'The sooner you get over men and develop an interest in sport the happier you'll be.' It does not take Dr Freud to see where I got those lines from.

There were deliberate gay overtones as the title *Big Girl's Blouse* suggests. Left to our own devices we created a show that was steeped in camp. We did sketches about the gay Olympics, and the girls invented a community television show called *What a Drag*, in which they were two women playing two men playing two women. Close to home for me, we did a sketch on the tabloid outing of gay celebrities. Increasingly, I wanted my real self to be present in my work.

The *Big Girl's Blouse* special was really well received and so we decided to do a series. Although the show was sketch-based, the characters of Kath, Kim and Sharon would appear in every episode with a story arc and the segment would be called *Kim's Wedding*. It followed their story from engagement through to nuptials.

The series was a terrific opportunity for us to let our imaginations and enthusiasms run wild. Suddenly the shackles were off and we could do what we liked. But the series struggled in the early ratings. The network didn't know what to do with the show, and, in my opinion, they programmed badly. It premiered up against a new ratings juggernaut from the US—a show called *ER* that starred a young George Clooney and Julianna Margulies. It ran for fifteen years and was nominated for 124 Emmys. By the time our little show came on, half an hour into the hour-long slot, viewers were already ensconced with George and Julianna. Interestingly, though, our largest demographic was men between the ages of eighteen and thirty-nine. A tough nut to crack, so to speak. It seemed we were breaching the divide.

*Big Girl's Blouse* slowly fizzled, but not without developing a cult following. And it gave us some enduring gifts. First was the belief that female-centric comedy could work. It also created the magic dynamic between the characters. There is a golden rule in situation comedy—nobody learns anything, nobody changes. Unlike film, which depicts the hero's journey, situation comedy is like Sartre's play *No Exit*: three characters locked in a room together for all eternity. Our characters were trapped not by a closed door but by their dysfunction. They formed, in psychological terms, a perfect narcissistic triangle. Kim was the narcissist, Sharon the co-dependent enabler and Kath the slightly vain, hapless mother who had created the monster. They were harbingers of what twenty-first century society, with its selfies and socially mediated neediness, was about to become. This would not be the last we saw of Kath and Kim. Or Sharon.

# HOME MOVIES

In 1997 I bought a camcorder, a small, sleek, sexy chrome thing that snuggled neatly into the palm of my hand. I thought I would use it to film little sketches and characters. And vaguely, off to the side of conscious awareness, I had a plan to film my father. I could sense he had a good story to tell, the way an angler can tell the size of a fish on the line. But something always held me back. Squeamishness? Fear?

I am, as we know, a ditherer. I know all too well the perils of action. *Aktion.* What can happen if you make the wrong decision. The corrosive power of regret. I listened—in our lounge room, at parties, at picnics, at funerals and whenever they were gathered together—to the old Poles, ruminating obsessively. Underneath it all the same terrible question swam ceaselessly like a shark. Had they done the right thing? Were they good people?

Few of us can bear to be thought a bad person. Luckily not many of us are put to the test. We will go to great lengths to prove our innocence, our guiltlessness, our blameless virtue. We even repeat our crimes just to prove that they were justified. And my father? How did he view himself?

'No matter how he assessed himself, I think your father is a hero,' a friend protests. 'You mustn't forget—and what can never be calculated—was how many lives your father saved through his actions.'

But we can never know who or how many. So his goodness lies in the realm of the incalculable. What *was* calculable were his sins. All committed in the name of a good cause, because it was the right thing to do.

Despite the fact he was on the right side, I don't think my father truly believed he was a good man. In his youth, he told me, he had no real understanding of mortality or moral complexity. After the war, as he matured, the absolute conviction of youth gave way to doubt. And then, when it was too late, a sharp needle of awareness punctured his denial. He had a terrible realisation: he could never undo what had been done.

My mother told me how, in the early years of their marriage, he would weep and beat his breast and wail, 'I am so guilty, I am so guilty!'

She would try to stop him. 'Peter,' she pleaded, 'for God's sake, please don't.'

No one understood him. Isolated from his friends, his family, his unit; separated by language and history—and seeing the pointlessness of his efforts—he did the only thing he could. He put it in a room marked 'the past' and then shut the door on it all. He shed his Polish skin and set about becoming a little Englishman. He cobbled together a kind of peace with what he had done. And he clamped down tight on all feeling.

My father's cool was not just an act. Over time he *became* his defence. Whenever he spoke about the war his language was stylised and removed. It was like listening to a cheap hood in a thirties movie.

He told me that the word for a Jew in hiding was a cat. A collaborator was a canary because they 'sang' to the Gestapo. Killing someone was 'rotting' them. His stories of the war were frozen in a no-man's-land between boyhood and manhood. Most disconcertingly, he would often talk of how he'd 'enjoyed the war', how he was the 'original war lover'.

Mum's friend Marie, who had lived through her own hard war in Holland, would shake her head. 'I don't know how Peter can say he enjoyed the war. I just don't know how he can say that.'

I didn't know either. Growing up I had glimpsed his capacity for cold-bloodedness. I was never afraid of my father but I began to wonder how much I was the child of his darkness as well as his light. It wasn't what my father did or said or told me. It was what he felt. At times it emanated from him like a force field. I was irradiated with his guilt. Whatever it was he had done I had to make my own peace with it.

I had always been the family bowerbird, scouring the house for old stuff no one else wanted, like Humpty Dumpty, trying to put back together the pieces of our broken family. Cravats and signet rings. A silver cigarette case. Now I had become the collector of stories. And perhaps, since I'd come out, there were fewer walls between me and my father. Like all children, I wanted to know who he really was. I was no longer a child. I was thirty-six. I was old enough to know the rest of it. Or so I thought.

My father was a man of many opinions: about history, politics, people. Dinners in our family were not the grim, silent ordeals they were in some of my friends' families. They were lively, vivacious free-for-alls. My father was no stern patriarch, he was chatty and expansive. But then suddenly he would clam up. 'No. You do not ask about such things. You do not talk about them.'

It was like swimming in a warm river and then hitting an icy cold patch. Through the fog you would glimpse the outline, the shores of madness. And somewhere along the way I began to harbour a sickening and irrational suspicion—had my father colluded with the Nazis? Did that explain his nauseating guilt? His apparent contempt for the little Jewish boy he sometimes mentioned? All the other old Poles loved to reminisce. But not my father. He had no patience for the talk. He was a man of action. Tennis, mowing the lawn, dancing. In the reverberating suburban silence I stumbled towards my own ghastly conclusions. Was he, in fact, a collaborator?

I wanted to know; I didn't want to know. Without realising it I plotted a course somewhere between the two. My father, unable to get any further with his own attempts at a reckoning, had simply closed the door on the past. And now I was about to open that door.

One day I approached him as he was doing the dishes. 'If it's OK with you I would like to get your story down on film, as a record.'

'Why?'

'Because I want to write a book about all this and I don't trust my memory. It's important I get all of the details right.'

He considered my proposal. 'All right.'

A few years ago I had the films transferred to an external hard drive. Today, as I plug it into my laptop, Mum and Dad's lounge room flickers onto the screen.

Dad and I are both in shot, sitting side by side at the formal mahogany dining table. Operating the camera is my beautiful friend Miche—one of the least judgmental people I know. I knew that when the truth came out I could trust her. Dad looks reassuringly suburban in a busily patterned crew-neck jumper from Kmart and oversized glasses. Still, on screen my breathing judders like a braking juggernaut. I sigh constantly, struggling to get air into my fear-constricted chest. I was still smoking in those days; I light up, taking a shallow breath. Mum brings in marzipan finger cakes and coffee. Judging by the light it is early afternoon.

Just before Miche began filming my father waved his finger at me. 'I will talk about this once. And then I will never speak of it again.'

And so he started. He talked for six hours about his life in Warsaw more than half a century earlier. Time twisted and turned and performed its magic trick and yet again I had the sensation of meeting my father for the first time. He was a strange liminal creature, half old, half young. He dragged out the atlas and the huge magnifying glass he and Mum would use for reading the paper when they couldn't find their glasses. He pored over the map, remembering names and places with quite shocking accuracy.

I wanted the narrative to be neat and chronological. I wanted to know what it felt like as it all unfolded. So I started at the beginning.

'What happened,' I ask, 'when the Germans entered Warsaw?'

He smiles cheekily. 'The first German I ever met slapped my face.'

'What?'

'There were three German chaps. They had a motorcycle with a sidecar. And I was standing on the street. And one of the Germans went'—he demonstrates, beckoning with his finger—'and he asked me directions. I knew enough German to know what they were asking me and I said, "*Ich weiss nicht*." And he looked at me and my eyes, it must have been in my eyes, he saw that I was lying. And he slapped my face. So I said to myself, "You son of a bitch! I will never forgive you for that!"

'After a while so-called normal life resumed. There was school, there was soccer. People started to rebuild, using old bricks. But then they really started to put the screws on. In 1940 the Ghetto was declared and people had to move again. You had to find yourself a place to exchange with the Jews. There were *Volksdeutsche* everywhere. Ethnic Germans who would sign up for extra rations—butter, bread, that sort of nonsense. They used to go to a place we called the Roundhouse, the round church for the Protestants and Anglicans. They were recruiting there.'

'When did the resistance begin?' I ask.

'It was started immediately by ex-army officers. They knew even before the collapse of the campaign that they were going to lose so they hid caches of weapons in the forest outside Warsaw. I joined at the beginning of '41.' He casts his mind back, catching the memory, hauling it in. 'I had a few friends and, umm, I organised them in a little group.'

I realise this was the 'private army' of which he has often spoken.

'And with that group I went from one place to another. For a while we were with what they used to call the Grey Ranks—old men and boy scouts. We were given "small diversions". With chalk you would draw the Fighting Poland symbol on the pavement. We used to go to the cinema—there was a saying, "Only swine go to the pictures during war" because at that time only German films were showing—and we used to let off stink bombs and all sorts of things. I saw a lot of films that way. And then, remember Pawiak? That prison?'

'Yes.'

'Well, I used to go there and write, "We will revenge Pawiak." But I tell you what, standing at night with only half an hour to curfew and writing on the wall…' He shakes his head. 'Scary. I always carried a gun. But I was lucky. I was maybe luckier than anybody I know. Because I wasn't all that heroic either. I was just stupid.'

He stares straight ahead, as if stunned by his own idiocy. 'After all, what is heroism? What is cowardice? I wasn't afraid. I wouldn't consider myself a hero.'

'You were an idiot,' Mum says, listening in.

'Do you think you weren't afraid because you were so young?' I ask. 'And didn't really know?'

'Well, there are not many things I am afraid of now.' He laughs. 'Apart from crocodiles.'

'Tell me about baptising Jews.'

'We got the birth certificates and all the necessary papers for them, filled them in, blah blah blah.'

'Where did you get those from?'

'Oh, we had people who were stealing them from Warsaw City Council. So the Jews had to pay, there was no way out. (Apart from Wacek, of course, we gave him everything for nothing.) Because you had to pay everybody: the one who stole, the one who forged. And then we had to think about the names of priests—preferably those that died in concentration camps and no longer existed—to sign the certificate so there would be no comeback.'

One of Dad's pals in his private army was caught by the Gestapo. He was given a beating and then revealed the name of Dad's partner in crime, Tomasz. 'Tomasz was interrogated but he never gave my name, so I was lucky again, you see. So Tomasz was a real friend.'

'And he was what age? Fifteen or sixteen?'

'Yes. We were all the same age. We all went to school together. I always said, if the Germans came to our district and took all the kids between fifteen and twenty and shot them they would probably make one or two mistakes. Otherwise we were all guilty.'

'Did your parents know what you were doing?'

'No. At that time nobody knew. Because I wasn't with the unit yet. You didn't want to tell too many people what you were doing anyway because you never knew if they might be tortured. You never knew, whether it's your mother or father, if they could stand the beating. And you wouldn't know yourself whether you can stand it, so best not to know too much.'

When I watch the film back I remember how Mrs Pieczak described my father as the bravest of the brave. But my father did feel fear. Once,

I was reading through the few odd pages of his attempt at a memoir. I stumbled across something in Latin: *Nec Hercules contra plures*. It is an old Polish proverb: Even Hercules is afraid when confronted with too many enemies.

It wasn't death that terrified him. It was the constant threat of torture. Your self-worth was measured against your body's ability to withstand agony. Your pain threshold, the sensitivity of your skin and teeth. Your own safety relied on one thing—your loved ones' ability to withstand torture. In wartime loving people is dangerous.

On film we continue talking. 'Tell me about your private army before you joined the unit. What did you do in that group?'

'We used to go and disarm Germans, take the arms and sell them to the underground.'

'How did you disarm them?'

'Well you just…' He points his finger at my face like a pistol. 'Take the gun and…'

He is still in boy's own adventure mode. One minute he is talking about stink bombs and the next he is pointing a pretend gun in my face.

He has often told me that he was recruited into the unit because he had a special skill: 'I was good at getting guns.' So in a city where guns were at a premium, this was how they got them.

'Then I worked with the communists for a while. You see we were only young, you must understand, we were only fifteen or sixteen. Politically we were completely and utterly immature. So we drifted from one thing to another. Wherever there was the possibility of shooting Germans or doing some damage we were quite happy to do it for anybody.'

'So can you remember how you got your first gun?'

He stops. There is a long silence. Suddenly, the boy's own adventure has evaporated. He fiddles, fidgets, rubs his ears twice, gazes up at the heavens, covers his mouth with his hand. Without realising it I have blundered into the darkest part of the forest. His finger rubs his lips, as if it might be able to erase what he is about to say.

'I took it from a German woman. It was like a toy.'

'Was she a…soldier?'

'Oh, I knew her. She was *Volksdeutsche*.'

So she was ethnic German, but not a German citizen. They were called *Reichsdeutsche*.

Watching now, I remember how my mind was racing and I felt physically sick. I was beginning to understand what he was saying and I wanted to tell him to stop. Why didn't I? Was it shyness? Curiosity? Or a kind of dissociation: a feeble attempt to normalise a bizarre situation? There I was, sitting in a lounge room in suburban Melbourne listening to my father talk about killing people at point-blank range. (You can tell none of this from my face which remains a mask of impassivity. I had learnt the lesson well.)

His hand moves to the side of his face, shielding him from the gaze of the camera. He has switched into medical mode: objective, detailed, accurate.

'Little five millimetre calibre…' He is smiling, a strange, apologetic smile. His voice is steady but his hand is still covering his face.

'She lived not far from where I did, actually. I had it right to the bitter end. You see many of these *Volksdeutsche* we went to school with, and the first thing all these little shysters got was a gun. Most of them were a couple of years older than us. So they were little Nazis and the first thing they did was to get themselves enlisted in *Kripo* or the Jewish department, which means they were going and fishing out Jews.'

'Nasty work.'

'They all had guns so we used to take them from them. And if they recognised us…kinda…killed them.'

He looks at me sheepishly. It cannot be undone. I smile back.

What are we supposed to do in this situation?

'It was either them or us.' Now he is back to picking up crumbs from his plate—a fidgety sign that he is in control again. 'And of course the problem was that the underground didn't like it because you see if you shot a German...' He eyeballs me. 'There were repercussions. You see they used to shoot hostages.'

And suddenly I am terrified for his soul all over again. My father is bathed in blood and there are no rituals, no soothing waters to cleanse him. I understand now that this was where the guilt came from. Not from colluding with the bad side, but from what he had done in the name of good. It is clear he had never helped the Nazis, and I feel like a fool for even having entertained the notion. *Rozumiesz.*

There is something else I have to know.

'How old were you when you shot...killed your first person? Can you remember?'

He looks stricken. I panic. I wish I could snatch that question back. He rocks back in his chair, scratching his head. 'I don't know.' He laughs a hollow laugh. 'Can't remember.'

And it is gone. Whatever he is feeling slips away as though it had never been. If I did not have this filmed record, I would doubt that I had ever seen it.

'I had no compunction whatsoever. No qualms of conscience, nothing. I didn't get any buzz out of it. Nothing.' His hands are splayed like Christ the Redeemer. 'I said, "Right."' He points his finger at me like a gun again. '"Finish. It's either you or me."'

Outside the shadows are lengthening, turning mauve as the darkness closes in. His mood now is much more sombre. All the talking has taken a toll. Reckoning has crept in.

'I'm not interested in the past. I'm only interested in tomorrow, and the next day. After that...doesn't matter really.' He looks down the barrel of the camera. 'There are some things that I've done that

I'm not proud of. I'm not ashamed. No qualms of conscience. I sleep quite soundly. I don't think I ever harmed anybody who didn't deserve it, at that time. But, as I say, life was all black and white. No shades of grey—well, I couldn't see shades of grey. To me you were either a Pole or you were scum. And then as you grow older you realise that a lot of people were subjected to all sorts of pressures, all sorts of threats and all sorts of things that you think, well…'

He means torture. He squints into the distance as though he might find…what? Answers? Justice? Wisdom?

'How would I react?' he asks straight at the camera. 'You see you don't know your reaction until you are actually there, until you are confronted with the circumstances. There were people swearing what they wouldn't do. And when it came to the crunch…they bloody well did it.'

When we finished filming I took the five tapes of my father's confession and placed them in my bookshelf. It was another sixteen years before I could bear to look at them.

# DOGWOMAN

Shortly after filming Dad we made the second Babe film, *Babe: Pig in the City*. This film took much longer—fourteen months in total—and it crashed into the rest of my schedule. I was working with Gina and Jane again. We were developing a new show called *Something Stupid* and this time Marg Downey and Glenn Robbins had joined us, along with our old colleague from the Last Laugh days, Mark Neal.

This show contains some of my favourite sketches, including *Hostile Designs*—our attack on what we considered to be human unfriendly architectural trends—with me as Vincent Hostile and Jane playing my wife. There was a groovy new hotel in town that was so angular and inhospitable that several of our friends had injured themselves on the sharp furniture. So we made our characters design things like spherical coffee tables and pyramid-shaped chairs—not too much of an exaggeration. My other favourite was Simone Nuntheweisser, an intrepid BBC journalist. I had formed an obsession with foreign correspondents—the grammar and tropes of the form as well as the content. And as I watched over and over, I had the gloomy realisation that they never shed any real light on the events they reported. And what they did report was just an endless cycle of the same things: another South American coup; more Palestinian youths throwing rocks at Israeli tanks. It was like Groundhog Day. And so Marg's anchorwoman (the slightly accented Anke Persson) would sign off saying, 'Where no news is new news.'

Once again Kath and Kim and Sharon had a regular berth in the show, this time in the build-up to Kimmy's baby.

During the filming of *Babe: Pig in the City* I fell in love with the animals. There were a lot of primates on set, mostly chimpanzees and orangutans, and a capuchin monkey. Primates are not to be taken lightly. We were all given training beforehand in how to deal with them. Basically, never, ever look them in the eye. Mickey Rooney had a lot of scenes with the chimps and he was a little wary. He'd worked with chimps a lot during his old vaudeville days and he knew how aggressive they can be. That said, hugging a chimpanzee, having it wrap its arms and legs around you and lay its head on your breast is one of the most magical feelings in the world. It is like the Bible never happened and we are once more part of the animal kingdom.

But it was the orangutan Mitra who stole my heart. In between takes Mitra would clamber across and casually sling his long arm over your shoulder like an old drinking buddy. He would take your hand in his and, his gentle gaze never leaving yours, lift it to his lips. Mitra was chivalrous. He was also an exceptional actor—far better than me. Acting is all about the eyes. Mitra's eyes were sad and wise. He would look at you, his eyes blinking softly. There was no threat or challenge there. No judgment. It was as if he already knew everything about you anyway, like a wordless sacrament of confession and absolution.

He knew exactly what was going on. He participated in this human nonsense, he knew we were fools. He knew he could crush me with one hand. Looking into those eyes there was no way you could doubt that he had a soul, an uncluttered soul that was millions of years old, that had travelled through many incarnations and forgotten none of the lessons.

Inspired by Mitra and the other animals, I got my own little dog—a beagle whom I named Jane Austen because she had the same brow line. It was a rash, ill-advised pet-shop purchase. I bought her for her adorable little face and sad pleading beagle eyes without a thought for breed behavioural characteristics. I didn't care. I adored her. I found her naughtiness trying but hilarious, especially when she was a puppy. When she was nearly two she followed her nose off the edge of a forty-metre cliff and broke her leg in six places. I had to film and so my father nursed her back to health, walking her every single day as the vet had ordered. I was relieved that she was in such capable hands.

When Jane went through a particularly difficult phase I got in a dog whisperer who introduced me to the concept of 'down the lead', the idea that any problem a dog was having had been transmitted by the owner or handler. I asked if, theoretically, a dog's bad behaviour could be deciphered and traced back *up* the lead.

'Oh yes,' he concurred. 'You can tell an awful lot about an owner from their dog's misbehaviour.'

It seemed to me that dogs, if read right, might be a key to unlocking the secret life of humans. A kind of conduit to the unconscious: a 'tell', like in poker. I decided this was an excellent premise for a murder mystery in which a genius dog trainer fixes the dog and in so doing also solves a crime. And so *Dogwoman* was created.

I wrote, acted in and produced it along with Roger Simpson and Roger LeMesurier. My friend Tony Ayres was the script editor. It was my first big solo venture and it tanked. There were people who loved it but the ratings were not good. It was not a commercial idea. It should have been done at the ABC but they didn't have the money to get the production values right. This failure haunted me for years. I have had many other failures—*Bligh, Babe: Pig in the City, The Spearman Experiment,* I could go on—but this one really knocked me around. It was my first baby, the one I really cared about, and I had fallen flat on my face. It took me a long while and a lot of work to get my confidence back.

But something magical did come out of that show, or rather from the wrap party at my house. There were four hundred people and among them was Kristen—we kissed that night and were together for the next eight years.

Jane Austen was still playing up so I rang Dad, knowing that he loved her as much as I did.

'She's being a little bugger! The trainer says she is testing me.'

'Well, don't get too attached,' he said with melodramatic heaviness.

'Why?'

'Because you might have to put her down.'

'What?'

'I said…'

'I *heard* what you said. I am not having my dog put down!'

'You cannot afford to be sentimental, Maggie.'

'She's a *puppy*!'

His tone became irritatingly lugubrious. 'I love Jane too, but you have to face facts.'

'What the fuck! What is *wrong* with you?'

Silence.

I couldn't understand how he could love something and yet be prepared to kill it. Or maybe I could.

# THE LITTLE JEWISH BOY

My grandparents took in Jews to keep them safe during the war. Their home became a halfway house. Whenever my father talked about his family hiding Jews he always spoke about my grandmother.

'My mother was a brave woman,' he said when I filmed him. Coming from him, this really meant something.

'Was Jadwiga scared?'

'Strangely enough, she wasn't. She kept that Jewish boy and we used to get annoyed with her. And yet she kept him for several months. Kid crying, screaming, could only speak Yiddish. Had to speak Yiddish to him. Despite that she kept him.'

'Who was his mother?'

'Wife of my father's friend. Big. Tall. Curly-haired. Jewish guy. His nickname was Airplane on account of his huge wingspan. All the gold teeth—he was a right prize for the Germans if they caught him.'

I wished he wouldn't speak like that. I always winced at the insensitivity. But I was beginning to see a pattern. He would always get hard-boiled like this when the conversation took a turn towards subjects that stirred up uncomfortable feelings. In the midst of such horror perhaps the only thing to do is to cut away all sentimentality. Or maybe it was the influence of all those Jimmy Cagney films he saw with Wacek before the war.

'This Airplane chap knew my father because he was a fence. And even though my father was in the police force Airplane knew he could trust him, and so he came and asked my father to hide his family.

'He and his wife were in their forties so the kid was an absolute little shyster. He used to have tantrums. And all in Yiddish!'

On the film I see my hands go to my head, aghast.

'And we used to say, for God's sake get rid of...And you see it sounded very anti-Semitic, until such time as you realised what it meant. To keep a Jew. In your house. Instantaneous death. On the spot.'

'Or off to a concentration camp?'

'No! They just shoot you...together with the Jews. So the risk was incredible. So anybody who tells me about what it was like...' He shakes his head. 'My mother was a very brave woman and she loved children. She used to cry and say, "He's just a child!" But eventually it got to the point they had to go. If I remember rightly, one of the neighbours said to my mother, "Mrs Szubańska, you better get rid of that child or we'll all be in trouble!" The neighbours had heard the child singing in Yiddish. It was no longer safe for any of them. Because what happens if you are my neighbour and the Gestapo come to you and say, "Did you know they had a Jew?"' He eyeballs me. As if to say, *Don't judge. What would you do?*

'If you saw a Jew you were supposed to report to the Gestapo, and say, "I saw a Jew there." If you were in the vicinity when the Germans caught a Jew they would say, "Did you know?"

'When Wacek escaped from the ghetto—that's Wacek, my

childhood friend—he came to my house. Andrzej was very angry with Wacek: "You are endangering everybody in the unit if you get caught!" If Wacek got caught he would have caved in to torture. So Andrzej told Wacek, "We will get you the papers in twenty-four hours and then you have to go." And even then, this chap stopped me in the street and said, "You've got a cat in your house"—because that's how they referred to Jews—and I said, "You say one word and you'll have a cold arse tomorrow."'

He sounds like Cagney when he says this.

'People don't realise what it was like. Poland was the only country where the penalty for hiding a Jew was the death sentence. There were not many Poles that dared to hide Jews. And some of them used to charge them a hell of a lot of money and hid them underneath the floorboards'—his voice is full of contempt for these Poles—'and they used to take everything from them. Some of these people were selling Jews.'

'Who? Poles?'

'Oh well, there were just as many rotten Poles as any other nationality!'

'And who were they selling them to?'

'The Gestapo. For various favours. They were smuggling food to the ghetto through the sewers, and one way of making a lot of money was to take the merchandise for which the Jews had already paid, steal it, and then tell the Jews that they got caught and that the Gestapo took the merchandise.

'But mainly they were trying to catch Jews because they always knew the Jews who came out of the ghetto had a lot of money.'

I am wary that my father has fallen into lazy anti-Semitic thinking—the assumption that all Jews have money. But he explains that the Jews who were smuggled out of the Ghetto often carried gold or precious stones with which to buy safe passage. Which of course made them prey for unscrupulous Poles.

'My God!' On the screen I am horrified. 'Doesn't paint a very pretty picture of the Poles!'

'They were no worse than anybody else. That's how it was. The Jews did the same to each other. Don't kid yourself. There is always an element that will do anything for anything.

'My mother took *nothing* from these people, but eventually, quite rightly, she had to say, "Sorry but, you know, now people are starting to talk." But it was *impossible*. The kid was *impossible*!'

'Were you there when she told them?'

'No! I wasn't in. I just popped in one day and I said where is…I forget the name. She said,' his voice is low and sad as he imitates her, '"Oh," she said, "They're gone." And then you rely on one fact—that if the Jewish mother gets caught that she doesn't bloody well shop you to the Gestapo and tell them that she spent however long at such and such a place.'

There were some Jews whom the Germans tortured to find out the identity of the Polish Catholics who had hidden them. My father had not even a hint of disapproval in his voice about this. 'Some of these Jews were very brave,' he said matter-of-factly. 'And the kid wouldn't have known because he was only three or four.'

Given what was at stake, why did my grandmother Jadwiga do what she did? What made her risk not only her own life, but also those of her children, my father and my aunt? What makes a mother put the life of a stranger ahead of her own life, ahead of her children's lives? And how did my father feel about that?

I never had the heart to ask him those questions.

# KATH AND KIM AND SHARON

I was asleep when the phone rang. It was Kristen. Her voice was strained and urgent. 'Have you heard the news?'

'No. What's happened?'

'Islamic terrorists bombed the World Trade Center last night.'

As so often happens in my life, tragedy and comedy conflated. Later that morning we had the first production meeting for *Kath and Kim* at the ABC offices in Elsternwick, a Jewish area not far from where I live. As I walked towards the building I noticed that there were more security guards around the Jewish college across the street and the Holocaust Museum down the road. It felt wrong to be going about the business of making jokes on such a day. But comedy is our job. We started working.

We were all keen to pick up on the momentum that the characters of Kath, Kim and Sharon had created in *Big Girl's Blouse* and

*Something Stupid.* The segment had developed a small cult following and we felt there might be an audience for a longer show. Writing had begun some months earlier and initially I contributed. But then I was approached to do *The Crocodile Hunter: Collision Course* with Steve and Terri Irwin. The girls were very supportive, so off I went to have my adventure.

What I actually found was not an adventure story—it was a love story. Lots of couples love one another but don't like one another. Or they make a deal to tolerate the worst aspects of each other. But sometimes great souls merge. And that was Steve and Terri. They adored one another. They were engaging, funny, generous. Terri may look like a preacher's daughter but she has just about the bawdiest sense of humour I have ever encountered. And Steve was just like he was on screen. He had prodigious energy. We were filming six days a week—common practice—and it was exhausting. On our days off most of us would lie facedown on our hotel beds. Not Steve. He would be up at the crack of dawn, concreting the zoo.

Anyway, when I came back Jane and Gina had hit a number of obstacles in their attempts to get *Kath and Kim* onto the screen. Despite our combined track record with *Fast Forward* and *Babe*, the show was not a lay-down misère. The received wisdom was that Aussies did not like to watch homegrown sitcoms. There had really only been one success over the years, the Seven Network's *Hey Dad*. And we were coming off the back of *Big Girl's Blouse*, which had been deemed a failure. The ABC had lost faith in the production and, reportedly at the behest of the managing director Jonathan Shier, had threatened to pull the show. But Rick McKenna, Gina's partner, is a fighter. And fortunately the girls had two champions on the inside: Sandra Levy, Director of Television; and Robyn Kershaw, Head of Drama. Robyn is a frilly dynamo and cultural powerhouse. She had been general manager of the Belvoir St Theatre company in Sydney.

If the comedy department at the ABC did not believe in the show, the drama department did. So the girls shifted the show sideways, giving it the unique distinction of being the only comedy to be produced by a drama unit. As Robyn told me later, 'I would have crawled across broken glass to get you girls.'

*Kath and Kim* went into production in 2002 and aired in May of that year. As with every show I've ever been in, it started out slowly. Comedy usually does, the most famous example being *Seinfeld*, which almost got yanked off the air before it gained audience traction. The critics were unsure. There was a lot of discussion about whether we were just a bunch of snooty inner-city latte drinkers sneering at the suburbs. It completely missed the point. *Kath and Kim* is *born* of the suburbs. Suburbia is who we are. Even when we flee the suburbs we are defined by them: our characters were just thinly disguised aspects of us.

Suburban people—the supposed butt of the joke—loved it instantly. People would stop me in the street: 'You girls are *exactly* like me and my friends! We love it!' They loved seeing their lives represented and they loved laughing at themselves. They loved it in droves.

By the end of the first season we knew we had a hit on our hands. The ratings were huge. It was the most-watched show of the night with 1.63 million viewers and, what really matters to programmers, was the most-watched show by viewers under forty. The ABC commissioned a second series. It went on to become the most successful comedy in Australian television history.

With her little wagon hitched to the show, Sharon's star ascended and she became the most popular second-best friend in the country—second fiddle being a place I felt very comfortable with.

People frequently ask me where Sharon comes from; I often wonder myself. In truth Sharon is the most vulnerable part of me. I suspect that vulnerability has always been present in my work but it found its most perfect expression in Sharon. It was around this time that I started to top the Q scores, an independent measure to determine what and who the public finds familiar and appealing. Basically, a huge scientific popularity contest. And I had won it. If only the outcast, lonely me of my teens could have known. Mass communication is a fascinating thing. Powerful and mysterious. It is where the collective unconscious rises and meets. It is where souls touch.

Sharon was conceived in *Big Girl's Blouse* but she fully emerged in *Kath and Kim* when I was going through one of the most intense stages in my therapy process. Finally, late in 1999, I had started therapy. I had to. The darkness was closing in on me again and I didn't know if I could handle another bout. Also I was starting the relationship with Kristen and I knew that if I didn't get help I would fuck it up. Painstakingly, over a period of several years, I named and reclaimed feelings that had been left out in the cold for decades. Emotions rose up like zombies and threatened to suck my brains out. It was in therapy that I finally began to untangle the rats nest of intergenerational trauma, to understand my father's legacy. And that was when the nightmares started. I would find myself in a grey, muddy landscape, pockmarked with holes and quicksand. A barbed-wire fence ran along the field, preventing escape. I was a small child hunkered down in one of the holes. An old man was beside me. He was trying to tell me something, but I couldn't hear or understand him. Off to the side, near a hedgerow, was a large mound of dirt in which small children were buried in the cold earth. I could see their limbs protruding. And I knew, with the certainty you have in dreams, that this was hell.

I would wake up crying and choking.

Neither the therapist nor I knew what these dreams meant. But I persisted with the sessions and, over time, therapy changed my acting. Within the safety of therapy I felt I could explore areas of feeling I could have never ventured near in acting class. And it altered Sharon's resonance. Life had often been a steep climb for me, one I'd attempted unsecured. Now I had holds and ropes: there was someone belaying me. And it all found its outlet in Sharon.

Gina and Jane were writing the character, playing to my strengths and cannily exploiting my weaknesses. But whatever she was saying, Sharon always vibrated with bass notes of pain and loss. She is the heartbroken Irish in me, the scarified Pole—but also a product of my optimism. Sharon is one long unguarded moment. She wears her heart on her sleeve and is full of hope and love and the dream that, if she just keeps trying, things will work out and people will be nice to one another and love will prevail.

While I was playing Sharon I was also in the longest, most stable relationship of my life. And this was changing me in subtle ways. Kristen made me feel adorable and beloved and how could that not translate to the screen?

At the end of 2002 *Kath and Kim*—a comedy—won three Australian Film Institute awards under the tough drama category. Best Drama Series, Best Screenplay in a Television Drama Series. And I won Best Supporting Actress in a Television Drama.

# MOLOTOV COCKTAILS

In March 2003 the Coalition of the Willing invaded Iraq. My father and I were watching the war on television. He pulled his blanket around his shoulders and settled back into the Jason recliner. 'Ye gods. I remember that feeling. When those tanks turn and point their guns at you, when they have you in their sights. I wished there was a hole in the ground, some tiny crack I could crawl into. But there is no hole deep enough.' He shuddered, and there was the tiniest flicker of something. A faint echo of fear.

My father was adamantly opposed to the invasion of Iraq for tactical as well as moral reasons. 'Bloody idiots,' he would mutter. 'How many body bags will it take before they realise this war is a bad idea? The Americans will get bogged down and they'll never get out.'

'The Americans have a pretty powerful war machine, Dad. I wouldn't like to be on the receiving end of it.'

'We Poles had nothing and still we were a thorn in the side of the

Nazis for six years. The biggest war machine in Europe, but still they couldn't get rid of us.'

'Yes, but what should you do about the terrorists?'

'*One man's terrorist is another man's freedom fighter*. The Nazis considered *us* to be terrorists.'

My father knew that even in his war, a just war where Hitler had to be stopped, the balance of good and evil was no simple thing. He also knew that a mixture of adolescent testosterone and ideological fervour is the most explosive Molotov cocktail on the planet.

I commented once that the *aktions* must have been well organised. He sat up on the couch. I had not seen this look before.

'I was good at it. Good at organising the *aktions*.' And there it was. The bastard emotion. Hard, shining, gleaming pride.

Was this the stone of madness? His pride in his efficiency as a killer? It seemed he was simultaneously proud and ashamed of what he had done. Maybe that was what he couldn't forgive himself for.

Like an old man looking out to sea he saw in the invasion of Iraq the same bloody tidal wave of history roaring towards the world. The parades of patriotic God-summoning, with their flags bobbing about, looked to him just like a Nazi war rally. 'I look at them and all I see is the bloody Germans. *Gott Mit Uns*. What's the bloody difference?'

He was too ill to get out on the barricades and protest against the war so he started a letter-writing campaign. He asked me to proofread his letters. He would fuss over them, fretting that his English wasn't good enough, desperate to be persuasive. His pen would hover over the page when he wrote, fidgeting. He had fallen victim to his own standards.

So I went over, ready to revise his efforts. Clutching his blanket, he came out of the den with a manila folder. The stent the doctors had recently put in his kidney had given him golden staph and now he was indelibly cold and the blanket was a semi-permanent fixture.

Like a nervous schoolboy he took the letters out and showed them to me as if I were his English teacher. A little bit of me feared that they would be crazy rants.

They weren't. They were immaculately punctuated, beautifully worded, elegiac pleas for peace. Tears came to my eyes.

'They're beautiful, Dad. You don't need to change a word.'

The *Age* published one of his letters. But of course it made no difference.

# THE STONE OF MADNESS II

I frequently had to travel for work, but I would always call my parents from wherever I was in the world and we would talk for hours about all sorts of things. I would always tell Dad many times that I loved him. His father had never told him that and had died before there was any chance for the conversation to happen. I didn't want anything left unsaid. Slowly the tone of our chats began to change. They became more intense, more raw. They spiralled deeper. The man who had dispensed death was now about to face his own. Chunks of his subconscious that had remained submerged for decades began to break loose and float to the surface.

I was in Adelaide filming *Dr Plonk* with director Rolf de Heer. Rolf had discovered some unused black-and-white film stock in an old fridge and so, naturally, he decided to make a silent black-and-white slapstick comedy about the end of the world. As you do. Rolf is one of the most interesting filmmakers this country has produced and I agreed to do the role without a moment's hesitation.

We had finished filming for the day and it was dark by the time I got back to the hotel. I called Mum and Dad as usual; we spoke for maybe two hours. Dad's English was excellent, but when he was excited or emotional he often spoke in fragments. He would say things like, 'You must put the thingy in the whats-it.' To which I would reply, teasing, 'You know, a noun or two might help.' This funny little tic became worse when you ventured into unknown territory. He would speak elliptically, assuming knowledge you could not possibly have. And I think there were some things it was just too hard for him to say. So his vocabulary, like a discreet servant, would obligingly withdraw.

That night something changed. Our conversation had drifted, pulled on unseen tides, and now we were far, far out to sea. It was like I was talking to a different man. This was not Clive of Poland. There were none of the carefully crafted stories. This was raw. He was saying things he had never said before, using words he had never used before. Maybe it was the nearness of death. Or perhaps he sensed that I was up to it now, strong enough to be able to hear. But it wasn't just us who changed—time changed too. As my father sat on one end of the phone in Melbourne while I was eight hundred kilometres away in Adelaide, the door to the past creaked open. And I was there—with him. In Warsaw. I was talking to my father as a young man.

So here we were, careening towards the conversation that I had both dreaded and craved my whole life. The conversation in which he would tell me what had really happened, what he had really felt. What he had really done. I felt both privileged and terrified. What if he had overestimated me? What if he told me something that I would never recover from? What if it was all too much for him? I was full of pre-emptive guilt that the pain would be unbearable; that it might kill him.

Our talk plunged on late into the night and I realised that I had to take notes in case I forgot some vital detail. I pulled out the hotel biro and notepad and started writing. After we hung up I transcribed some of the conversation onto my laptop, along with my thoughts and reactions. But it was late. I had an early flight the next day so I decided I would finish transcribing when I got home. I shut down and left my notes on the bedside table.

The next morning as I packed my suitcase I reached for the notepad. It was gone. I frantically searched through the drawers. What had I done with it? I was certain I'd put it on the bedside table. I grabbed the bin, upended it and scrabbled through the contents. I checked the bedclothes over and over. A cold sweat crept over me. 'I've lost it. I've fucking lost it!' I started to cry like an orphaned child. I thumped my head with my fist. 'You idiot! You fucking idiot!'

The phone rang. My car was waiting.

I flung the bedclothes on the floor. Nothing. It was nowhere. Vanished. There was a knock—the porter come to collect my bags. I let him in, he took my things, we left and I shut the door. Knowing that my notes were lost and I would never find them.

When I got home that night I wrote down as much as I could of what was still fresh in my memory. These are the notes that survive.

*Saturday 12 August, 2006, 7.00 p.m.*
Conversation with Dad. Starts like every other conversation since we had the extra phone line put in.

'Wait a minute I'll get your mother.'

Mum gets on the line. We three-way chat, then she leaves Dad and me to chat alone. He has just finished his last radiotherapy treatment. He has shat himself a couple of times. Conversation about gastrolyte, spirulina and protein shakes. I offer advice because I love him but also because I feel guilty that I am not there. Why do I feel this internal pressure to mother him? Despite his intelligence, capability and self-assurance there is a kind of boyish incompleteness about my father, as though he had not been quite finished. And in a sense he wasn't. His childhood was robbed from him when he became a boy soldier and he spent the rest of his life trying to regain a lost youth. But I suspect a much deeper yearning lies beneath—that of a young boy for his mother and father. Perhaps because I look like his late mother he projects her onto me. Or perhaps I became like her because of his projection.

We talk about current events, the Middle East, the mujahideen. He takes pride in knowing the name and pronouncing 'mujahideen' correctly. He wants to apologise. 'I had no youth. That is why after the war all the soccer and tennis because they were all the things that I never got to do.'

'Yes, and maybe a way of keeping your demons at bay.' I want him to know that I understand and forgive him for all the tennis madness and the rest of it. It was not his fault, he was only a child.

'Possibly,' he says, 'I don't know. I lived as a man. I had girlfriends. I never lived where I had a girlfriend and I never had a girlfriend where I lived.'

I don't understand this. Was he on the run? Where were his parents? And is he telling me that he had lovers before Mum?

'I say one thing for them, the whores were always good to us.'

'The who?'

'Prostitutes. The ladies of the night. They would always look after us. Give us a place to kip if we needed. And they would tip us off, where were the Germans.'

Is he saying he slept with prostitutes? Or with the other women in his unit? His weirdly antiquated terminology—'ladies of the night'. Is that because he has not said this before or out of deference to my sensibilities, and the fact I am his daughter?

'Why did you start your own private army?'

'I couldn't stand what was happening to the Jews. When I saw them killing the Jews and the Jews jumping into the flames…they threw their kids in and then jumped in after them so the Germans wouldn't get them.' He falls silent. 'I couldn't stand to see that. The little kids.'

He says the word 'stand' as though he is spitting something foul from his mouth. So this is a glimmer of what he really felt.

'You saw little kids killed?'

'Yes.'

'What happened?'

'It was another time. There was a little kid. Maybe six or seven. Typical Jewish kid. He looked like that photo, you know of the kid with the bag of something and the cap and his hands in the air?'

'Yes, I know the one.'

'Well, he looked like that. He had a bag of potatoes or something. And this German bastard—the kid had crawled almost all the way through the barbed wire, you know—let him get all the way through and the kid looked back…he knew. And just when he nearly got there the German bastard, with a smile on his face, picked him up by the scruff of the neck and shot him.'

I am weeping down the phone. I'm trying so hard not to sob my heart feels like it might stop beating. My face is soaking wet. I feel guilty and self-indulgent for crying. But maybe, I think to myself, maybe somebody has to cry for that little kid. And for my father. Dear God, surely somebody has to do the crying.

'And there was nothing you could do?'

'Of course not!' And then, 'I just bloody stood there. But I thought, if there is a God, how could He let that happen? But later the situation was reversed.'

'What do you mean?'

'I saw the German again and this time I had the gun. I said, "I saw what you did, you bastard.'"

'What did you do?'

'I shot the bastard.'

And in that moment I realise that I am no pacifist.

'Good on you,' I say. 'Good on you, Dad.'

He dismisses me. 'Ach! Many people were brave, but very few were noble. I don't want to be some kind of hero. I'm not proud. I'm not ashamed. I don't want you to feel sorry for me. There are only two things I want for you—lose weight and never feel sorry for yourself.'

I tell him I understand.

I ask him, 'When did you first get a gun?'

'I always had guns before the war. I had my own .22 and a revolver. My father's service pistol was always on his desk. I think that was how I learned discipline. My friends always knew it was there.'

'What?'

'I had a lust for guns. There was this one particular gun, a German Walther. And I wanted it. There were two brothers, the Schmidts.'

There is a loud hissing sound in my head, like a kettle. It is the sound of my own blood roaring through my veins. My head feels thick and heavy, as if someone has poured quick-dry cement into my skull. I can feel myself listing. Everything slows down.

'And,' I say.

'So. One of those Schmidt boys had a Walther.'

I understand what he is saying. He killed those boys. They were his first. And they were boys. This means that he was killing long before he was officially involved with his unit. He can only have been about fifteen.

And this is the bit where my mind goes blank. It is like we both go into some kind of traumatic fugue state. He cannot speak properly and I cannot hear properly. It is as if we are trying to talk in the centre of a tornado.

Then he suddenly changes direction and says the strangest thing: 'You see, all my life I have been terrified that one of my kids would grow up to be a traitor.'

'A traitor. What do you mean?' I ask. But he doesn't really seem to know either.

We chatted for a while longer, I told him I loved him and we rang off. Soon after that I called the Polish priest, and two months later he died. It would take me years to figure out what he was trying to tell me.

# A LION IN SUBURBIA

After Dad died I moved in with Mum to keep her company. Those three months were the longest we had lived together since I was seventeen. And it seemed that every week another of her friends died. It was an octogenarian massacre out there.

'Did you go to Iris's funeral?' I asked.

'Nup. Och, God hen, I just can't *face* another funeral,' she said wearily, her voice a combination of guilt and relief. Like a naughty dog. My mother gets very upset at funerals. She can't control herself and doesn't want to be a bother. I'm the same. After Dad died it was like the tap had been turned on and we couldn't turn it off.

We were sitting in the Jason recliners in the TV room. She was in hers and I had inherited his. Slowly I was turning into my father. We were drinking tea and watching the UKTV channel. The gloomy *Coronation Street* theme tune dirged on.

'Jesus Christ! I cannot *stand* this dismal shit. I thought that was why we left England—to escape those grimy council rows. How can you watch this?' I asked.

'I like it.'

'I know you do. It makes me want to slash my wrists.'

'All right, what do you want to watch then?'

'Anything. As long as it's not *Coronation Street*. Or *Midsomer Murders*.'

We settled on something less inflammatory: the early news. After a while Mum said, 'Jesus! It's nothing but ads for insurance and boxes to be buried in!'

'Do you believe in heaven and hell, Mum?'

'I don't know, hen. But if there *is* a hell there are a lot of people in it.'

The anaesthetic of denial and incomprehension had worn off and I felt much worse than I had immediately after my father's death. I had a little narrative that consoled me: 'His was a good death,' I told myself. 'We'd had all the important conversations. He is not really gone, his spirit is everywhere, in the wind and the trees.'

Two months later, this children's story was ripping apart like an old sheet in a strong wind. He was gone and he was never coming back. As much as a feeling, it was a cognitive assault beyond my comprehension. I guess this is what is called a spiritual crisis. I felt like my namesake Mary Magdalene who stayed by Christ's tomb weeping and waiting with spices to anoint his body. Only there was no body. Just ashes.

A week later I was sitting cross-legged in a spacious suburban mansion, now converted into a Buddhist centre, listening to a talk about conflict resolution. On the floor was a lurid turquoise carpet and at the front of the room a gaudy array of images of beloved lamas and Buddhist prayer flags and tinkling bells and pots of sweetly smoking nag champa. A young Buddhist monk entered in his dark red robes and took a seat at the front of the room. I would have loved for this to be the place where I could lay down my burden.

Like many westerners I am drawn to Buddhism, to the smiling face of the Dalai Lama, to his compassion and his openness. His belief that happiness is possible. I am moved by the tragic plight of the Tibetans. And I love the ritual, the incense and bells—vestiges of my Catholicism, no doubt. And of course the chanting. That sonorous thunder that comes from somewhere deep in the earth and rumbles up through every chakra.

The words of the teacher penetrated my reverie. 'Think what terrible karma it would be,' he said, 'to come back as a lion.'

'What? I love lions,' I thought. 'They are magnificent beasts! Is nothing sacred?' My father's star sign is Leo. I pictured my old dad as a lion let loose in suburbia.

Then I thought about *Animal Planet*. About what it feels like for the impala as the lioness runs it down and pounces on its flank. I thought about the YouTube clip of the revolt of the wildebeests at the watering hole in Kruger National Park. The lions isolating the weakest baby member of the vegetarian herd. Going in for the kill. And the spine-tingling moment when one of the herd stops and, in a moment of giddy defiance, a big 'fuck you' to Darwin, turns back and charges at the lion, tossing it in the air like a rag doll. Was it magical thinking, or were we witnessing a watershed moment? I thought about that furry little rabbit riddled with myxomatosis, its head sinking to the ground. I thought about my tennis opponents. I thought about the people I have had fallings-out with. Old lovers, hurts, pains, dreams of revenge. Small transgressions, crimes against humanity, prey become hunter. Is it all the same wickedness?

Thou shalt not kill.

I was afraid for my father's soul and had come to the Buddhists because I wanted someone to reassure me that it would all be all right. That he would not burn in the eternal flames of hell.

People were asking about how to deal with relationship issues and conflict in the workplace. 'But what if someone has a gun to your head?' I blurted out. 'What if it is a case of kill or be killed? What then?'

Stunned silence. I had plunged everyone into the deepest parts of my head. I felt flustered and ashamed, as if my psychological slip was showing. Even when I write comedy, this relentless question is there on my shoulder. Even when I went on holiday with my girlfriend in blissful Fiji I managed to find a book about the horrors of cannibalism.

The gentle monk thought. His silence ballooned out and filled the room like a bubble at a birthday party.

'I don't know,' he said at last.

I felt a strange desolation.

He thought a while longer. 'Well, perhaps karma might be your guide. Perhaps you might decide to consider what is best for the karma of the other person and for yourself. And perhaps you might decide that it is better for your karma if you were to die rather than to kill. But you may also,' he shifted on his cushion, 'consider the karma of the other person and try to do what would be best for *his* karma. Clearly it would be bad for his karma to kill you. You might say to him, I will not kill you. I understand that you feel you must kill me. But I will not kill you.'

I understood that survival was not the main game in this room. The thought experiment of reincarnation shifts everything. Whereas if you believe you only have one lifetime, survival matters. It makes you grabby.

I didn't think I could live up to this standard. Did that mean I was a bad person? Was I what was wrong with humanity? Some part of me kicked back violently. My father had risked his life out of altruism but he had also killed, and now these Buddhists were raising the bar even higher and I wanted to scream, 'How dare you judge him! You have never been put to that test. How dare you!'

But of course the Buddhists *have* been put to that test. In Tibet and in Burma. Those extraordinary nuns and monks let the blows rain down on their heads, were subjected to torture and unimaginable cruelty. And how did they respond? With compassion. They pitied their abusers because they knew the terrible karmic consequences that lay in store for the evildoers. Is that what my father meant when he said there were many brave people but few noble ones?

Most morality draws the line at self-defence. What my father and grandparents did was selfless and altruistic. It did not increase their chances of survival. In fact, helping Jewish people meant that they might now suffer the same fate as those they were trying to protect.

What is the right thing to do? I asked myself. What should we do?

Who would know? Does such a wise soul even exist?

The class ended. We gave thanks and we picked up our cushions and collected our shoes.

Six months later I was invited to meet the Dalai Lama himself.

It had all started with a phone call.

'Hey, Mags…'

The director Simon Phillips can make a single syllable sound naughty and cheeky and full of forbidden fun. 'Mags, I'm doing an adaptation of a Broadway musical about a bunch of kids competing in a spelling bee and I want you to play an eleven-year-old boy named Barfée and…'

'I'm in.'

*The 25th Annual Putnam County Spelling Bee* is a warm, funny, heartfelt Broadway hit. It's a beautiful piece that tracks the emotional journey of a bunch of lonely spelling geeks as they compete in a spelling bee.

My character, William Morris Barfée, was a grumpy spelling savant—fat, nasty and friendless. This presented me with a genuine acting challenge and the opportunity to explore the male psyche. Could I make people forget that I was a forty-six-year-old woman? Could I make people love this hurt, caustic, unappealing little boy? And, even more challenging, would they stay with the journey of my character as he falls in love? I would have to find what Armistead Maupin calls 'the genderless neutrality of the human heart'.

The opening night went off. The play was going to be a hit. Sometimes you can feel it. Being in a hit show is an incredible rush. I imagine it releases the same kind of euphoria a surfer feels inside a huge barrel wave.

*Spelling Bee* was one of the most joyous, hilarious and satisfying experiences of my life. For some reason I found it very easy to inhabit the skin of an eleven-year-old boy who is going through puberty. I didn't alter my inner emotional landscape or my psyche one little bit in order to play Barfée. I just took the nerdy, obsessive part of me and dressed it in shorts and a school tie. And not for the first time I wondered—are we really as different as we think we are? Is the divide so great? I became very intrigued with the whole idea of drag and the possibilities it might reveal.

For its Sydney run the show moved to the Sydney Theatre Company. On the morning of our opening night in Sydney I got a phone call from a friend who was the producer of Geraldine Doogue's radio program. 'Hi, Mags. Look, Geraldine was at a preview of your show the other night and she absolutely loved it and she was wondering if you'd be interested in being on a discussion panel tomorrow morning with His Holiness the Dalai Lama? It's part of the Happiness and Its Causes conference. Malcolm Turnbull pulled out last minute.'

'Absolutely,' I said and immediately rang Mum. 'The Dalai Lama! I'm going to meet the freakin' *Dalai Lama*!'

The hoopla that surrounds the Dalai Lama is extraordinary. He is the closest thing to a living Jesus for agnostic westerners—the repository of all our hopes and dreams for a better world. And I am as affected by it as anyone. I felt a vague question forming in the back of my head that perhaps His Holiness would be able to answer.

Opening nights, especially of successful shows, mean late nights. I had virtually no sleep and the Happiness conference was starting at 8 a.m. I raced to the entertainment centre and was whisked into the make-up room. As I sat being powdered the convenor rushed me through some basic protocols. 'You should address His Holiness as "Your Holiness". Try to keep your feet in a neutral position flat on the floor pointing forward. It is considered very rude to point your feet at His Holiness.' Then we made our way into the auditorium. I was introduced to Geraldine Doogue and the three other panellists, Linda Burney, Clive Hamilton and Gordon Parker. And then His Holiness, the Dalai Lama arrived with his translator.

His Holiness came up to greet us. He had a white silk khata scarf, a gift symbolising compassion, for each of us. The whiteness represents the goodness of the giver. He smiled, placed the scarf around my neck and took my hands in his warm ones. I expected something magical to happen but nothing did. Nothing obvious anyway. As he would say of himself, he is a simple Buddhist monk. He was funny and warm, a little hard to understand at times, as he does mumble a bit. I got the feeling that he is no pushover. And that what we project onto him is our own banal conception of what a holy man should be.

A voice started up in my head. *He may be a simple monk, but he is also a prince and a rock-star guru fêted by the most powerful and coolest people in the world. He is surrounded by adoring followers. How hard can his life really be? How would he cope with three screaming kids under the age of five? That's a real test of how Zen you are.*

What was I doing? This was the Dalai Lama! I was putting the Dalai Lama through the moral hoops! I was testing him. I was testing him because I felt he was testing me. Judging me. Finding me wanting. I felt like he could see right through me. Like he knew the darkness of my heart.

I knew I was missing the point. That some neurotic complex was scrambling my rational processes and that he was doing nothing of the sort; that this madness was all of my own making. A counter voice argued back: *Snap out of it, Magda! You are verging on rude. Why are you doing this? What the hell is eating at you?*

And then I realised.

I needed His Holiness to tell me the right thing to do. I wanted a blueprint for goodness. But more than that, I wanted redemption and forgiveness for my father, the lion in suburbia. This was the baggage I wanted to lay at the Dalai Lama's innocent feet. And I thought, His Holiness must have to cope with this crap all the time. All of our desperate needs and wants and fantasies. All of our damage. Yet he continues to stand his ground, to smile and be infinitely kind and compassionate. And that was when I understood his magic. It is both simple and profound—he is a sane, emotionally healthy human being in a mad world.

The Dalai Lama was sitting there right next to me. I felt a tussle between my own agenda and the need to be of service, to ask the questions I felt the audience might like to hear.

The question burning a hole in my head was the old one. 'Was my father a good man?' He killed because he believed it was the right thing to do. But was there another way? What do you do when you are invaded by Nazis? Could you stand by and watch a small child be killed?

This was what I wanted to ask the Dalai Lama. 'What would Jesus do? What would Nelson Mandela do? What would you do, Your Holiness?'

But of course that is not the question I asked. I did not lose my head completely; I knew that my job that day was to provide a voice for the people listening. So instead I asked him a question on their behalf: if we are going to change the world, how should we teach children?

And although it was not exactly the question I wanted to ask, perhaps I got the right answer anyway: 'Firstly, maximum affection.'

His Holiness and I chatted back and forth for a few minutes. The session went on a while longer. He elaborated on the need to train the mind and the heart, to prepare oneself so that in tough times the best reaction would ensue. And he emphasised the paramount importance of warm-heartedness. Then we wrapped up and said our farewells.

I stood there, my question still blazing in me. I watched as he walked off the stage and disappeared into the darkness. No miracle took place. I wasn't Lazarus. But it was as if the Dalai Lama had placed a small, subtle seed in my heart. And there it began to grow.

# LOSING WEIGHT

'Wow! You won't be able to play Sharon anymore.'

A chill ran through me. I had just shown a friend a photo of me, slimmed down to my lowest weight while an ambassador for Jenny Craig. I took it in the mirror one day as proof—she could not believe how I looked. It wasn't a studio shot, it was on my phone and in bad light. But it captured me in a way that was even more astonishing because it was real. I looked like a different person.

By the age of fifty most women are supposed to have become invisible. But, bizarrely, I found myself swimming upstream when in 2009 I appeared on the cover of *Australian Women's Weekly* in a sexy black dress. The response was instant and overwhelming. Word was I was hot. Never in my whole life had I been called hot. Now people would yell compliments at me in the street. Where once I had dreaded walking past building sites for fear of unkind remarks, now I was showered with appreciative catcalls. Drivers in white vans would screech to a stop and yell out, 'Well done, Magda!'

I looked at the picture on my phone and I wondered, 'Is my friend right? Can I still play Sharon?' The perpetually put-upon, unlucky-in-love second-best friend and victim. Would my altered external appearance change my inner reality so much that my soul would have a different vibration? What would it mean if I were to lose Sharon? The thought rattled me.

Aside from the catcalls, the message from fans was mixed. 'Congratulations on your weight loss, Magda!' they cried. 'But don't lose too much weight!' they hastily cautioned. 'You'll still be funny, won't you?'

I felt like some kind of public utility. People had a stake in me. Clearly the link between fat and jolly is alive and well in the public imagination. The question was, did I still believe it?

My weight loss began in 2007 when my friend Ted Horton approached me to do Jenny Craig. Ted is an advertising adept—we did the Jetstar ads together and the campaign had been hugely success-ful. He is smart and he knows how to get the best out of people. He trusted me and encouraged me to co-write my spiels.

But when he first asked me about Jenny Craig my reply was short and not so sweet: 'Not my style.'

A year later, after a sleep specialist told me I had sleep apnoea and the most chaotic sleep architecture he had ever seen, I was back on the phone to Ted. 'I want in.'

So I started on the program. It was like magic. The weight peeled off me like an onion. I went from 122 kilos to 83. It was hard work, of course; it required discipline. I got a trainer and everywhere I went I toted my vacuum-packed Jenny Craig food, feeling like a Sherpa. This dedication no doubt added to my sense of self-efficacy and my self-esteem.

But there were bad days too. Very bad days when I fell off the wagon. On those days it was as if all the tormenting thoughts harangued me at once. I berated myself. I felt worthless and useless. The therapist would try to talk me down. Sometimes it worked, sometimes it didn't.

And, despite what people may have wanted, I became a different person. I became aware of myself as a decorative object: a bauble. I felt I had to live up to the stylised version of me that people saw on the magazine covers. A friend said of the *Women's Weekly* cover, 'It looks like you but it's not you. It's not the you I know. It's like it could be your relative or something. A cousin.' In truth I had morphed into a close resemblance of my Polish cousin, Magda.

It was like I was a magic trick. The shape shifter who played around with costumes, make-up, identity, had transformed in real life. Was this the real me?

I couldn't stop perving at myself in shop windows. I had to struggle with myself to go out the door without make-up on—I had never been one of those women. I started scrutinising myself in the mirror, noticing every flaw, every blemish. My job and my worth became how I looked rather than what I did. What's more, I started to find myself becoming oddly static. Posed like a still life. In fact, I did fear that I would lose my sense of humour.

Despite the weight loss I was not thin. I was still in the medically obese category. But people, both men and women, flirted with me much more. I can't be sure if this was because of their changed perceptions or mine. The sexiness of fat women is like a dirty little secret. Perhaps now that internet hacking threatens to expose our deepest fantasies, the truth about fat women will be revealed.

I didn't capitalise on my newfound sexual cred, though. I had lost my armour and I felt exposed. There is an expectation that when you lose weight you will become more sexually desirable and therefore more sexually active. You feel almost *obliged*.

But sexual attraction is enormously complicated. What is the relationship between the person we love and the package they come in? Sexual desire is the desire to touch another's body, to feel aroused by its form. What if that form changes? It cuts both ways. The world is full of fat people who have lost weight only to lose their love as well. On a plane once I met an attendant who lost a heap of weight and then split up with his wife because she insisted that he stop. But once he had tasted the elixir of health he simply could not go back. 'She didn't understand,' he said sadly.

The whole experience was reality bending. I did unthinkable things. For example, I ran.

I hadn't run in years. But when I got down to eighty-three kilos I ran. I was with a bunch of girls camping at Cape Leveque, a three-hour drive along tooth-shattering corrugated roads north of Broome in Western Australia. If they had beach resorts on Mars they would look like Cape Leveque. Ruby-red rocks, bone-white sand, turquoise sea, azure sky. The exact same kind of stark beauty I was bewitched by when I was a little girl.

There is a gang of us, a loose coalition, that has gone camping for thirty years and more. A bunch of lezzos and straight-lady fellow travellers. We're an eclectic lot. Doctors, magistrates, marine biologists, forensic psychologists, science reporters, human rights advocates, Kakadu rangers, advisors to the World Health Organization. And a comedian. There is never a shortage of good conversation. And this year we had all decided to go to Cape Leveque.

At mealtimes we would all gather in the communal hut, which was perched right above the rocks. As the sun dropped down into the Indian Ocean a huge pale moon rose in its place, illuminating the beach like a ghostly sporting arena. Spontaneously we all ran down to the beach and started kicking a soccer ball around, dodging the waves and the rocks.

And I ran. Actually it was more of a sprightly jog, like a toddler on tippy toes. And surprisingly fast. I was ducking and weaving. Shoving the other girls aside and giving as good as I got. I discovered I am a naughty soccer player. I like to play dirty. I jostle a lot. With the damp, hard sand underfoot, with the waves crashing onto the beach in the cool light of the moon, I ran. I ran and ran and ran and laughed so hard I wet my pants.

It was exhilarating. But I also felt the unbearable lightness of my own being. I am used to having a lot of ballast, a serious gravitational mass. This new me felt insubstantial. I felt displaced. Like I might just float away. And terribly sad, and afraid that this would be fleeting.

Which it was.

# IRELAND

In the midst of all this I was approached to do *Who Do You Think You Are?*, a reality television program that takes people in the public eye and traces their family history. It is like being publicly led blindfolded through the closet full of family skeletons. Unbeknown to me, they had uncovered something juicy about my grandfather, Luke McCarthy. In order to find out what it was I would have to go to Ireland.

I *never* wanted to go to Ireland. How many times had people insisted that when I went to Ireland I would love it? I would feel, they said, that I had come home. What with the cosy pubs and the wistful whimsy and everyone being a born storyteller. On account of the Blarney. Let's not forget the Blarney!

And the bog-Irish bigotry and the buggery and the un-Christian brothers. And the kneecapping. Let's not forget those either. I did not want to go to Ireland.

But I had agreed and everything was planned. A strange and

completely disproportionate fury arose in me. I just wanted it to be over quickly. I had not much interest in my maternal grandfather. But in the end, it was Ireland and the story of my grandfather Luke that finally cracked open the hard shell around my heart. In Ireland a lost and precious part of our family was found.

I rang Mum and told her I was going to Dublin.

'Oh, Dublin.' Mum's voice turned sad and soft with fondness. I was astonished. I never knew she felt like that about her father's home town. Her voice faltered and she started to weep. In an instant Ireland became something else altogether, a place of loss and longing and stories. A home, a hearth, a land before exile.

'Oh, Dublin. The city of the most beautiful speakers of the English language,' she said in her own soft Scottish brogue. 'Och. Oh hen, I really wish I could come with you.'

'I wish you could too, Mum. I wish you could too.' And now I was crying as well. 'Are you all right, Mum?' I asked.

'I'm fine, Magda,' she snapped. 'Don't make a big deal out of it.'

I was never told anything much about Luke. But my mother's eyes—beneath the humour—were haunted by a deep, fretting sadness. Behind the querulous hypervigilance, the nitpicking, the irritability, there cowered a terrified child. A child full of panicky uncertainty about everything. I wanted to reach back and grab her hand and pull her through time and…what? I wanted to hug my mother when she was a child, to tell her everything was all right.

Unlike the innumerable photos of my Polish family, there are only a handful of photos of Luke in the album: a rectangular-faced, tallish, thin man with soft and slightly fretful eyes set either side of a hawkish nose. His suits are ill fitting and cheap. He was a shoemaker.

There is a photo of him standing next to my grandmother, Meg, and in front of them are their two tiny tots—my auntie Mary and my mother. They are wearing identical velvet dresses. My mother is an adorable wee thing. Her older sister is moving forward, inquisitive, while Mum, only about two years old, hangs close to her mother's skirt.

My mother's stories of her father were all about how funny he was. His tales, his jokes, his antics. Of how in adulthood, on one of the very rare occasions when he drank, he walked into the pantry of the mirror-image house next door thinking it was the toilet and took a piss all over the pans. I knew only a few scant facts about him. His shop was owned by the Earl of Elgin and the earl himself one day came to visit and shook my grandfather's hand. My family was proud of that. I knew that he had a brother, maybe two, one of whom was a chronic alcoholic. Luke himself was, eventually, teetotal. I knew the youngest daughter, Betty, died of pneumonia when she was only two and he never got over it.

But I also knew about the terrible temper. Mum would rarely talk about it but Auntie Mary called him 'the auld bastard' and Uncle Dominic said my mother was the only one who had the courage to stand up to him.

McCarthy means 'son of the loving one'. Luke revered his mother, the devout and saintly Mary Jane. All we have of her, my great-grandmother, is a small religious card with her writing on it. Half of it is in Gaelic. My grandfather gave Mum a set of rosary beads that had belonged to Mary Jane but somewhere along the way my mother lost them. Just as many years later I lost the precious rose gold wedding band that my mother had given *me* and that had been my grandma's.

My grandfather never spoke of Ireland. When he died he left behind nothing but questions. Why did he never mention Ireland? And why did he have to leave Ireland in such a hurry? Was it, as my mother suspected, because he had been a member of the IRA? The *Who Do You Think You Are* crew wanted to film Mum. She was not too thrilled about it. She is shy and old-fashioned about secrets and family business. But as the camera began to roll, painful truths tumbled out of the old woman. As she looked at the pictures of her father she began to reminisce about Luke's shell shock. 'Oh yes, my father was in hospital on and off for years. He used to wake every night screaming.'

I was stunned. This was the first time my grandfather's shell shock had not been made light of. I imagined their tiny house and a small child wakening to the screams of her father's tortured soul. A different grandfather appeared. It was a bizarre sensation—I never met my grandfather and now I felt like I never met him twice.

On the plane to Dublin the flight attendant recognised me and fussed over me. At the end of the flight he beckoned, 'Come with me, doll.' He took my hand and led me through to the galley. 'Here, your hands will feel *amazing* after this.' He gave me a sachet of salt. 'Cover your hands with this.'

I dutifully spread the salt over my skin.

'Now, some lemon. And finally the bubbly.' And with that he poured the remnants of a bottle of the most expensive French champagne over my hands. 'Now rub! This is the best exfoliation you'll ever get. Your skin will feel softer than a rose petal.'

'My God! Is this OK?'

'It's fine, darl, we have to chuck this stuff out after each run. It'll be wasted anyway.'

I don't really like champagne so I was happier to wash my hands in the stuff than drink it but this kind of Caligulan decadence is not really my thing. Still, I appreciated the kindness of his gesture. I gazed out the window. Thousands of feet below, brisk winds whipped the Irish Sea into sharp peaks. How many times had my relatives batted back and forth across these waves? Scots and Irish, fleeing and pursuing. How much Irishness was still in me?

It was December and the sky hung so low every time you took a breath you could taste the gunmetal grey clouds in your mouth.

I was taken to meet Elizabeth Cuddy, the genealogist for *Who Do You Think You Are*. Elizabeth had a copy of a census form from 1911. It had been filled in by Mary Jane. I noticed that she had the exact same feathery handwriting as my mother. There was my grandfather Luke's name. And a column that read *Births*. Mary Jane had written *13*, then crossed it out, and replaced it with a *3*.

I was confused. 'What does that mean?'

Elizabeth looked at me. 'She had thirteen children but ten of them died.'

'Ten. She lost *ten* of her children?'

Later, Elizabeth told me this was a very high number even by Irish standards. I have known families to be bent, buckled and broken by one such loss. It is worth noting the statistics do not count stillbirths or miscarriages. So these were children born alive who died later. This is what it means to come from a poor and powerless family.

I felt winded. This impersonal bit of bureaucracy was the only thing to bear witness to Mary Jane's suffering. I felt like I was behind a pane of unbreakable glass watching ten children die of poverty. Was this why I had always dismissed the thought of Ireland? Passed down through the generations, without my even knowing it, had we all braced ourselves against this terrible loss? In a flash of insight I understood why my mother clings like a python, then turns and snaps like a crocodile when we get too close. Sheer numbers of people and years, bearing down on us—on both sides—creating people who had never learned the happy knack of easy attachment. Driven by the fear of loss, we swing wildly between clinging too hard and not hard enough.

Was this the gift of my Irish inheritance—the ability to survive loss, but at the cost of loving easily? This, presumably, is the legacy of many other families too. But when I began to sob uncontrollably—inexplicably—it was for *my* family. For my parents, my grandparents, my great-grandparents and beyond. And for Mary Jane's ten nameless children buried in the cold Irish earth. And maybe also for myself. Because I wondered, in that moment, if this was why I have never had children of my own.

That night I went back to my fancy Dublin hotel and ordered room service.

But when the meal arrived and the waiter removed the silver cloche from the plate and said, 'Enjoy!' I couldn't. There they were… potatoes. The symbol of Ireland's tragedy. As I lifted the fork to my mouth, images of those ten dead children were swimming through my head. I'm sure I sound like a bad joke, a parody of misery. But I could not swallow that bloody potato. It stuck in my throat, choked with sobs.

The Irish in Ireland have moved on. My grief was an anachronism: it had no place there. But where does it belong?

There I was, the famous face of a weight-loss campaign, my hands exfoliated with two-hundred-dollar bottles of wine, sitting in a posh hotel in a land where my entire family but one had been wiped out by poverty. It was like a Monty Python sketch. Of the thirteen—or more—children Mary Jane gave life to, only one survived into adult-hood and reproduced. My grandfather.

It was 7 December 2009. That night I wrote in my diary: *How will I tell Mum?*

During your *Who Do You Think You Are* journey you are not supposed to have contact with family and friends, but stuff that. First I rang my brother and my sister. They were sympathetic but there on the other side of the world the effect was not so devastatingly immediate for them. And then I Skyped my friends, including my friend Teresa. Her Irish great-grandfather was sent to Australia for allegedly trying to kill a British officer after he saw the man beating a horse. In fact, he punched the officer in the face and went back to the pub to finish his Guinness. Moments later he was arrested and transported to Australia. Teresa whistled down the phone line. 'Gee,' she said, 'I knew you were Irish. I didn't know you were *that* Irish.'

I started to feel woozy, wobbling. My great-grandmother Mary Jane and the ten children she buried in unmarked graves…Was this the dream I'd had? Children buried in mud. In my sleep, in my dreams, was this where the Royal Road to the Unconscious had led me? To my Irish DNA and all these poor dead little ones?

The next day we drove down to County Laois to where Luke had lived with his family in Factory Street. The name said everything. From the outside the whitewashed, thatched stone cottage where Luke and his family had lived was a cliché of cosy charm. But fifteen people had lived there, in two rooms with dirt floors. The census had classified the house as *Ruins*. But still the family had to pay rates.

This was where the ten children had died, and no wonder. I couldn't imagine trying to maintain hygiene in such a place. But what story did Mary Jane tell herself? Did she feel she was a bad mother? As she read her beloved Bible over and over did it comfort her? Did she feel she was like Job? Or like the Virgin Mary, who lost her own dear child? Did she weave the sad strand of her story into the sorrowful national narrative of invasion, oppression and impoverishment?

I thought of all the jokes about dumb Irishmen and I wanted to scream. It is the same story the world over—justice inverted, victims blamed for their suffering, their grief and trauma turned into a joke. A nation of proud people reduced to self-loathing shame, willing to pay rent for the privilege of living in 'ruins'.

A seismic roar of Irish rebellion rushed through me. The rumour that Luke had been a member of the IRA seemed entirely reasonable, judging by the blood that boiled through my veins. I suddenly found my Irish temper. Righteous anger with nowhere to go. Trauma backed up on itself and turned into drinking and violence. It is, after all, called Ire-land.

How much loss and pain can an individual bear? How long before it sours you, and turns you into the person you were never meant to be? By the time he was seventeen my grandfather Luke had lost ten brothers and sisters and his father. He found an unlikely means of escape: prison.

At sixteen, Luke was well on the way to a boozy end. Elizabeth Cuddy showed me a charge sheet. Drunk and disorderly; drunk and assaulting a policeman; two weeks' hard labour for being drunk and threatening a woman; drunk and disorderly; drunk. Drunk, drunk, drunk, drunk, drunk.

There is some light relief.

He moved on to a life of crime. Well, he tried to. He and his friends broke into a shop and stole some tobacco and bacon and so on—and then they attempted to crack the safe at the Protestant church. But the rasp snapped in the latch and the next day Luke was found, dead drunk, on the banks of the river, his feet still immersed in the water. He was sentenced to three years in prison. He did two and when he was released he went straight into the army. There were no other prospects for a young convict. He could read and write, but the only way out of one hell was via another. He was sent to the trenches in northern France.

My family had no idea where Luke had fought or with what division. But Richard Moles, the war researcher for *Who Do You Think You Are*, had discovered that he was sent to the army base depot at Étaples with the 16th (Irish) Division Infantry. There he was taught how to survive the trenches, before being posted to the Inniskilling Fusiliers on account of the fact that they had suffered such heavy losses from gas poisoning.

Luke was at the Somme, then Passchendaele. I spent a day with

Richard in the National Museum of Ireland, looking at image after image of a grey, shell-pocked hellscape. These were not structured trenches as I had imagined. These were nothing more than holes in the waterlogged mud. Richard explained that the land at Passchendaele is a reclaimed swamp, the water table only half a metre below the surface. The waters crept up, filling the holes. It was as if the earth itself was against them. Muddy holes filled with piss and shit and rotting corpses: body parts of the living and the dead. Men would slip off the duckboards and vanish, swallowed up by the liquefied earth.

Pits with mud. Quicksand. Hell on earth. It was utterly heart-rending. But I didn't know what to say because here, in black and white, were photographs of my nightmares. I was so disoriented I could hardly speak. Hollow-eyed men with murdered souls stared at the camera. The thousand-yard stare.

That night I wrote in my diary: *The crew think I am nuts. I keep muttering about having a genetic memory. I am quietly freaked out about this. It is the most peculiar sensation.*

Finally I rang Mum and told her about her father and the little ones. I told her Luke had been in prison. 'Needs must when the Devil drives,' she said.

She was calm about it, but later she told me she was very upset for her father's suffering. She is a much tougher bird than me. 'Well, you know, times were hard back then. That was common.' Was I too soft, too privileged? Yet again I was unsure which was the mad response—feeling or not feeling. And which response was more useful—mindfulness or denial.

We left Ireland and headed to Scotland where Luke had been sent to for his rehabilitation from the shell shock. We drove to Musselburgh in East Lothian, to Edenhall where Luke was hospitalised. As I sat in the chilly cab, silent icy fog crept down the hill towards us. Dank cold filled our lungs. The cab wound through the trees along the driveway and a gloomy edifice loomed like Lowood orphanage in *Jane Eyre*. This was where Luke had recovered after the war.

There was no Mr Brocklehurst waiting to greet me at the top of the stone stairs but a middle-aged woman with strawberry blonde hair. This was Yvonne McEwen, who has spent the last thirty years researching Edenhall and studying the effects of trauma in wartime. Her own grandfather suffered shell shock, also after serving at the Somme and Passchendaele. Coincidentally, in the same division as my grandfather.

We started to chat. I was about to tell her my jumbled theory that trauma is passed down through families. 'You know, Magda,' she pre-empted me, 'I think this stuff is passed on genetically.'

'Yes!' I spluttered. 'I've been saying that over and over.'

Can it be that some dim memory of trauma is carried in our genes? Yvonne and I spent the day talking between takes about nervous complaints and strange presentiments. 'And of course,' she said, 'there's the smell.'

'What smell?' I asked.

'The burning smell. In the back of—'

'The throat.' I clutched her arm. 'All my life I have had a weird burning smell in the back of my throat. I never knew what it was. What do you…?'

'Cordite. I think it is cordite.'

Yvonne showed me footage of 'hysterical gait'—men transformed into nightmare versions of marionettes whose grotesque movements are manipulated by some psychotic puppet-master.

Shell shock. A term I had heard all my life became superabundant with appalling meaning. My mother's family stood in its cold shadow. I rang Mum to tell her what I had learned. She had a different view.

'You want to know what life with my father was like?' my mother said. 'He was fun.' My mother didn't want Luke to be reduced to victimhood, to be seen as a miserable, broken, angry man. In other words, he was more than just his shell shock and his convict past.

I don't know what sort of treatment Luke received in hospital, if it was humane or harsh. Yvonne informed me that the cures in those days were often more cruel than the diseases. Hysterical mutism, for example, was treated with electric shocks. But perhaps Luke had a gentler rehabilitation. 'All around there were magnificent gardens and the men would work in them,' Yvonne told me.

When I described the subsistence farming at the hospital to Mum, tears welled up in her eyes.

'Yes, yes! We had lemon trees and plum trees and apple trees and rhubarb. My father always said, "When I die bury me under the apple tree."'

A whole life blossomed before my eyes. A life of careful and attentive nurturing. A patient, gentle life.

As my mother insists, Luke's tale isn't all sad. The Irish are champion talkers, and my grandfather Luke McCarthy was the king of the talk. He could talk you into anything. And then he could talk you right back out of it. His words held you hostage. He would rile you up into a bloody rage and then, at the height of apoplexy, make you laugh. He robbed you of the high-octane fury needed to propel you out of his velvet inertia.

And so it was that nothing would ever happen. No plan ever hatched. No scheme ever came to fruition. The humour, the Blarney, the talk. Designed to dull the pain and make you never leave. There is a famous family story of how, not long after he and my mother were married, my father and Luke got talking late into the night. Silver-tongued Luke proposed a business venture and fired my father up about it. Bursting with enthusiasm, making promises to one another, they went off to bed. The next day my father rose early, ready to execute the plan, and Luke just laughed. Nothing ever came of it. My father never believed another word my grandfather said after that. He liked him but he would grumble, 'Ach! The McCarthys! All talk. They never *do* anything. They just bloody talk around and around and around the thing until they talk themselves out of it.'

I was finding patterns. Me and Yvonne. Me and Mum. Just as my mother's father was constantly in and out of hospital, so was mine. The difference is my mother lived through it twice. When my father became ill, it must have been hard for her to go through it again. She was present, loyal as ever, but some small and vital part of her stepped back from the family. Throughout her infancy her father spent years away from home in that hospital. And when he was home he was an unexploded bomb in a small house full of children. They suppressed their childish energy, walking on eggshells for fear of detonating him.

But kids will be kids, and there was a story she often told me. When she was maybe six years old she went down to the burn, the creek at the end of their street. She tried to pole-vault across it as she had done many times, but this time her nerve failed her and she was plunged into its muddy waters. The dress her mother had made, the special dress for visiting her father in hospital, was ruined.

'Even at that young age,' Mum told me, 'I knew, I knew I had done something wrong.' When she told me this her face caved in, stricken with remorse. Actors can never replicate this look. Meg didn't punish her, but 'Oh! The look of disappointment on my poor mother's face.' Now, today, more than eighty years later, my mother still feels the stinging sense of guilt.

History repeats. That story of how, when I was six, I got blood on my best dress before a trip to take Dad to hospital. Mum slapped my leg in hasty anger. I understand now, of course, that it was herself she was slapping. Her life-loving, disobedient six-year-old self. We are bookends, she and I.

History repeats, love and loss. Dad with the tiny coffin on his knee.

Luke going to mass every day. His little girl Betty dying of pneumonia.

This is Job. This is Nietzsche's 'eternal recurrence'. This is the wheel of Samsara.

I am part of this circle, with my Irish talking-paralysis on the one side, and my Polish romantic impulsiveness on the other. The hand-me-down trinkets of family and trauma. This culture clash of competing responses to calamity. And I am beginning to realise that there is no right answer, no proper response. So you had better learn to forgive yourself.

# THE SEWER

By the time I arrived in Warsaw for the Polish segment of *Who Do You Think You Are* I felt like a walking bruise, sensitive to the lightest touch. We landed after dark and drove to my aunt's apartment to film her. It was only a few days before Christmas and I had never seen the city look so beautiful—a wonderland of snow and golden fairy lights. I thought, 'Good for you, Warsaw!'

There was a delay while the cameraman set up lights in Danuta's apartment. It was minus sixteen degrees. As I sat waiting in the car downstairs, icy-cold air crept deep into my guts and bones. My skin was chilled like a plate of liver just out of the fridge. 'This is what death must feel like,' I thought. 'Cold like this is a daily brush with death.'

Finally the lights were ready and I entered the same clanking lift I had first been in nearly thirty years before. As it lurched up to the seventeenth floor I felt my heart fill with the same inexpressible sadness I had felt all those years ago.

My aunt was too old to rise out of her chair to greet me. Her knotty hands fluttered up to my face. '*Magdusiu, kochana.*' We kissed and hugged. We sat holding hands while I asked her about our family. My aunt explained how my grandparents' home was a hub of resistance activity during the war. Along with guns and ammunition they hid documents and forbidden underground newspapers in the cellar in their apartment on Miedziana Street. When an *aktion* was to take place the members of the unit would come and sleep on quilts on the floor.

And she told me more about the little Jewish boy. They hid him for three or four months. He cried and she would try to comfort him. I wanted to know more but conversation was difficult. My aunt was old, and bursting with so many unheard stories. Her talk wandered aimlessly and she digressed at length about my grandfather's fistula. I asked what my grandparents were like.

'Saints! They were saints! My parents helped a lot of people.'

She said my father was 'very brave, very. He was a young man. He executed all the orders, whatever was necessary. *Vultures*—that is the only way to describe those who betrayed others! They betrayed not only Jews but also those who worked for their fatherland.'

The isolation of communism had preserved her rhetoric in its pure form. She displayed none of my father's tortured self-doubt. It made me wonder if Dad had been too hard on himself. Perhaps the empathy he felt for the collaborators he killed was more than they deserved.

The next day I met with two former members of my father's unit, Ryszard Bielański and Lucjan Wiśniewski. Lucjan told me that Dad was a natural leader. And a 'party animal'. Neither surprised me. They both told me about the extraordinary risks my grandparents took. Until this trip I hadn't realised just how courageous they really were.

At the Warsaw Uprising Museum I met the Deputy Curator, Paweł Ukielski. He told me that my father is now considered a hero of the resistance. And the flag of Unit 993/W, stained with the blood of his comrade Hanka, who was shot as she smuggled it through the streets, hangs in pride of place in the museum. Despite his philosophical indifference to others' opinions of him, I think my father would have been pleased to know that.

Late one night, after filming, my cousin Magda and I went back to the apartment of her son Jan and his wife. We chatted about family, about the more challenging character traits that her mother Danuta and my father shared. And we wondered what role trauma had played in creating them. What toll their courage had taken. That night Magda told me that our grandfather and her father had smuggled guns into the ghetto.

I wondered why, all those years ago when I was reading Leon Uris and had asked my father what the Poles had done to help the Jews, he didn't tell me about this. Perhaps he didn't know. Perhaps he thought it unseemly to trumpet such acts of valour. Perhaps he was resigned to being misunderstood and had simply given up trying.

I had so many questions. How did they get these guns? Did my father get them? My father had always told me he was good at getting guns. I knew now what that involved. But my cousin had no answers.

We went to Ryszard's house, where we met his adorable wife Grażyna. She is old and little, with mousy grey hair and a sweet expression like a beloved character from *The Wind in the Willows*. Despite the fact that she had a broken arm, the table was covered with a dazzling array of homemade Polish cakes and delicacies. Ryszard gave me a bundle of my father's letters. It felt like a communication from beyond the grave.

Everywhere I was haunted by ghosts—my father, my grandparents. Ryszard took me to the Evangelical Cemetery where he and my father had assembled on that first day of the Warsaw Uprising, 1 August 1944. My father's twentieth birthday. The cemetery was covered in thick white snow. It looked beautiful, like fondant icing on a wedding cake.

Ryszard told me how, in retaliation for the uprising, the Germans became even more brutal. They torched buildings and people. In just a few weeks 200,000 people were slaughtered. My father had been fighting in the Old Town. With the city in flames and Germans blocking every exit the only way out was through the sewers. From his letters, it seems my father and a comrade were charged with the responsibility of deciding who got to go into the sewer and when.

By the end of the uprising the Paris of the East was a giant pile of rubble. Knowing that Poland had lost its chance at freedom, my father slipped through a manhole and into the cesspit. When he went into that sewer he was a man with a country, a family, a future. When he climbed out he had lost everything.

'What was it like in the sewer?' I asked him one time.

'Hunched over in the pitch black,' he said. 'Shit lapping up to your chin and every so often your foot would crunch through something.'

'What?'

'Well, the body of someone who hadn't made it.'

This was the way to survival, to freedom. Trudging through shit and corpses.

'Why couldn't you use a torch?'

He scoffed at my ignorance. 'Don't be stupid! The Germans see you and *whoof*! Drop a carbide bomb.'

For the same reason the journey had to be made in total silence.

'How did you know where you were going?'

'There were guides. Girl scouts, boy scouts, just kids. Young sportswomen in their teens.'

'Why sportswomen?'

'Strong. Good power-to-weight ratio. They could lift their own weight to climb out at the other end of the sewer.'

All day these kids—they called them 'sewer rats'—took people back and forth through these rivers of shit. Like Charon the ferryman of Hades they dwelt in the dark bowels of the earth waiting to take the living across to the other side. Through *Who Do You Think You Are* I was able to meet one of them. He told me that sometimes he would have to stay in the pitch black for five hours. Alone. Silent. Waiting for his next group. He was fifteen when the war ended. A veteran.

It was the only time my father admitted to being scared. He lost his grip on the man in front of him and wandered a few metres down the wrong path. 'Ye gods, Maggie. I went into an absolute funk.' Many people died that way. Alone in a stream of human excrement. On this occasion my father retraced his steps and reached out and clasped the belt of the fellow in front of him. He was lucky.

The *Who Do You Think You Are* team had organised for me to go into the sewer through which he and the other fighters had escaped. It turned out to be just around the corner from where we were staying. Council workers had opened up a large slab of concrete. There were footholds, small iron half-rectangles built into the wall to form a basic ladder. Post–Jenny Craig I was still trim and fit, but this was trickier than it looked. The soles of my boots were covered in slush. Just in case, the team had placed a tripod over the manhole and a rope dangled from it to a harness attached to my waist. I was not tackling this sewer alone—it would be an assisted passage.

And so I climbed down. I had heard about this sewer for years, and now I was in it. It was perfectly clean and only slightly claustrophobic. I asked the filmmakers to turn the lights off and felt the walls close in around me. But no simulated stunt like this could ever give a true sense of what it is like to run for your life though a working sewer.

Once again my father eluded me.

# COMING OUT

The experience of *Who Do You Think You Are* really knocked me around. More than anything it made me question myself. How would I respond if tested? Would I be able to follow in the path of my ancestors and find the courage to do the right thing?

The test came sooner than I expected. Late in 2010 an email landed in my inbox. It was from Stephan Elliott, the enfant terrible of Australian cinema and the director of the camp classic, *The Adventures of Priscilla, Queen of the Desert*. He was asking if I would make a statement in support of same-sex marriage. He already had Hugh Jackman, Olivia Newton-John and Guy Pearce on board.

I had three choices. I could ignore the email. I could respond but not mention my own sexuality. Or…I could come out. I wanted to come out. But I did not want to flame and burn. I did not want to be a victim, or a coward or a martyr. There were long conversations with my agent and my family. With my friends, with my therapist.

My mind raced forward to thoughts of my deathbed. The things I would regret. And when a voice started up, quietly at first, I had the feeling it was my forebears calling to me: 'This is the right thing to do.'

I felt a powerful sense of opportunity. This was my chance, in some small way, to help make history, to change it, and possibly to change lives.

I told my agent to tell Stephan that I was planning to do more than make a statement: I was going to come out of the closet. It was now just a question of when, and how.

As 2011 wore on my impatience grew. Finally, like a pregnant woman who has come full term, I could stand it no longer. It was time to get this baby out. So I rang Kerryn Stricker-Phelps, a close friend and the ex-president of the Australian Medical Association. Kerryn and her wife Jackie are veteran gay campaigners; Kerryn had been trying to get me to come out for years. She wanted me to experience the freedom she and Jackie felt. Kerryn arranged for me to talk with Alex Greenwich, the convenor of Australian Marriage Equality. The moment I spoke to Alex I knew he was, as Kerryn had assured me, a 'safe pair of hands'. We all started thinking of when.

'Valentine's Day next year,' Kerryn suggested.

'Perfect.'

Alex suggested *The Project*, which was live to air, so there would be no question of the interview being edited. He had worked with them before and had found them to be very supportive. Alex made the call and the producers agreed.

I rang Barb and Chris and asked them if they and their families would be in the audience that night. 'Yup,' said Chris.

Barb got teary. 'Of course, Mag, I'd be so proud to be there.'

'Do you think Mum'll be OK with it?'

'I don't know, Mag. She's very different from us. We're more like

Dad. Sometimes you just have to do the right thing. But I'm sure she'll be fine.'

I rang my mother. 'Mum, I've decided to come out.'

'Oh, aye. When?'

'Next Tuesday. Are you OK with that?'

'I'm an old woman, Magda. What harm can come to me? But are *you* absolutely sure you want to do this, hen? Just…I worry. You know there are some old biddies out there who will turn off the television when they know.'

'I know, Mum. It's time.'

'Och, hen.' I could hear her voice faltering. 'You don't have to do this.' She took a deep breath, 'You don't owe us. If anything *we* owe *you*.'

And now we were both crying.

My sister and I were wrong. My mother absolutely knows the right thing to do. But she also knows the price can be high. My Irish friend's response was the same. It's the Irish survivor in them. 'I don't know, Magda. My instinct is to tell you to keep your head down. Don't do anything that makes you stand out.'

'Mine too. It is just that it's become unstoppable. I feel like I'm on a runaway train and the train is me.'

'Well. You are very brave.'

'I don't feel it. Not at all.'

The question was—what was I coming out *as*? Lesbian didn't feel right. It was not the full picture. Bisexual implied a kind of half 'n' half, which was not accurate either. Saying gay without mentioning I had slept with men made me feel like I was fudging it. The day before the interview I bemoaned my dilemma over coffee with a friend.

'So how would you define yourself?' he asked, and that's when I found the answer.

We decided it would be a good idea to put out a press release supporting same-sex marriage before the show. So I wrote a statement, making deliberate use of the first person plural pronoun.

> We pay taxes, fight wars for this country, nurse you when you are sick, make you laugh, sing and dance for you, play netball for you, star in your movies, cook your meals, decorate your store windows. And, chances are, gay people designed whatever it is you're wearing. All Australians, including gay Australians, should have exactly the same rights, including the right to love, marry and take care of our partners.

We issued the press release and waited. If it all turned into a media circus I knew my home would be no sanctuary so I decided to stay at a hotel with Barb and Mum. We picked Mum up in a limo. She was excited. A little nervous. We had a lovely dinner in our hotel room and then all went to bed. It was the last night I would go to sleep with a large percentage of the country thinking I was straight. I had taken the leap. And this time I was sure I was not falling—I was flying.

The press took the bait. The next morning it was all over the papers and radio. There was a lot of speculation about that 'we'. Phone calls started coming in. I turned off my phone and let Alex field calls. Then Mum, Barb and I went to the day spa to prepare for our big night.

When we arrived at the studio my entire extended family—brother, sister, niece, nephews and in-laws—and numerous friends were there to support me. As I chatted to the lovely make-up girls I realised, with some self-consciousness, that they knew I was gay without me having to tell them. It was now out of my control.

On the panel that night were Charlie Pickering, Dave Hughes, Carrie Bickmore and Steve Price. I didn't want this to be like a normal television interview with me pushing a barrow. I wanted it to be a moment of connection and understanding, something that cut through the clichés. I wanted, if I could, to help people to feel what it is like to be gay and the pain it can cause.

I was possibly the most nervous I have ever been. My breathing was constricted but I could still make a sentence and even a joke. When the guys asked me how I identified I replied, 'I am absolutely not straight. I wouldn't define myself as bisexual either. I would say I am gay-gay-gay-gay-gay-gay-a-little-bit-not-gay-gay-gay-gay. Unfortunately there's not actually a word to describe me so I have to express myself through the medium of the dance.'

Over the next nine minutes I tried as best I could to make people feel in their hearts the rightness of our cause. I had only one chance to get this right. I looked out into the audience and saw my whole family. My eighty-eight-year-old mother, sitting there with her halo of snowy white hair. And she nodded to me. In that moment I just needed to be loved. I needed my mum, with her partisan ways. My mother, the lioness, protecting her cub. I prayed to the Poles for courage, to the Irish for Blarney.

And then it was over.

We all made our way back to our hotel and gathered in the bar. Thousands and thousands of well-wishing messages poured in. More friends came to celebrate with us including Helen, Miche, Izabella and her sister, some old friends from uni and some of Helen-Mary's kids. I was sad that Helen-Mary herself couldn't be there. She had died several years earlier. Jane and Kristen couldn't make it but sent their love.

The next morning I ran into Mum and Barb's room in my terry-towelling dressing-gown and we sat on Mum's bed reading the papers, and it was all good.

A few days later I was at Mum's when the phone rang. It was one of her posse of octogenarian gal pals, a very nice woman but super

Catholic. After Mum got off the phone she said, 'Angela sends her love.' Her brow puckered and her lip quivered. 'I thought I might lose her.'

And with a terrible pang I realised that I was not the only one taking a risk. Mum did not have many friends still alive. She could not afford to lose any of the few she had left. But she had never so much as breathed a word of her own fears.

# WOMEN'S CONSPIRACY

I was not feeling what I was supposed to be feeling. I was like a nervous hostage who's been held captive for fifty years: institutionalised. Accustomed to the confines of my closet. The door had swung open, but I daren't walk free.

The phone rang. My dear, camp friend Mark Trevorrow. 'Jeez darl, good on ya love! I'm so proud of you. How do you feel?'

'I feel a little shaky actually.'

'Ha! I bet ya do! And are ya thinking to yaself, *What the fuck have I done!* But, you know…' He laughed. *'It does get better.'*

Over the next few days the peaks and dips of the roller-coaster became steeper. I had no resilience. I was as brittle as an osteoporotic bone. Everyone kept saying, 'You are the perfect woman for the job. The public loves you. If anyone can pull this off, you can.' God knows, I said those things myself. But it wasn't the public I didn't trust. It was myself. At dinner a friend told me about her famous athlete friend who killed himself after coming out, and I felt the wrecking ball smash into me. It was all I could do not to groan.

I felt hyper-visible. The weight started piling back on.

Fat. My most trusted companion. I crawled back into the thick folds of it, grateful for its constancy. It welcomed me back, without even the slightest reproach. I suspected the weight gain was a peace offering to the universe, a sign that I was still the same non-threatening Sharon. Why couldn't I just let myself feel proud?

I decided I needed to get out of Australia for a bit and arranged to meet up with my friend Stella in Warsaw. Stella has a striking Amazonian appearance and a cool Athenian intellect. I have known her for over thirty years, we were at uni together, but it is only latterly that our 'Polishness' has drawn us together. Now, in our fifties, having completed the task of assimilating, we were going back to assess the damage. I knew that the Europe in my head was a fossilised relic. It was a phantasm conjured by my childhood self. Perhaps I could lay that ghost to rest.

This was probably the last time I would ever see my aunt Danuta. She was in her nineties now and her memory, once prodigious, had become an ancient parchment, cracked and brittle. This would be my last chance to check the facts. All the old warriors were dying.

Warsaw was as hot and steamy as Bangkok. Stella and I were holed up at the Bristol Hotel, the same one that I dined at the night Rajmund taught me how to drink vodka.

We met Magda's son Jan and his beautiful wife, also called Magda, for dinner at U Kucharzy. It is always strange for me to be surrounded by so many Magdas.

Jan looked at me with his doleful, comic eyes. 'It will not be easy with Grandma Danuta,' he warned me. 'Even a year ago would be better but now her mind is *pffft*!'

'That's OK.' My throat tightened.

'It is good to have your questions prepared in advance. Do you know what you want to ask her?'

'Yes. I do.'

It was thirty years since my first visit. Aunt Danuta still lived in the same small apartment. It was still crowded with chinoiserie. Uncle Andrzej had died several years back. Danuta's hair had lost all its golden lights and now was cold grey. She rolled up her trousers to show me how bad her legs were. Her skin, made transparent with age, was so thin now it was just the idea of skin. You could see bones beneath it and her shins were stained purple with huge bruises.

I gave her a box of chocolates and we chatted for a while. Then we set up my iPhone and Danuta began to speak. But it was slow progress. Not everything she said made sense. We were watching the landscape of her memory vanish with each step we took towards it. Old age had sandblasted away many of the details that create narrative flow, that weave stories. Now her memory was distilled to its pure, cinematic essence. Mostly what remained were images—vivid images—and feeling states. She stopped and raised her trembling hands to the sides of her head. 'The fear. I remember the fear.'

My aunt was involved in what they called 'women's conspiracy', sly acts of subversion. She was a courier. Her job was to distribute the *bibuła*, the underground newspapers. She told us that Jadwiga had bought another small shop expressly for the purpose of hiding and distributing these pamphlets. Danuta would be given a delivery route around the city. The route was changed regularly so as not to attract attention. The reduced calorie regime imposed by the Germans had made her slender form even slighter. Paper, even thin paper, is heavy. 'I weighed only forty kilos. I was carrying a thousand pamphlets. They were so heavy.'

Danuta was a great beauty. Honey-blonde hair and green eyes, and a fresh, healthy, Ingrid Bergman kind of feel about her. Without any vanity she said she suspected that on a few occasions her looks saved her. 'We would go out, a bunch of pretty girls just having a night out, and the Germans thought nothing of it.' She was on her regular route when she saw a German soldier. 'I can still see it, the leg coming out of the lorry.' It was night-time but not yet curfew. 'He came out of the lorry. He saw me. And he looked at me, right at me. The blood drained out of my face. I started sweating.' But he didn't see that. What he saw was a pretty girl. The German looked her up and down, smiled at her. And let her go.

But the damage was done. Something snapped in her. She made her way home. When she arrived back at the apartment she 'looked like death', her parents said. They put her in a hot bath and made her cups of tea.

Uncle Andrzej looked at his wife trembling in the bath and said, 'No more.' Surviving the Nazis meant acting every single day of your life, taking fear and hiding it behind a mask of innocence and calm. Danuta, now that she had lost her nerve, was a threat not just to herself but to everyone. She was no longer fit for women's conspiracy.

But there were other things she could do. Things that took even more courage.

I asked her about the little Jewish boy. 'Who was he? Can you remember his name?'

Jan translated. 'She thinks the mother was called Hella. And the boy was Jurek.' And for the first time he became real for me.

Jurek had blond hair and blue eyes so they put him with Danuta because she had blonde hair and green eyes. She could have been his mother. He slept in her bed. The boy would cry and weep pitiably for someone called Irka. 'My Irka! They took my Irka!' My aunt imitated him with a thick Yiddish accent. The little boy spoke no Polish. Danuta shook her head. 'How could he? He had spent most of his little life in hiding. He would sing little songs in Yiddish.' When he wept my aunt would hold him in her arms and take him up to the window to look out at the sky.

I remembered the old pictures of Warsaw streets. The balconies festooned with the hanged bodies of Poles like my aunt.

The way my father remembered it, his mother was beside herself for days, weeping and fretting, unable to bring herself to tell them to go. I could hear his voice.

'She said, "Dear god, I can't. I can't! He is a child. Just a child!"'

'What did she say? Were you there? How did she tell them?'

'I don't know, Magda! I wasn't living there anymore.'

'But where was your father?'

'I don't know. I can't remember! For God's sake, this is fifty bloody years ago! I just know she was crying. My mother loved kids.'

I felt a desperate need to know. As though I could share and somehow diminish Jadwiga's harrowing grief. It makes no sense, but that's how I felt.

'No.' My aunt was emphatic. 'No. The parents made the decision. It became too dangerous. They came and took him away.' The final parting was rushed. Little Jurek clung to my aunt. They wept. And then they left. After that we don't know what happened to them— Airplane and Hella and Jurek.

My father had drawn his own conclusions. 'I'll say this much for that Jewess,' he told me. 'She must have been brave.'

'Why?'

'Well, she didn't squeal.'

'What do you mean?'

He looked at me as if I had learning difficulties. 'She didn't squeal. She didn't *talk*.'

'I'm not stupid, don't look at me like that. I know what squeal means. I don't understand what you're saying.'

'We lived.'

'So?'

'So she didn't tell the Krauts where she had been.'

'What, would she have gone and reported you?'

'When they got her! She didn't tell them.'

'She didn't get away? You mean she was caught?'

'With a nose like that? Of course. The Germans weren't stupid, they would know she was a Jew.'

'But why would she have told?'

'Because some of the Jews did.'

'Why? Why would they do that?'

'Because the Germans would torture them.'

We took our leave from my aunt. I hugged her tight. Such a little woman. As Stella and I travelled back in the taxi we spoke about Danuta, marvelling at her courage but also her ability, in the midst of all that horror and fear, to still be able to care and be loving. We left Warsaw the next day. It was the last time I ever saw Danuta.

# TREPANNING

I am on the phone to Barb. 'You might not want to hear this.'

'Well, try me,' she says.

I take a breath. 'I know what it means—that bizarre sentence. I finally have figured it out.'

'Which sentence?'

'The thing he said. "I was always terrified that one of my kids would be a traitor."'

'Oh. Right. That sentence.'

I have been thinking about that phone conversation I had with Dad in Adelaide, turning it over in my mind like a worn pebble. Did he mean that people like me—lazy, greedy, weak people—we are the cause of it all?

Because, it seems to me now, that was what it was all about. All the tennis madness, the 'killer instinct', the exacting standards. He was trying to cure me of weakness. In order to help me survive he thought he needed to expunge normal human frailty. To make me strong so there was no risk that, should the situation arise, I would line up on the side of weakness, of betrayal; that I would become a collaborator. They were the ones with no mental toughness—the chokers. He understood history. He knew the wild extremes to which it can swing. And that it repeats. He tried to make us strong like him because if we succumbed there was only one possible course of action. He would have to do his duty. He would have to kill us.

He was toughening me up so that he wouldn't have to kill me.

This, then, is the stone of his madness. In the depths of my father's soul there was a tiny part—cold and diamond-hard—reserved for his children. I thought this realisation would hurt me more but in reality I have always felt it.

Barb agrees. 'Yes, that sounds right.'

He crossed the world to get away but he carried the stone of madness with him. It was right there in his own head the whole time—the enemy within. With all of his might he tried to reason it out of existence. The decades spent trying to crush it with Englishness and rational thinking and belief in the scientific method had not even touched it. It was indestructible.

And I think: this is what war is. It is a universe in which doing the right thing is almost always simultaneously the wrong thing. And that is madness. Schizophrenics can know and not know that they are ill, and it looks a lot like lying. It isn't. It is a mind driven mad by irreconcilable truths.

The belief that you must, if necessary, sacrifice your own. It took me a long while to understand. Some infinitesimal but actual part of my father was primed to kill me because I was a weakling who would be a collaborator.

But even that was better than what I feared. Because my worst fear was for him: that he had collaborated. That was my stone of madness.

My father, as a boy of fifteen, had killed women and children in order to save women and children. And yet, as far as we know, not one of the people my family tried to save survived. Not one. Despite all their sacrifice and courage and love.

I never once saw my father cry for his Jewish friend Wacek Goldfarb. (For that matter I never saw him cry for his own family either. Some grief is just too great for tears.) But I know he risked his life for him. He risked being tortured for him. And he risked his immortal soul—I believe Wacek was one of the reasons my father started killing. Out of love for his friend. And because he couldn't stand the collaborators, the betrayers. Why did my family risk their lives to help Jews? It's as my cousin Magda said. 'Breeding.' Everything and everyone that went before them, their entire history, led them to that choice. It could not have been any other way. And besides, as she also said, 'To us these were not Jews, they were *our people*, Polish people.'

My father was at his best in friendships. He was devoted, loyal, honourable. He used to say, 'Wacek and I would go walking in the rain together and talk for hours. Hours and hours.' Many years later, in 1977, when it was safe for my father to return, he went looking for Wacek. He never found him.

I asked him about this. He brushed my question off with his usual detachment, laced with a slight irritation. 'Well, what do you expect. He looked like a Yid, a typical handsome Jewish man.' There was one tiny giveaway. 'Ach!' He picked off an imaginary piece of lint and straightened the crease of his trousers. That was it. The whole ghastly inexpressible everything.

Now I am like a stray dog, a middle-aged woman trying to salvage what is still useful. The words line up like a firing squad.

Martyr. Victim. Collaborator. Sacrifice. Nobility. Traitor. Duty. Hero. Courage. Love.

I hear the words of my therapist. 'You are not your father, Magda.

His guilt is not your guilt. His shame is not your shame. His courage is not your courage. You are a separate human being.'

I get it. Sort of. Not really. I feel suffused with his stuff: it's part of my fabric.

But this is not Warsaw. I have the privilege of being able to feel the feelings my father could not allow himself. On these safe shores, on this island, I can finally forgive myself for feeling fear. For feeling shame. For feeling weak.

I take out my hard drive and plug it into my laptop. I replay the film I made of him. And something he says leaps out at me.

'That's what I believe is real heroism. People who are afraid, have their pants full, and yet—they go and do something. Then you say, By God! It took courage to do that! But if you're not afraid, it's easy.'

And it dawns on me: that's me. He is describing me. That is what I have just done. How could I have forgotten that he said that? How could I not hear him properly? And I start to sob uncontrollably. For Dad. For me. For the whole damn lot of us.

# EPILOGUE

The very cells of my body feel different.

No one can possibly tell you what it feels like to be out. How empowering it is. You cannot know how it will change you until you are there. Like a fitness instructor trying to communicate to me what it feels like to be fit when I was 125 kilos, beached on the couch, watching TV.

Mardi Gras has come and gone again. This year I was part of the float for *Twenty/10*, an LGBTQI Youth Support Group for which I am now the official patron. As I stood with those beautiful young people—with their tattoos and piercings, their transgressive frocks and facial hair—I felt a surge of what can only be described as maternal pride. I marvelled at their courage and resilience. Some of them have terrible stories, far worse than anything I have had to deal with. I felt privileged to be their patron and protectress and for once I felt that I was doing the right thing.

It took me years but I got here. What did I learn from Poland? From Ireland? That the journey towards acceptance and understanding is a long and arduous one. That mutual respect can be destroyed and must be rebuilt on stronger foundations. That even though progress is a myth and history is a turncoat, you still have to believe in them. That for some of us the spirit endures. For others, it never recovers. And yet somehow we must live together honouring and respecting difference.

For more than four decades of my life sexuality was a huge issue for me. Then all that melted away, and it was amazing. The incredible freedom, when I am out having dinner with friends, of saying the word 'lesbian' proudly and openly. Now I love that word. I love the depth of its history, its associations with the ancient Isle of Lesbos and the iridescent love poetry of Sappho. I love the sensuous, exotic music of it. Now I can truly be myself. And being your real authentic self, when you have felt forced to hide your whole life, is the most beautiful feeling in the world.

Mum and I are back on the Jason recliners. Some of the Irish fight has damped down in us. We are gentler, kinder with one another. Some ghosts have been laid.

I wish Dad were here. I wish he were here to see it all turned out OK. I think he knew it would. I wish they were all here—Meg, Luke, Jadwiga, Mieczysław, Andrzej, Danuta. And I wish I could tell them how well he prepared me for life. He tried his best to shield me from the absolute worst that human nature can deal out. He gave me freely whatever he had. His wisdom and indomitable optimism. His belief that it is possible to change yourself. His uncompromising honesty and fairness. His incredible warmth and humour. His curiosity. His lack of bitterness. His love. And, the greatest gift of all, his love of life.

I wish he could have seen me come out. He would have been proud. But perhaps this had to be me and Mum. I needed her one-eyed clannish devotion. And we needed to find our own courage, in our own way. We who are not lions. The trembling sheep, the frightened horses, the impala at the watering hole—we had to take this next step.

And in our own faltering way we did.

# ACKNOWLEDGMENTS

There are many people I wish to thank, both living and dead:

Ryszard and Grażyna Bielański for their loyal friendship to my father and their incredible hospitality, and for the gift of my father's letters.

Celia Tait, Kay Pavlou and the gang at Artemis Pictures for taking me on my *Who Do You Think You Are?* journey. I had already begun to write this story but that experience changed my life and your research was an absolute boon.

To my various therapists over the years—thank you for helping me find insight. Alex Stewart, Marcus Fazio, Mish Coppel and Maureen Wheeler, thank you for the advice.

I am grateful for the long and sometimes wrenching conversations with my friends Pauline Rockman and Bernard Korbman, who took the time to educate me about the Jewish perspective and listened with patience and kindness as I tried to figure out my own legacy.

To the Kobylański family, thank you for being the conduit to my Polish heritage.

Stella Babirz and Dominika Balwin, thank you for accompanying me, literally and figuratively, on my journeys, and for all the translations.

My old pals Helen Grützner, Sue Ryan and Jane Crawley for being such all round good sports. To all my other friends who have put up with me banging on about this book for years, a big thank you.

Helen-Mary Sawyer and her beautiful family—Caro, Anna, Katrina and Peter. My indefatigable assistant Samantha Cameron who takes care of the real-world stuff so I can do what I do.

My dear friend Kristen Blöink for her gentle loving support. Miche Bonett-Horton for helping me to get down on film my father's story.

My agents Fiona Inglis and Ann Churchill Brown, who gave me the confidence to think that maybe what I was writing wasn't absolute drivel.

To my big and sprawling Scottish, Irish clan, all my wonderful aunts and uncles and cousins. Auntie Kathleen and Uncle Dominic I hope you are not offended by my version of events.

My family in Poland—Danuta, Andrzej, Magda Zawadzka and Jan Zawadzki and Rajmund Szubański. A deep and heartfelt thank you for your courage, hospitality and love. And for your stories.

My brilliant editors Michael Heyward and Mandy Brett who cut down to size the original sprawling behemoth I brought them. For their infinite patience—allowing me to pester them with my whining, nagging and general neediness—I am extremely grateful. As I am for their clear-sighted intelligence and all round good taste.

And my ancestors—my beloved gran Meg, Luke, Jadwiga and Mieczysław, three of whom I never even met but who, literally, made me who I am. Thank you for all that you have given me and I hope we can finally meet on the other side.

And lastly my family—deep love and thanks to my nieces and nephews and great-nephews: Sarah, Simon, Michael, Sarah, Max and Jacob, who carry our family's present and future. My beautiful sister Barbara and my steadfast big brother Chris, thank you for your companionship, support and love over the decades.

And of course Mum and Dad. The two great loves of my life. Dad, I hope you are up there somewhere, because now I feel I understand you a little better it would be great to have a big chinwag. I love you and miss you darling. And Mum, wee Maggie. Thank you for your love and courage and loyalty. And the gift of the Blarney. I adore you.

Magda Szubanski
August 2015